The Game Production Toolbox

The Game Production Toolbox

Heather Maxwell Chandler

CRC Press
Taylor & Francis Group
Boca Raton London New York

CRC Press is an imprint of the
Taylor & Francis Group, an **informa** business

CRC Press
Taylor & Francis Group
6000 Broken Sound Parkway NW, Suite 300
Boca Raton, FL 33487-2742

© 2020 by Taylor & Francis Group, LLC
CRC Press is an imprint of Taylor & Francis Group, an Informa business

No claim to original U.S. Government works

Printed on acid-free paper

International Standard Book Number-13: 978-1-138-34171-5 (Hardback)
International Standard Book Number-13: 978-1-138-34170-8 (Paperback)

Visit the Taylor & Francis Web site at
http://www.taylorandfrancis.com

and the CRC Press Web site at
http://www.crcpress.com

To Jack and Rafael—thanks for supporting me throughout this journey.

Contents

PART 2   Creating the Prototype

PART 4   Assembling the Game Team

Foreword

When we play a released video game of good quality, everything in the game seems to naturally make sense. We can be in awe of the game artistry, be impressed by its technological innovation, and reach a state of flow—losing track of time and external pressure—thanks to a refined gameplay. However, when developing a game, especially in the early stages, the game team is at the bottom of what can seem like an insurmountable mountain which they need to painfully climb. The top of the mountain is in a fog of war, making the end goal—what the game is going to be—out of sight, and the road is filled with obstacles. What awaits us on this journey? What path should we take? What caveats should we avoid? How can we pace ourselves, make the right decisions and trade-offs, and set up the correct priorities so that we can reach our goals and avoid missteps that could be costly or, worse, fatal to the project? Most veteran game developers have worked on a project that collapsed at some point in their career because focus was lost, the scope of the game exploded, or too many resources were wasted.

Not only does the game team need to have a clear understanding of where they are heading and how to reach this; they also all need to progress in the same direction. Aligning designers, artists, engineers, and the many other talents who are contributing to a game is a complicated choreography, danced to an unfinished tune, with an ever-changing beat on a slippery dance floor. Going with the flow in such conditions is extremely risky, and it's very easy to fall over. Not only is the game unlikely to reach its maximum potential without a strong process and framework—additionally, a lot of time and resources will be wasted. Making games is a difficult and chaotic endeavor, but it's a chaos that can be tamed and catalyzed. And that is the responsibility of the producer.

While Heather and I were working on Fortnite, I witnessed firsthand the critical role of a producer on such a deep and complex game. Considering all the design, engineering, and art challenges this project had, it was quite hard to stay focused on the most important tasks, prioritize what needed to be done, and not lose sight of what experience we wanted to offer our audience. Heather's work, along with that of the other producers on the project, allowed the team to progress when the tasks ahead felt overwhelming. Among the many other things Heather orchestrated on Fortnite, her work allowed her to establish a strong user experience (UX) pipeline on the project, which was key to allowing the team to stay true to the game pillars while adopting the perspective of our audience. This is why investing in game production is critical, and Heather shares her extensive expertise to offer us a perfect overview of what it entails, addressing all the aspects of game development. *The Game Production Toolbox* is not only a guide for producers and aspiring producers, filled with concrete tips and resources, but also a companion for any game developer, especially indie developers, who may not necessarily have the support of a strong infrastructure and large resources. *The Game Production Toolbox* is the book that will guide you along the winding path to the top of the game development mountain at a steady pace and without tripping over the many obstacles in your way.

Celia Hodent
Game UX Consultant
Santa Monica, California, December 8, 2018

Preface

Why This Book

When I started working in the game industry in 1996, I was pretty green. I had recently graduated from University of Southern California (USC) with a master's degree in Film Studies and was trying to figure out the next step in my career path. I was interested in working in the film industry but hadn't yet found something that I was passionate about or that was a good fit for me. Queue Activision—they recruited me to work as an assistant to the head of the studio, Howard Marks. My day-to-day activities included beta testing games in development; duplicating CDs so that people could test the games (digital distribution was not a common thing in those days); playing and internally reviewing competitors' games; reading magazines (!) like *Nintendo Power*, *Game Developer*, and *PC Gamer*; and a doing a variety of production tasks for the development teams.

After a few months, Howard asked me where I wanted to go in the company. Without hesitation, I said, "Producer" as I had discovered that my passion was for game production. To me, game production is a critical part of making great games. The role of production is to provide support to the developers so that they can stay focused on what they do best—coding, art, design, audio, etc. This support runs the gamut from giving people the hardware to do their job; mitigating different points of view when defining features; synthesizing the feedback that comes in from all places; making sure that all the moving pieces are progressing; and, most importantly, unblocking anything that prevents people from doing their work.

In my 20+ years in game production, I have worked with all types of people, games, platforms, and publishing models. I remember the thrill I felt when I saw my first game credit for Zork: Nemesis, and it's still a thrill when I see my name in the credits, most recently on Fortnite. What I've found is that *what* the producer does hasn't changed dramatically, but the tools, methods, and processes have changed *how* the producer works.

This book is my attempt to pull together all the things a producer needs to know in order to make a game production—a book I wish I'd had when I started my journey. It focuses on the nuts and bolts of production, and how you can organize and support the creative, technical, and business efforts that are all part of game development. This book isn't going to tell you how to design a game or what technologies to use—there are plenty of books and websites with that information. Instead, it provides techniques and insights into how to manage the chaos that is inevitable when making games. Production isn't about budgets and schedules; those are just ways to measure and track progress. Production is about understanding all the pieces that must come together, putting a plan together to make this happen, and providing support to your team as they execute the plan.

Who Needs This Book

This book is geared towards people involved in or curious about game production. People who are new to the field will find lots of information in here to aid them in understanding what is expected of them, how to fulfill these expectations, and generally how to herd the cats so they are all going in the same direction. Veteran game producers will find some nuggets here as well—especially if there are areas of production they are less familiar with, such as producing voiceover, localizations, managing a live game, and financing. Discipline leads will also enjoy learning more about production and how it can help them do their job more effectively. Leads can then take this information and work with their producer to improve processes, pipelines, feedback loops, and more for their team.

Since this game is geared to the production point of view, topics about the nuts and bolts of making a game—such as how to script levels, create characters, and design game loops—will not be addressed in detail. However, developers will gain a better understanding of how business choices, resource availability, and product quality have a direct impact on game design, art style, and technology choices.

How to Use This Book

This book is organized to roughly follow the production flow of creating, developing, and releasing a game. Game production is not a science, so creating a one-size-fits-all process is not realistic, but this book does overlay a general sequence of events that most games will pass through on their journey to the player. Your daily challenges won't be the same on any given day, but this book will help you understand what types of things you will encounter so you can be better prepared to overcome them. A good producer is always thinking ahead to anticipate what challenges the team will encounter.

There is a dedicated chapter for each major aspect of the game development process. While it is ideal to read this book from beginning to end so you can experience how the process flows, you can also skip around, and read specific chapters of interest. This book is divided into six parts:

- **Part 1—Overview:** This section provides basic information on the game industry, financing, distribution, publishing, production, and legal elements. Understanding these is important since they all impact how you approach the game production process.
- **Part 2—Creating the Prototype:** This section discusses getting started, establishing stakeholders, defining and fleshing out a concept, prototyping, and pitching the game.

- **Part 3—Establishing Requirements:** This section breaks down how to define the scope, budget, and schedule for your pitch. This is where you will gain a better understanding of the effort that is needed from a time, money, and game feature perspective.
- **Part 4—Assembling the Game Team:** This section focuses on how to assemble and organize your team, from hiring to outsourcing. It also discusses effective team leadership, including team building and team health.
- **Part 5—Making the Game:** This is the longest section and talks about how you can pull all the pieces together to actually make the game, including how you execute goals, prioritize work, implement feedback, and get a project back on track. There are also chapters focused specifically on UX, audio, and localization.
- **Part 6—Launching the Game:** This final section covers how to launch the game to your players, including testing, releasing, and maintaining its live health. Some information is also presented on marketing and community management, which are key elements to a successful launch.

Throughout this book, game industry experts offer some great advice based on their real-world production experiences. I hope you enjoy reading this!

Heather Maxwell Chandler
Principle Game Development Consultant
Media Sunshine, Inc
heather@mediasunshine.com

Acknowledgments

Writing a book always takes more time than I think it will, so I wanted to give a special shout-out to my editors, Sean Connelly and Jessica Vega at CRC Press, for their patience and support while I finished this one.

A huge thanks go to all the people who were interviewed for this book. Thank you for taking the time to answer questions and share your knowledge with others.

A special thank you to Celia Hodent for reading an early draft and providing lots of great feedback and insight on how to make it better. She was also kind enough to write the foreword.

Thank you to Ken Turner, who also took time out of his busy schedule to read this book and provide feedback. His suggestions improved the end result.

Author

Heather Maxwell Chandler is a veteran producer with more than 20 years of experience in the video game industry. During her career, she has led teams at Epic Games, Electronic Arts, Ubisoft, and Activision. As a Senior Producer on Fortnite, she worked closely with the development team on managing the development, the launch, and updates of the game.

She has managed the production of Indie and AAA titles, and has worked with a variety of intellectual properties. Aside from Fortnite, she has worked on more than 35 games, including Never Alone, Star Trek Rivals, Kingdoms of Amalur: Reckoning, Two Worlds, Monster Madness: Grave Danger, Heavy Gear, Apocalypse, Vigilante 8, and Shanghai: Second Dynasty. She also worked on seven titles in the Ghost Recon series, including Ghost Recon 2 and Ghost Recon: Advanced Warfighter.

In 2019, she was chosen to be an American Association for the Advancement of Science (AAAS) IF/THEN Ambassador, a program to support, encourage, and inspire girls' interest in STEM.

Heather is also the author of *The Game Localization Handbook, Second Edition* (Jones & Bartlett Learning, 2011), and a chapter in *The Project Manager's Desk Reference, Third Edition* (McGraw-Hill Professional Publishing, 2006), as well as three chapters in *Secrets of the Game Business, Second Edition* (Charles River Media, 2005). She has published numerous articles on game development and has lectured at the Game Developers Conference, NLGD Festival of Games, International Game Developers Association (IGDA) Leadership Forum, Future Play, North Carolina State University, and the Digital Game Expo (now known as East Coast Game Conference). She served as the chairperson of the IGDA Production SIG from 2006 to 2010. She graduated with honors from Vanderbilt University and earned an MA from the USC School of Cinematic Arts.

PART 1
Overview

In order to best define the game production framework, an understanding of the game industry and how a game gets from concept to release is important. Each chapter in this section provides an overview of one aspect. The chapters are:

Game Industry Overview;

Developer and Publisher Overview;

Legal Overview.

CHAPTER 1

Game Industry Overview

1.1 Introduction

Back in the early days of Pong, the development process was simple because one person was usually responsible for the design, code, and art of a game. If additional help was needed, the team was still fairly small and able to manage the workload without much production support. But as games became more complicated, with well-developed characters, worlds, and story lines, and technology that allowed for more graphically intense experiences and deeper gameplay mechanics, the player's expectations grew as well. Today, players expect a compelling, emotional, and high-quality gameplay experience, and will be very vocal online about their expectations and disappointments. In order for a game to meet these high standards, many people are involved in the game development process—not just designers, engineers, and artists but also investors, lawyers, marketing and PR people, community managers, QA testers, CS, and many more. The producer is expected to pull all these pieces together and make sure everyone is working together and everything is aligning towards the same set of goals. Any successful game faces many obstacles along the way, and games that have a producer at the helm are more likely to deal with these obstacles efficiently and effectively.

Thus begins the journey of the producer. While a producer doesn't generally contribute art, design, or code directly to the game, the production role is critical for getting a game to market. Someone needs to be "minding the store" to ensure that milestones are met, progress is made, and work is not blocked. If you are a new producer, you may be wondering what you've gotten yourself into because your team is expecting you to spearhead and navigate this process for them. If you've been in the industry for a while, you are probably aware of all the complexities that go into releasing a successful game but still have areas you want to learn about so that you can be more effective at wrangling all the pieces.

Before delving into the specifics of how to manage all these pieces, a general understanding of how the game industry works is useful. Managing the development of a game from concept to release is both a demanding and a gratifying experience. You and your team will put a lot of passion and energy into getting your game to market, and decisions you make about securing financing, determining your revenue model, and distributing the game all have an impact on the production process and ultimately the player's game experience.

1.2 Game Development Framework

According to the Entertainment Software Association (ESA 2018), the game industry generates tens of billions of dollars each year and has experienced double-digit growth on an annual basis for the past few years. This translates to a lot of games being made by development teams around the world. The teams can vary in size from a few to a few hundred people and can take anywhere from a few months to several years to commercially release a game. While the team sizes and complexities of the games may vary, the overall game development framework is fundamentally the same:

1. **Create the Prototype:** This initial phase is where you decide what game you are making, who you are making it for, and what the key gameplay mechanics are. The work done in this phase has a direct impact on the success of your game. You have more freedom to explore new things and make mistakes because nothing is set in stone. You can make a lot of decisions that will impact the quality of the game. The focus is on "finding the fun" through prototyping and feedback. Part 2 of this book delves more deeply into how you can make the most of creating your pitch.

2. **Establish Requirements:** Once you have an understanding of what you want to make, you need to plan how you are going to make it. How much time and money is necessary? What people are needed for the development team? Answering these questions now puts your game in a better position to succeed. Part 3 provides more specifics on how to create a budget, schedule, and overall production plan.

3. **Assemble the Team:** As you define what game you're making, you will need people who can help. How do you find these people? How do you organize the team? How do you keep the team happy and motivated? Part 4 answers these questions and more.

4. **Make the Game:** You have the money, the people, and the time, and now the team is ready to create the game. In a perfect world, this phase is simply executing your plan—all the questions are answered, all risks are mitigated, and you have everything you need to make the game from start to finish. The reality is that this phase will have its bumps and obstacles as well. The producer will be putting out fires, reworking plans, and keeping the chaos contained. Part 5 discusses how to navigate the ins and outs of making the game. This includes coordinating all the moving parts and determining when the game is done, and offers strategies for getting a project back on track.

5. **Launch the Game:** Finally, the game is ready for the players. Testing finishes up, third parties have signed off, marketing campaigns are in flight, and the players wait in eager anticipation. During the launch phase, the focus is on getting all the pieces in place for customer service, community management, and the live operations of the game. After the game is launched, expect to deal with player feedback, bugs, rolling out new features, and anything else that is needed to maintain the health of the game.

As you can see, there is a lot of planning that goes into making a game, and this is reflected in the process. Note that the first three phases are all focused on planning, answering questions, assessing risks, and generally defining the plan for how to make the game (including people, finances, and publishing partners). Skipping some (or all) of the planning can be tempting; you may want to jump directly to scripting levels, creating character models, and coding cool features since they are probably more enjoyable than planning. Don't fall into this trap! Save yourself time and headaches later by putting effort into planning and understanding everything that's needed to get your game in the hands of the players. In addition, there is a fair amount of planning for the game launch. Again, don't create more problems than needed by ignoring the importance of a launch plan.

The completion of each phase has a direct impact on the final quality of the game, so understanding the goals for each phase is important. By accomplishing the set of goals defined for each phase, you are setting yourself up for success in the next phase. If you don't understand what the goals are and subsequently don't complete them, you don't have a strong foundation for building a successful game.

For example, if teams start in Phase 1 with creating, prototyping, and vetting the concept, issues can be solved before they become bigger obstacles for the final game. If teams jump straight to Phase 4 and start making the game, they won't fully understand what is being made, which makes it harder for them to agree on the key goals and features. They may also start running out of money or time because they miscalculated the effort required to make a shippable game. There are many stories of games that were never released because the team couldn't figure out what game was being made, or they ran out of resources.

For purposes of clarity, this book walks through each of these phases from beginning to end before moving onto the next phase. In reality, the transitions between the phases aren't well defined; there won't be a clear beginning and end, things will be done in a different order, game features will be changed or removed, people will roll on or off of a project, a game will go through multiple iterations before launch—the list goes on.

Because the phases overlap at various points in the development cycle, thinking about game production as a series of iterative cycles is helpful. For example, your team may create a playable prototype of the basic game mechanics, test them, and then release them to a limited group for feedback. Based on this feedback, you may do a few more rounds of feature iteration and then release the game publicly.

Using an iterative development cycle also means that you will have game features in different stages of development. For example, you may launch a game as what is commonly referred to as a minimal viable product, or MVP for short. This means that the game is released with a minimal set of features that are sufficient for early adopters. As players interact with the game, the publishing team gathers feedback, then utilizes this feedback to improve the next set of features to be released. With this approach, there will always be one set of features in the planning phase, one in the execution phase, and one in the launch phase. If you have established a strong planning and development pipeline, you will be able to juggle all of these feature sets at their various stages of development.

Now that you have a general understanding of how the game development process works, let's talk about other factors to consider when making a game.

1.3 Financing Options

Financing is an important part of the game production process. While it is possible to create and release a successful game on a shoestring budget, or just on pure grit alone, financing can make the process much easier. There are lots of options available, especially for independent developers. An independent developer is one who self-funds their game development and does not rely on publisher funding. This model provides the developer with more freedom. Gone are the days when publishers were the main source of funding, which limited the types of games made and who could afford to make them. What follows is a brief overview of different types of funding; it is not an exhaustive list but provides a good starting point for your journey to secure funding. The funding is there; you just need to look for it. Also, consulting with a financial professional is strongly advised—a certified public accountant (CPA), financial advisor, and banker are invaluable to you in learning how to navigate the ins and outs, and select the funding that is the best fit for you.

1.3.1 Self-Financing

Self-financing is a popular choice, and the upside is being your own master. You don't need to convince anyone for a loan and are free to spend the money as you determine, and it's your choice if and when you pay it back. If you have personal savings or assets to liquidate or borrow against, you can also get money fairly quickly.

The downside is that you are taking on all the financial risk. Ideally, you make the game, release it, and make your investment back. In some cases, this doesn't happen, and you may find yourself in financial jeopardy. Minimize this risk by thoroughly exploring the pros and cons of self-financing and talking with a financial professional before taking on this huge personal commitment.

1.3.2 Credit Cards

Credit cards are another option for self-financing, but they are even riskier since the money will have to be paid back with interest and within a certain period of time. This option is tempting since getting a credit can be fairly easy, and there is no shortage of credit card companies to choose from. This method can be expensive if interest rates are high, and only the minimum amount is paid back each month. There is a possible risk of negatively impacting your credit score or declaring bankruptcy. If money is not paid back, it makes it harder to borrow money in the future.

Credit cards may be a viable option if you have excellent credit and can take advantage of 0% introductory rates. Also, if only a few thousand dollars is needed, credit cards could be a good way to go. Be diligent about paying them off, ideally before high interest rates kick in.

1.3.3 Bank Loans

Bank loans are a more traditional way to borrow money. To secure a loan, the banks will want to see a full business plan, including a financial analysis and information about your prior professional experience. The bank wants to know that you understand how to run your business, make a profit, and pay back the loan. Some banks may be wary of investing in games, so try to find a banker who is receptive, enthusiastic, and understands the industry.

The bank isn't concerned about development progress, game quality, or the release date. Once the money is loaned, they are hands off as long as regular payments are made. This can be a good option for a team that has a proven track record or just needs to borrow money to improve cash flow.

The Small Business Administration (SBA) is a wonderful resource. Their mission is to help small businesses get established, find funding, and grow. They work directly with specific banks to provide loans that are more accessible to small businesses. The SBA also provides a lot of support, education, and counseling to people who are starting up a small business, making it easier for you to put together a business plan and apply for a loan. You can find more information about this on their website: www.sba.gov.

1.3.4 Crowdfunding

In February 2012, Double Fine successfully used Kickstarter to fund an adventure game called Broken Age. This ushered in the era of crowdfunded independent games. There are a host of successfully released crowdfunded games, including Banner Saga and Shovel Knight. Crowdfunding is when you pitch your game to the public and ask for funding. In return, they usually get a copy of the finished game and other types of rewards, such as T-shirts, plush toys, and books. Generally, the process works like this—you determine a funding goal, start and end date for the funding period, and set up a project page with information on what the project is and how the money will be used. People contribute to the fund, and if the funding goal is met, you get to access to the money (plus any extra money contributed beyond the funding goal). The money is used to make the game, and when it is complete, the funders get their copy of the game (usually, before it is released to the public). If you don't reach your funding goal during the allotted time, you don't get any of the money, but you always have the option of trying again.

Kickstarter (www.kickstarter.com) is one of the most popular crowdfunding websites, with Indiegogo (www.indiegogo.com) following close behind. The nice thing about Indiegogo is that you can keep whatever funds are raised, even if the funding goal is not met. With each of these, people can learn about your project through demos, presentations, and videos posted on your project page. People choose how much they wish to contribute, and based on the contribution amount, they get some type of reward. They are not investors in the traditional sense since they don't have any ownership of the game and won't earn any returns from the game sales. Anyone is free to post a Kickstarter or Indiegogo campaign.

Fig (www.fig.co) is also a crowdfunding platform, but this one is curated, so your game has to be selected for the platform. It also allows contributors to become investors who get a return on game sales. In addition to providing the framework for crowdfunding campaigns, Fig provides other services to developers, including development advances and marketing support when the game is released. If you want to fund your game through Fig, you will need to apply for their program.

For crowdfunding, as with the bank, you must put together a business plan that includes information on budget, schedule, team members, and so on, and a full game pitch. While the bank is likely not interested in a full pitch, your potential crowdfunding investors are since they want to invest in games that excite them. See Chapter 7, "Pitching Your Game," for more information on what to include.

If the funding goal is met, you can access the funds pretty quickly after the campaign is over. Then, the fun really begins since you know you have a group of people eagerly waiting for your game to be launched.

Money raised this way is given in good faith by your contributors. You have convinced them that this is a viable game, it will be successfully completed, and they will get their expected rewards. You are accountable to them, even if things don't go according to plan. You need to provide your backers with regular updates on how things are going and be transparent about any obstacles along the way. If the game is never released, you may find yourself in a position where you have to refund all the money to your backers. Before signing up for any type of crowdfunding, make sure you understand all the risks involved and are prepared to be accountable for any issues that occur.

JASON DELLA ROCCA, CO-FOUNDER, EXECUTION LABS

The Opportunity Mindset: What Investors Are Looking For

Game developers are great problem solvers. Whether it is squashing a tricky bug deep in the enemy Artificial Intelligence (AI) logic or streamlining dialogue trees, developers are tackling problems constantly. A particularly challenging problem many developers face is the lack of development funds. When faced with such a problem, developers set off into the world to find those that can help with their lack of funds problem.

The sad reality is that no one cares about your lack of funds problem. Well, maybe your mom does…but it is unlikely that she can foot the bill for your amazing Multiplayer Online Battle Arena (MOBA) killer.

Investors fund opportunities. That may seem obvious enough, but it is a critical mindset shift needed by developers to pitch what they are doing as a legitimate opportunity to investors. There's a big difference between "Can you give me money so I can finish making my dream game?" and "The teaser trailer for my dream game already has a million views, this is your chance to invest in something that has fans eager to play."

If investors are looking to fund opportunities, how do we know what kinds of opportunities they are looking for? Different types of investors are looking for different types of opportunities. For starters, this requires you to think deeply about what kind of opportunity you have in hand. There are three main categories of opportunity: noncommercial projects, commercial projects, and companies.

Noncommercial Projects

To be clear, noncommercial means projects that are intentionally noncommercial and not failed commercial projects. Examples could include a game to raise money for cancer research or a game used to generate awareness of the lack of clean drinking water in Africa, or a purely artistic project for an art installation at a museum. The list goes on and on, and speaks to the power and diversity of the medium of games.

In these cases, the funding sources tend to be governments, foundations, arts councils, and the like. They want to provide funding for these projects to get made and usually run a submission-type process or will commission specific works.

If you are deliberately working on noncommercial projects that have some specific vision or goal that aligns with these types of funding agencies, then you can get funding for your work. It is a very diverse and broad category, and sources will vary widely depending on where in the world you reside.

Commercial Projects

Many developers will fall into this category. You are working on a cool ninja adventure game for Steam, and you are trying your best to build a community and create a commercially viable game. This usually implies that you are using a premium pricing model and treating your game as a fixed product (e.g., 20 levels or 15 hours of gameplay to complete the game). The commercial potential can usually be best represented as a linear revenue curve.

In this case, investors are putting money into your project and will take a share of future revenue in anticipation of the game generating more revenue than it cost to make. The largest source of project funding is game publishers. However, anyone providing funds against future revenue (like your uncle or certain government funding schemes) is a valid source of project investment.

Aside from their overall assessment of the marketability and revenue potential of your game, they are gaging your ability to deliver it (more or less) on time and on budget. So, if this is your first game, it is unlikely that a publisher will invest based on a pitch deck and some cool concept art. Your game will need to be much further along in order to convince them that you know what you are doing and that you can execute.

Companies

Game studios are another viable target for investment if you are working on something with highly scalable potential. Investors in this category tend to be angels or venture capital (VC) funds. They are looking to invest directly in your studio, handing your funds in exchange for a percentage of your shares. This means that the investors become part owners of your studio (usually with a minority stake). Since they are part owners of the studio, they care most about the long-term growth and value of the company.

For the economics of company investing to work, you need to develop projects that have exponential potential. This usually implies online, multiplayer/ social, highly streamable/watchable, "endless" gameplay that altogether drives a thriving community around your game. Think Fortnite, Rocket League, Counter-Strike, Hearthstone, and League of Legends. In theory, these games can be played forever and can generate unlimited revenue. Now, just because you are making a MOBA doesn't mean you will make limitless money…but at least you have that chance, if the game starts to take off.

In these cases, investors are looking at the quality of the leadership team and to what extent they believe you have the ability to build a scalable business. Since their payoff comes when they "exit" the business (i.e., when their shares get bought by a larger company or by a much bigger investor down the line, or when the company goes public), they need to believe that your project(s) and vision will grow the value of their shares over time.

In the end, no one cares that you need money. They all care about opportunities. Each investor defines opportunity differently: an opportunity to help with cancer research, an opportunity to ship a game on Steam and generate strong sales, an opportunity to back a studio with long-term vision to scale and build shareholder value. Starting the funding process by thinking about YOUR opportunity and which investors align with it best will dramatically increase the chance that you can successfully pitch your opportunity (and, in turn, solve your lack of funds problem). This sidebar barely scratches the surface of the complexities of funding. Search online for conference lectures and articles for more insight on the topic.

1.3.5 Investors

Investors exchange capital for equity in the game. This means that they own a percentage of the game sales, with the hope that the sales will pay back their investment, plus more. The percentage they own is negotiable but may be dependent on how much money they invest, or how much clout or other support they bring to the project. The benefit of working with investors is that they often provide more than just financial support. Since the value of their investment is directly tied to the success of the game, they will provide mentoring, business guidance, and connections to others who can help make the game successful. This section provides a general overview of some common types of investors.

1.3.5.1 Friends and Family
This is pretty self-explanatory. Friends and family may be the group you can convince most easily (or not) to invest in you. As with any investor, they will want to see a business plan and game pitch. They may provide funding with no strings attached, may loan money with favorable interest rates, or may decide to become actual investors with a share in the company.

1.3.5.2 Angel Investors
Angel investors are people who are passionate about what they invest in. They want to both invest money and have an emotional connection to the project since they are not solely driven by making a profit. Angel investors come in all forms, from friends and family to a small business owner looking to diversify to an independently wealthy person who loves games. Other game companies might also provide angel investment. For example, Chucklefish is a developer based in London that invests in other indie game companies. You can find out more on their blog: https://blog.chucklefish. org/funding/. Indie Fund is another example of a group that provides angel investments and support to independent game developers. You can find out more about Indie Fund on their website: https://indie-fund.com/

1.3.5.3 Venture Capital (VC)
Venture capitalists are more willing to invest in risky ventures, especially if there is potential for a huge return on investment. This type of funding is more difficult to secure as games are risky and less predictable than other

types of industries. Venture capitalists who are not familiar with games may also be less helpful from a strategic perspective. In addition to finding a worthy project to invest in, VC firms are also looking at who they are partnering with. They want to work with people who are open to receiving feedback and being coached. If you are not interested in compromising your vision or changing how you work, then VC funding might not be the best choice. But if you are willing to adjust your vision and plan based on their feedback, there is potential for a successful project and working relationship. Here are a few examples of VC firms who specialize in games:

- **Altered Ventures:** www.altered.vc/
- **Makers Fund:** https://makersfund.com/
- **London Venture Partners:** www.londonvp.com/

You can always do some research to find more.

1.3.5.4 Accelerators and Incubators

Accelerators and incubators are other investment resources. As far as similarities go, both of these groups offer more than just financial support. They offer office space, mentorship, education, connections, and a highly collaborative working environment. If you are part of an accelerator or incubator program, expect to go into an office on a regular basis to work with your team. This is likely a shared office space with other teams working on different projects. Admission to these programs is competitive, so, as with the other funding discussed, a business plan and compelling pitch are must-haves. The nice thing about accelerators and incubators is that you are working alongside other projects who have the same business goals. You can get a lot of support with this arrangement and have a ready supply of testers on hand.

While there are a lot of similarities, and the terms are sometimes used interchangeably, there are some key differences. An incubator is focused on supporting new companies. Imagine you have a strong concept and business plan, but you don't have a demo or any other proof of concept. The idea might also be risky in the short term but have potential as a long-term success if it can grow slowly and is focused on long-term goals. You can partner with an incubator to get support to develop your concept and refine your business plan. Incubators usually have government or educational support, and may not actually provide funding. Instead, they provide support, training, office space, and connections to get funding. NC Idea (http://ncidea.org/) is an example of a group that offers incubation assistance for start-ups. Their goal is to promote economic development in North Carolina.

Accelerators are for companies that are already operating as start-ups. They are past the "new company" phase and are in active development on their projects. They need financial and structural support so they can grow more quickly. Accelerators usually operate on a specific timeline in order to push companies to move faster. For example, the accelerator program may last for three months and culminate in some type of graduation, pitch process, or demo day. From there, companies may decide to provide further support, based on what they saw on graduation day. Accelerators will also take an equity stake in the company in the hopes that it will turn into a successful investment. GameFounders (www.gamefounders.com/) is an example of an accelerator that focuses specifically on games. There are more options out there, so do some research to find them.

1.3.6 Grants

Grants are a popular and sought-after form of funding because grant money doesn't have to be paid back, and there is not a group of investors expecting a return. Once you secure grant funding, you control how it is spent. The catch is that grants are only offered for a narrowly defined type of project, and they are highly competitive. Most grants are funded by government or academic institutions, and they are looking for projects that serve underrepresented groups, do something innovative, or provide some type of positive impact.

If you want to get a grant for your game, your chances are much higher if you are working on a game that has an educational focus. You will need to go through a rigorous grant-writing process, and again, you will have to detail your business plan and game pitch. The following organizations are just some of the places that offer grants:

- **Epic Megagrants:** www.unrealengine.com/en-US/megagrants
- **National Endowment for the Art (Artworks Media Art Grants):** www.arts.gov/grants-organizations/art-works/media-arts
- **European Games Developer Federation:** www.egdf.eu/funding/
- **IndieCade Foundation:** http://indiecade.org/
- **ESA:** www.esafoundation.org/application.asp
- **Lego Education:** https://education.lego.com/en-us/grants-and-funding
- **National Science Foundation:** www.nsf.gov/funding/aboutfunding.jsp
- **Institute of Education Sciences:** https://ies.ed.gov/sbir/
- **Games for Change:** www.gamesforchange.org/

RAY CROWELL, DIRECTOR OF VENTURE CREATION, SAVANNAH COLLEGE OF ART AND DESIGN (SCAD), FINANCING RESOURCES

When considering how you are going to finance your game, you really need to dive in and learn the lexicon. There are constraints, restraints, and risks, beginning with how you even structure your game company (e.g., choosing an LLC vs a corporation). You need to understand capitalization or "cap" table management, how to calculate valuation, and generally how to understand what favorable terms mean to you in the short and long term. There's an exhaustive list of books and blogs to read, podcasts to listen to, and influencers to follow on social media.

Follow These:

@inflectionconf by @FrankDenbow
https://medium.com/@harryalford3
https://medium.com/@melissaperri
https://blog.leanstack.com/
https://a16z.com/
https://blog.asmartbear.com/
http://www.onstartups.com/
www.forentrepreneurs.com/

Listen Here:

www.thetwentyminutevc.com/category/podcast/
https://a16z.com/podcasts/
www.gimletmedia.com/the-pitch
https://marketingschool.io/

Read These:

Running Lean and Scaling Lean by Ash Maurya (Portfolio, 2016)
The Four Steps to the Epiphany by Steve Blank (K&S Ranch, 2013)
Rocket Surgery Made Easy by Steve Krug (New Riders, 2009)
The Principles of Product Development Flow by Donald Reinertsen (Celeritas
    Publishing, 2009)
Inbound Marketing by Dharmesh Shah and Brian Halligan (John Wiley &
    Sons, 2014)
Traction: Get a Grip on Your Business by Gino Wickman (BenBella Books, 2012)
Designing for Growth by Jeanne Liedtka and Tim Ogilvie (Columbia Business
    School Publishing, 2011)
Value Proposition Design by Alex Osterwalder (Wiley, 2015)
Rework by Jason Fried and David Heinemeier Hansson (Currency, 2010)
Shoe Dog: A Memoir by the Creator of Nike by Phil Knight (Scribner, 2016)

1.3.7 Early Access

Early access is a model that is specific to games and shouldn't be relied on as the main source of funding. The upside to this model is that you can release your game before it is fully debugged or has all the features fully implemented. This allows you to start generating revenue sooner, have some flexibility with your finances, and get player feedback on how to make the final version more enjoyable. Early access should not be considered if you don't have a playable version of the game. If this is the case, you should explore other funding options.

With this model, you must have a playable game that is worth the price the players pay to access it. Players know that the game is buggy but playable and that all the features are not fully implemented. Players enjoy this because it allows them to be more involved in the development process; they can provide feedback and suggestions, and help debug. Once players have access, they won't need to make additional payments to get updated versions of the game.

Minecraft and Subnautica are examples of games that were successfully funded this way. Before Minecraft became a billion-dollar franchise, it was initially released in 2009 on a feedback forum called TIGSource. Eventually, the developer moved it to a dedicated website where people could pay to download beta versions, and the rest is history. Subnautica debuted as an Early Access game on Steam in 2014, with the full version released in 2018.

There are several options for developers who want to use the Early Access model. The most popular one is Steam, which is an online publishing and distribution platform for games on PC and Mac. Participating in the Steam Early access program is not hard; you can find out more at their website. You will need to pay them a percentage from each copy sold, so account for that in your financial plan. Microsoft, Sony, and Google also offer Early Access programs. You can get more information from their developer's websites or by talking to your account managers.

DEVELOPER WEBSITES

Android Developers: https://developer.android.com/distribute/console/
Apple Developers: https://developer.apple.com/
Epic Games Store: www.epicgames.com/store/en-US/about
Humble Bundle Developers: https://www.humblebundle.com/developer
Microsoft Developers: www.xbox.com/en-US/developers
Nintendo Developers: https://developer.nintendo.com/
Sony Developers: https://partners.playstation.net/
Steam: https://partner.steamgames.com/doc/home

1.3.8 Publishers

Finally, it's time to talk about publisher funding. For a long time, working with a publisher was the only way to make a game and get it distributed. This has changed dramatically in the 21st century, and as you can see from the previous sections, there are now many alternatives to publisher funding.

Publishers like Activision Blizzard and Electronic Arts have defined their release calendar years in advance—much like movie studios. They have a set number of major releases in any given year, along with smaller releases throughout the year. Internal development teams are typically responsible for creating the blockbuster games, while independent game developers may get publisher funding to create some of the other games. There are large and small publishers out there, and they are all looking for good content they can fund, market, and distribute. While the publisher may provide funds up-front, they will expect a percentage of the game receipts in order to recoup their investment and make a profit.

There are huge benefits to working with a publisher. Essentially, you are partnering with them to create, market, and distribute your game. Chapter 2, "Developer and Publisher Overview," goes into more detail on the role of the publisher and what to expect out of this relationship. As with other types of funding, the publisher has an expectation that you will deliver on what you signed up for. When you pitch a game, they will expect to see— you guessed it—a business plan and game pitch. In many case, developers may also expect to see a demo of the game. Consider it your calling card to demonstrate what your team is capable of doing.

There are a few things to consider before partnering with a publisher. First, consider who will own the intellectual property (IP) of the game. If a publisher decides to finance a game, they may also want to own the IP so they can continue to create sequels and content updates for the game, even with different development teams. Second, understand that the publisher is pretty involved in the development process. They will have opinions and feedback on the game, and some of the feedback needs to be implemented, even if you don't agree with it.

You can connect with publishers at conferences, such as E3 (www.e3expo. com) or the Game Developers Conference (www.gdconf.com). Look at who publishes some of your favorite games, and try to make connections with someone in the business development department or the studio. Going to game development meetups and participating in game jams and festivals are also good ways to connect with publishers.

1.4 Revenue Models

Now that you know a bit about funding, it's time to think about how you can recoup your investment. Most developers expect to sell their game once it is done, and the profits will be used to pay for the initial funding. If the game is successful, the profits can also pay for future funding. The chosen revenue model (aka monetization) will have an impact on the game design, and Chapter 3, "Getting Started," has more information on how. This section focuses on a high-level review of the most common revenue models.

1.4.1 One-Time Payment

For a long time, games were sold like any other item—you went to the store, paid for the game, and took it home. These days, this is just one way in which to monetize a game, and you don't even need to go to the store since most games are now digitally distributed. Section 1.5 goes into more detail on various distribution options.

A one-time payment is when a set amount of money is charged for each copy sold. This makes sales forecasting easier since there is a direct correlation between selling more games and making more money. This model is also the most straightforward—people pay money, get a game, and own it forever. If a game is stand-alone and won't have additional content later, a one-time payment is a good way to go. You don't have to alter the design significantly (as you need to for a free-to-play game), and you don't need to worry about constantly providing new content to keep the players coming back (as subscription games need to do).

The downside of charging up-front for a stand-alone game is that not everyone will buy it, and it may not sell as many copies as anticipated. There is a lot of free content available, and paid games have to compete with this. The game has to be enticing enough for players to part with their hard-earned cash. If you have an interesting concept that is well executed and are charging the right price, players will likely invest in the experience.

1.4.2 Subscription

A subscription-based game is one where players are charged a monthly fee to access the game content. This model depends on getting and maintaining an active base of subscribers. The content needs to be valuable enough for players to want to continue paying the monthly fee. World of Warcraft is an example of a subscription-based game. For games like World of Warcraft, it is important to provide ways for players to invest deeply in character creation and leveling so that they continue to find value in paying for the monthly subscription.

Other types of subscription-based services are modeled after Netflix. A monthly fee is charged, and you can access an entire library of games. Services like GameFly (www.gamefly.com) are based on this model. Sony and Microsoft also offer a monthly game subscription service. If your game is part of this service, you will get some percentage of revenue (this is, in addition to other places where you sell the game).

1.4.3 Downloadable Content (DLC)

DLC is when additional content is created for a released game. It is used to add new character outfits, story lines, or features to the game. If the game is subscription-based, the DLC is made available at no extra charge. If the game is a stand-alone purchase, the publisher may offer the DLC for free or charge for it, depending on how much new content it contains.

DLC is a good way to extend the life of the game. It can also be cost-effective to develop because you can mitigate the technical risks by simply adding new art, audio, or quests (for example) to an existing code base. This can reduce the amount of development effort and testing needed. Sea of Thieves uses the DLC model. They initially released the game for a specific price and then offered (at least at the time this book was written) the DLC for free.

Some game publishers utilize a variant of DLC, referred to as "episodic" content. Episodic games are released as smaller, discrete installments of a larger game, and players pay for each episode. For example, Telltale Games published the Walking Dead this way. Players purchased the first episode, which had less content and cost less than a full game. The hope was that players would enjoy the first episode and would purchase each episode that followed until they had experienced the entire game. Episodic content can be a good model if you have a strong, story-based game that can be divided into chapters. You can also test the waters before making a huge development commitment—if the first episode does not sell well, you can assess whether spending time and money on developing the second episode makes financial sense.

1.4.4 Free-to-Play

Free-to-play is a model that's become extremely attractive in the past few years. Players can download the game and play for free, with the revenue coming from microtransactions. Microtransactions (also known as MTX) are when players can purchase items, such as cosmetics or XP boosts, in the game for a small amount of money. Usually, these items are not required to play the game but instead enhance the gameplay experience by providing new content or a faster way to complete objectives. Microtransactions, if done well, can be extremely lucrative. The key to making money with this model is to have strong gameplay loops that mesh well with the microtransactions. Out of all the financial models discussed, this one will have the most impact on the gameplay mechanics. It is estimated that Fortnite, one of the most profitable free-to-play games ever, made over a billion dollars in its first year just by selling character skins and other cosmetics that have no impact on the actual gameplay. League of Legends and Candy Crush are other examples of successful free-to-play games. Most free-to-play games don't have that level of financial success. It can be very difficult to profit from microtransactions since only 2%–3% of your entire player base is likely to make an in-game purchase. So, if you don't have millions of players in the game, it becomes harder to make a profit.

One of the downsides of the free-to-play model is that there is a stigma that these types of games are cheaply made, have shallow gameplay mechanics, and rely on a few big spenders (aka Whales) to make money. This may have been the case when this model first emerged, but games such as Fortnite and League of Legends show that this model works well with AAA quality games. There are also concerns that free-to-play models lead to pay-to-win scenarios, meaning that players can pay for additional skills or gameplay advantages. This makes these players more dominant in competitive online games and gives them a distinct advantage over players who aren't spending money.

Developers considering a free-to-play model need to spend time iterating on the gameplay mechanics to create an experience that doesn't take advantage of players or reduce the importance of game skill. There are several useful books and websites that provide information on the best practices for designing for this transaction model, so do your research to understand how to best utilize this model with your game.

1.5 Platforms

A game platform refers to the hardware on which the game is played, such as a computers, consoles, or mobile devices. Each platform type has differences that will impact the design and monetization of your game, such as controller inputs, technical limitations, and screen size.

Each platform will also have a different operating system, based on the hardware. For example, Microsoft and Sony each have console hardware, so their individual software requirements are going to be different from each other. This also means that if you want to release a game for a Microsoft console, you will need to work directly with Microsoft to get the game published and distributed.

When games are released on multiple platforms, think about what design elements work best with a given platform, and design accordingly. The game should provide a consistent experience on all platforms but also take into account the platform differences in order to provide the best experience.

1.5.1 Personal Computer (PC)

PC games are played on a personal computer with a Windows, Linux, or Mac Operating System (OS). PCs have a lot of processing power, random access memory (RAM), and hard drive storage, which allows PC games to display more realistic graphics and animation. The keyboard and mouse input system allows for a lot of player-input control since there are more buttons to map actions, and the keyboard and mouse configuration allow for more accurate targeting and shooting. PC games have the lowest barrier to entry for developers since they are easily accessible and don't require permission from a third party to develop on it.

The operating system of your PC also impacts which games you can play. Common operating systems are Windows, Mac, and Linux. If your game is going to support all of these operating systems, you will need to include this in your production plan as additional engineering is needed to accommodate each of these platforms. The good news is that if you are using a third-party engine, some of work to support multiple platforms is done by the engine.

1.5.2 Console

A console is hardware that plugs into the television and utilizes a controller for the main gameplay input. There are options to attach a keyboard and mouse to consoles, but most people play with the controller. Development and distribution of console games is regulated by the console manufacturers Sony, Microsoft, and Nintendo. When developing for consoles, you must take into account players' using a controller instead of the point and click interface of a PC. Processing power is more limited on consoles, so a fair amount of engineering work is required to create a game that runs within the memory limits, has good graphics, and runs smoothly at a high frame rate. When converting a PC game to the console platform, you will need to account for these types of differences.

1.5.3 Mobile

The mobile platform includes phones and tablets with touch controls. As with console, the technology limitations impact graphics and performance. You may need to have lower resolution art assets, so they are small enough to be used with a mobile game. The touch interface comes with its own set of challenges—you have to rely on taps, swipes, and tilts to interact with the game interface. The mobile user interface (UI) must be more simplified so that players can engage with it more intuitively. The small screen size also needs to be accounted for, which means reducing the UI elements as much as possible. In addition, mobile games are designed around shorter play sessions, so the player can pick up and play a few minutes and put it down just as quickly.

Like PCs and consoles, the mobile platform has different operating systems. The two most popular are iOS and Android. iOS is the Apple operating system and is used in iPhones and iPads. Android is the Google operating system and is used in a variety of devices. If you are releasing games on mobile platforms, you will need to distribute them through the digital storefronts managed by Apple and Google in order to get them in front of your audience.

1.5.4 Virtual and Augmented Reality

The VR platform requires some type of headset that completely encloses your eyes so that you can become fully immersed in an artificial digital environment. VR setups require more space so that players have room to move when they are interacting with the game. VR games need to account for different controller functionality, and some of the same memory and performance limitations that consoles have. As with consoles, there are differences in the VR hardware, so if a game is going to work on multiple types of VR setups, then multiple ports of the game are needed. VR games have their own set of design challenges, particularly in how the players interact with the game and the immersive environment.

AR games overlay audio and visual elements onto a real-world setting to create an interactive experience. This is a different experience than VR, in which everything in the game world is artificial. Pokémon Go is an example of an AR game—the game uses real-time locations and then overlays the Gyms and Pokémon into the locations. AR games tend to enhance the players' real-world experience with the addition of gameplay.

1.6 Distribution Options

As with financing, there are a myriad of distribution options that don't require a traditional publisher. In the past, developers needed a publisher to actually create the boxed product—replicating discs, printing boxes, assembling the pieces, and distributing it to stores. This type of distribution was cost prohibitive for a developer without a publisher. These days, digital distribution has become the norm, and boxed product is becoming less important. If developers have access to digital distribution platforms, it is much easier for them to self-publish or partner up with a smaller publisher who can support the distribution and marketing efforts.

Most of these distribution options are offered by third parties and will take some percentage of sale in order to offset their costs. At the time this book was written, the typical revenue split was 70% to developers and 30% to the distribution platform or publishing partner.

1.6.1 Steam

We discussed Steam earlier when talking about Early Access. Steam is the most accessible platform for PC and Mac developers—large publishers, small publishers, and self-published developers launch games daily. Games distributed through Steam have access to millions of gamers looking for entertainment. In addition to game distribution, Steam also provides access to payment methods, social features, discussion boards, and other things developers need to successfully market and distribute their games. Steam takes a percentage of the game sales. You can't launch console or mobile games on Steam; this platform is only for PC and Mac games. Anyone can sign up for a Steam account and get a page set up for their game pretty quickly. The submission process is straight-forward, and the game does not need to comply with a specific set of third-party technical requirements. The developer controls when to submit and launch the game.

1.6.2 Epic Games Store

Epic Games Store's digital storefront was launched in 2018, so it is not as feature-laden as Steam at the time of this writing. As with Steam, this storefront is for PC and Mac games only. Epic is adding features to the store on a regular basis, so it will eventually have equivalent features and functionality to Steam. The biggest advantage to publishing a game on the Epic store is the revenue split. When it was launched, the typical revenue split was 88% to the developers and 12% to Epic. In addition, if you used the Unreal Engine for your game, the revenue split was 93% to the developer and 7% to Epic. At the time of this writing, getting approved to launch a game on the Epic store is more difficult than launching on Steam, but as more features and functionality are added, this may change.

1.6.3 Third-Party Storefronts

Apple, Google, Microsoft, Sony, and Nintendo all support digital storefronts that cater to their specific platform. Like Steam, they provide a full infrastructure for marketing and distributing games. The difference is that you must apply to become a licensed developer on these platforms, which can take some time. Once you are a licensed developer, you get access to developer-specific hardware to aid in development. You also get access to the SDKs, which contain software development tools used for developing games on a specific platform. Each company has their own proprietary SDK.

In addition, there are platform-specific requirements that the game must fulfill before it can be approved for distribution. Most of the technical requirements (TRCs or TCRs) involve specifics on how the game handles platform-specific content, such as official terminology, common system messages, and friends' functionality. Once the game is ready for distribution on one of these platforms, you submit it for approval. The game is reviewed and tested against the TRCs. If the game passes these checks, it is approved for distribution. If the game fails these checks, the developer fixes the issues and resubmits. This approval process can take several weeks, and if the game has to be resubmitted, more time is added to the launch schedule. Like Steam, these storefronts will take a percentage of the game sales, which can be as high as 30%.

1.6.4 Humble Bundle

Other types of digital distribution include Humble Bundle. Humble Bundle is a digital distribution platform for games, books, and other digital content, which also contributes money to charity. Several products are bundled together at a flexible price. Buyers can choose how much they wish to pay and how the money is divided between charity, the developers, and the company. If you are interested in participating in this program, you need to contact Humble Bundle as they only accept a limited number of games per year. Visit their website: www.humblebundle.com/developer for more information.

1.6.5 Self-Distribution

There is also the option to set up your own website for distribution. At minimum, the website must be able to accept online payments and offer an easy way for players to download the game. Including areas for CS, community forums, and news gives players the resources they need to get technical support and to participate in the community. One of the biggest benefits of distributing a game on a stand-alone website is that a third party isn't receiving a percentage of game sales. However, the money spent to maintain this website might offset that savings.

The other downside to self-distribution is that it will be harder for players to find out about your game since it won't be visible on any of the mainstream digital platforms, like Steam, PlayStation Network, or Xbox Live. You will need to create a robust PR and marketing plan in order for your game to stand out against the competition. If you don't have adequate funds for marketing, this will be challenging. Even if you do have enough money for a strong marketing campaign, it will be difficult to cut through the noise of the games releasing on the other digital platforms.

1.6.6 Boxed Product

Before digital distribution, boxed product was the only way to distribute a game. Boxed product is less popular now because it is more efficient and cost-effective to distribute a game digitally. Boxed product distribution is more expensive since you have to pay for cost of goods (COGs), which is essentially the cost of replicating a disc, printing a box, printing paper inserts, and shrink-wrapping. In addition, there is a cost associated with shipping product to the stores, and in some cases, a stocking fee is needed to get the game on store shelves. Boxed product distribution is most accessible to major publishers who can support the additional costs. This is not something an independent developer can easily do. When you work with a publisher, they will usually pay for the COGs, distribution, and stocking costs. This is another benefit of using a publisher to get your game to market.

1.7 Conclusion

Understanding how games are financed and distributed is useful when embarking on a journey to make a game. Some of the game design and development choices will be directly impacted by this. If you are an independent developer with a small budget, participating in an Early Access program might be the best way to get your game out there and generating revenue. If you are a larger developer that is funded by a publisher, you likely have the luxury of spending more time on development, creating a game that will be distributed on multiple platforms, and getting a large marketing push. Having a wide range of revenue and distribution models allows for a variety of funding, platform, and distribution combinations, so that game teams of all sizes, budgets, and publisher connections can make and release a game. The next chapter delves more deeply into the roles of the developers and the publishers.

CHAPTER 2

Developer and Publisher Overview

2.1 Introduction

Developers and publishers each contribute something important to the process of launching a game—developers are responsible for turning a concept into a playable game, and publishers are responsible for the distribution and marketing, and sometimes financing. The functions vary for publishing and development, depending on the type of game, the team size, the budget, and the overall goals. For example, Stardew Valley was developed solely by Eric Barone over the course of 4 years with support from a small publisher. Eric made the game, and the publisher supported him with marketing and distribution. On the other hand, Riot Games, the developer and publisher of League of Legends, has thousands of people focused on the development and publishing effort. With a large team like this, Riot can have a development team focus specifically on creating and launching a single hero for the game, while another team can focus on creating some other game features. From a production standpoint, understanding the functions of all parts of the game team is critical since the producer is responsible for wrangling both development and publishing tasks.

2.2 Function of Developer

A developer is typically focused solely on making the game, which comprises art, design, engineering, audio, UX, and QA testing. Their day-to-day tasks involve designing and implementing game features, and they have little contact with the publishing departments. The exception to this are discipline leads as their input and expertise are relied upon to help publishing build a strong marketing and release pipeline for the game. In a well-integrated game team, the developers work collaboratively and rely on each other's strengths to make the best choices for the game. Engineers, artists, and designers work very closely together to make sure the game is cohesive and fun, and hits a specific quality bar. The input and feedback from all these disciplines working together is invaluable in making the best game possible.

The producer is somewhat of a hybrid since their function sits between the developers and the publishers, and is focused on bridging the communication between the two. For more information on functions in the game industry, and advice on how to learn the necessary skills for these functions, check out *Surviving Game School and the Game Industry After* by Michael Lynch and Adrian Earle (2018).

2.2.1 Art

Artists create the concept art, animations, 3D models, 2D textures, and any other graphic elements in the game. As technology becomes more powerful, artists are able to create anything from simple 2D textures for a platform game to fully immersive virtual worlds. They also create all the amazing special effects that are necessary to create "wow" effects, such as explosions, power-ups, and water droplets. If a game is art intensive and needs a lot of content, the artists on the team might outnumber the other team members by 2 to 1. For example, Fortnite releases new character skins and accessories on a regular basis, and all of these need to go through a full art production cycle before they are ready for the game. This includes creating concept art, 3D models, textures, animations, and special effects, which means the art team needs to be large enough to have multiple art assets in active development at the same time.

If the development team is small, the artists on the team may be generalists, which will mean that they have the ability to create different types of art assets. They might be able to create a character concept and have the skills necessary to take it from an image to a fully animated 3D character. For large development teams, artists may choose to specialize in an area and become very skilled at it. Setting up an art pipeline for a large team is more efficient if different people are focused on different parts of the pipeline. The most common art roles are the following (note that some companies may use different titles for similar roles):

- **Art Director:** They create and manage the artistic vision. They work with other project leads or directors to shape the overall scope and requirements for the game from an artistic standpoint.

- **Lead Artist:** They manage the day-to-day work of the art team. They provide feedback and mentoring, which allows the art director to stay focused on the creative elements. In some cases, the lead artist will also contribute content to the game (if there is time). They work with other project leads or directors to shape the overall scope and requirements for the game from an artistic standpoint.
- **Concept Artist:** They create concepts for game objects, environments, and characters that the other artists use as a reference when making the game assets.
- **World Builder:** They build the game world that the characters and objects inhabit. This is sometimes considered a design position because the level layout has a direct impact on the gameplay (and vice versa).
- **2D Artist or Texture Artist:** They focus on creating all the 2D art or textures for the 3D models. They may specialize in a particular area, such as vehicles, environments, or characters.
- **3D Artist or Modeler:** They build all the 3D models in the game. As with 2D artists, they may specialize in a particular type of area.
- **Animator:** They focus on creating all the animations in the game, including fully rendered animations (highest quality) and in-engine animations (used for interactive sequences). An animator may choose to focus on animation or rigging, and may also focus on a particular type of animation (facial, characters, objects).
- **UI Artist:** They create the art needed for the user interface (UI), including buttons, boxes, and drop-down lists, and other elements that appear in the game.
- **Technical Artist:** They focus on the technical side of asset creation. They work closely with the engineers to push the technology so that more impressive art can be included in the game. They also help the engineers build art tools that can streamline an artist's workflow.
- **Marketing Artist:** They focus on creating assets used by publishing and marketing, including logos, website design, key art, gameplay video, and anything else marketing needs.

2.2.2 Design

The main function of the designer is to create an engaging and immersive gameplay experience. Like artists, there are all types of designers—some are generalists, and some are specialists. They are responsible for creating all the "verbs" in the game, that is, things a player can do and interact with. This includes the control scheme, game systems (combat, trading, leveling up, etc.), narrative and story, character backgrounds and personalities, missions and objectives, level layouts, and so on.

You've heard the saying about too many cooks spoiling the soup. Designers are in the soup pot and receive a lot of feedback while making the game from all corners of the company, including UX Lab, QA, other team members, publishing, and senior management. Designers must be skilled in addressing feedback and incorporating what works for the game and makes it better. There are several types of designers. Here are some common roles:

- **Creative Director:** They create and manage the overall vision for the player experience. They focus on carrying this vision throughout the entire game. They work closely with the art director. They work with other project leads or directors to shape the overall scope and requirements for the game from a design standpoint.
- **Lead Designer:** They manage the design team and their day-to-day work. They provide feedback and mentoring. If there is time, they may also create art assets. They work with other project leads or directors to shape the overall scope and requirements for the game from a design standpoint.
- **Level Designer:** They create the level layout, mission, and objectives that the player experiences in the game. They work closely with the World Builder to bring all the art and design pieces together.
- **Narrative Designer:** They create the characters, setting, and story. They work closely with the Level Designer on the game missions to ensure that everything is narratively cohesive.
- **Writer:** They specifically write all the dialogues and in-game text. Sometimes, the Narrative Designer is also a writer (and vice versa).
- **Systems Designer:** They design any game-wide systems, such as combat, scoring, character skill progression, and AI design.

2.2.3 Engineering

Engineers (aka programmers) take the designs and turn them into something playable. They are responsible for creating the technology for every aspect of the game, including physics, performance, AI, graphics, scripting tools, audio, lighting, player movement, and so on. They also work closely with the art team to create technical solutions for enhancing the game's artistic style. For example, they create technology that makes it possible for game characters to leave real-time footprints in a snowy environment. Without engineers, a game design is more difficult to translate from an analog format to a digital one. Here are some of the common engineering roles on a development team:

- **Technical Director:** They define and communicate the technical goals and standards for the game. They work with other project leads or directors to shape the overall scope and requirements for the game from a technical standpoint.
- **Lead Engineer:** They direct and manage the engineering team. They work closely with the Technical Director. They work with other project leads or directors to shape the overall scope and requirements for the game from a technical standpoint.
- **Network Engineer:** They focus on networking and multiplayer features.
- **Graphics Engineer:** They specialize in getting the most out of the game graphics from a performance and pipeline creation standpoint. They work closely with technical artists.

- **AI Engineer:** They create the AI behaviors of the NPCs. They work closely with system designers to define this behavior.
- **UI Engineer:** They create the functional UI screens. They work closely with the UI artists and UX designer.
- **Tools Engineer:** They work with the development team to create different tools for the development pipeline: for example, a tool that designers can use to create stats for an in-game character and import these into the game.
- **Build Engineer:** They create the tools and pipeline for checking things into the game and then compile game builds. They will also automate the build creation process as much as possible.

2.2.4 Audio

If you play a game with the sound turned off, you quickly realize how much audio enhances the experience. Audio is one way to provide the player with feedback on what they are doing in the game and is an important component of the player's enjoyment. Large game development teams usually have an in-house audio team that handles all aspects of sound design and implementation. Smaller teams may choose to outsource some of this work if the game doesn't have a lot of audio needs. Common audio positions include:

- **Audio Engineer:** They focus on the technical aspects of sound design and implementation. They work closely with the audio designer.
- **Sound Designer:** They design the sound effects, music, and voiceover for the game. They work closely with the writer and the narrative and level designers. They also process and implement the audio assets in the game.
- **Composer:** They compose the music for the game. They may also be responsible for licensing music instead of creating original content.

2.2.5 User Experience (UX)

UX is mainly about making sure that the design and business intentions are experienced as intended by the target audience of a product, system, or service. UX practices employ knowledge of cognitive science and psychology, as well as user research methodologies (e.g., playtests and analytics), to ensure that the game has good usability and engaging. This encompasses the player's experience with the game and how they interact with the systems and content. It also includes the signs and feedback that occur when the player takes an action in the game. For example, if the player pushes the correct button, they should receive positive feedback on this action, perhaps in the form of a color change, sound, or both. For more details about game UX, please see Chapter 15. Common UX positions include:

- **UX Designer:** They design the layout, flow, and functionality of all the UI screens and player interactions in the game. They work closely with designers and artists.

- **UX Researcher:** They focus on researching how well the game is meeting its UX objectives. They develop research plans and UX tests, and recruit people to come in and play the game. After the UX tests, they analyze the data, extract insights from it, and create a list of recommended UX changes for the game development team.

2.2.6 Quality Assurance (QA)

QA testers are the last stronghold between the development team and the players. In an ideal world, nothing is released to the players without being thoroughly tested by the QA team. They focus on finding any bugs, glitches, or errors that would negatively impact the player's experience. They are somewhat unsung heroes, who spend countless hours playing the same parts of the game over and over to ensure everything is working as intended. The size of the QA team depends on the amount of content that needs to be tested and how many platforms need to be tested concurrently. QA teams may be subdivided to focus on specific areas of the game. For example, one QA team might focus specifically on testing the UI, another team might focus on the gameplay in a specific set of levels, and another group might test a specific platform. Chapter 18, "QA Testing," goes into more specifics about how to organize testing as part of the production cycle. Typically, the main QA roles are:

- **QA Lead:** They manage the day-to-day efforts of the QA team. They create the testing plan and organize the QA team to execute it. They work with other project leads or directors to shape the overall scope and requirements for the game from a testing standpoint.
- **QA Tester:** They check the game functionality against the test plan. Also, they do playtesting and ad hoc testing to uncover things that players may discover after the game is released.

2.3 Function of Producer

Since this book focuses on production, understanding what a producer does in more detail is useful. Production, like any other discipline, is a craft that can be learned and improved upon with experience. Some people may be more suited to the role than others because production requires a strong combination of both organizational and leadership skills. The producer works closely with people by helping them get the necessary tools and resources; guiding groups towards consensus; resolving conflict; and, in some cases, addressing performance issues. If you don't enjoy working directly with people, the producer role may not be a good fit for you.

So, what does a producer do? There's no set definition as each team may define the production role and responsibilities differently. At the most basic level, a producer pulls together all the disparate parts needed to develop and launch a game, keeps the team on track, and removes any obstacles that prevent the team from hitting their goals. They are also the information hub for any questions people have about what's going on with the game, the plan for future content, or how feedback is going to impact the project. A producer's job is never the same on any given day as there are always unexpected fires to be extinguished. Creating a schedule and budget are a small part of the job; these are the tools the producer uses to track progress. While it may be easy to think of the producer as a project manager marking tasks off the list and harassing people about deadlines, if the role is done well, it is much more than that.

Producers are not usually responsible for creating game assets, prototyping features, or writing stories because they are primarily responsible for keeping the team motivated and on track. Oftentimes, their feedback on design, technical, or artistic aspects of the game is a lower priority since they are not deeply involved in some of the creative or technical decisions. However, if a game decision involves something relating to overall scope, schedule, and budget, the producer's informed opinion holds a lot of weight. In situations where parties disagree about what the best decision is, the producer is expected to gather information from stakeholders, synthesize this information, make a recommendation, vet the feasibility of the recommendation with the leads, and then communicate the final decision.

Sometimes, there are hybrid producers who also do design, engineering, or art. This can create some interesting conflicts as it may be hard for a designer to put on a production hat and reduce the scope of the project by cutting a feature. So, if you are a producer with another role on the team, be aware of what biases you could bring to making production decisions.

BEN SMITH, SR. PRODUCER (PARTNER DEVELOPMENT), PUBLISHING PRODUCER CHALLENGES

As the publisher producer, the hardest thing to do is appropriately represent BOTH sides of the project: publisher and developer. Go too far towards repping the publisher's needs and goals, and you're not a value add. Go too far towards repping the developer's needs and goals, and you're going to be accused of going native and lose credibility with the publisher. I'll be honest—I'm not sure I ever managed to completely walk this tightrope. The only advice I can give is that you need to develop and focus on relationships in both organizations to an equal extent and do whatever it takes to add value to them both. Ultimately, you're responsible for the product, even if you're not building it directly, and both the publisher and the developer need your help to make it. Otherwise, your role wouldn't exist.

2.3.1 Background and Training

In general, producers have a particular area in which they are most skilled, such as managing technical projects, managing people, improving processes, managing creative groups, and so on. Some producers started out as engineers, designers, artists, or QA testers, and transitioned over to a production role (likely because someone observed that they were good with people and getting things organized). Some producers worked in a different industry, usually in a project management role, and were able to transfer their skills to the game industry. So, while they come from a variety of backgrounds, these are some common skills every producer should have:

- **Leadership:** Do you understand the game's vision, and are you able to communicate this to the team, keep them focused on the goals, build consensus, and motivate them to do their best work? Are you empathetic? Do you listen to your team? Are you able to take a risk, make an unpopular choice, or make things better than when you found them? These are the skills a strong leader has.
- **Communication:** Are you able to explain things clearly, diplomatically, and in a timely fashion? Are you able to give constructive feedback and deliver bad news in a transparent fashion? Do you know the different audiences you are communicating with, and do you tailor your message to them?
- **Organization:** Are you able to build consistent processes that are easy for people to follow? Can you break down all the steps needed to accomplish the goal? Are you able to track all the details and actions that are needed to complete each phase of the game? Are you able to create a plan that details what needs to be done, how long it will take, and how much it will cost?
- **Serving Others:** Are you serving your team, or do you expect them to serve you? Do you empower the team to make their own decisions and work autonomously? Are you open to suggestions and feedback, and do you make changes based on this? Do you create a working environment for your team that allows them to be their most productive?

As far as formal training goes, there are very few educational programs geared specifically towards a career in game production. There are a lot of game design, interactive media, and game technology degrees available, and the list of schools offering these degrees is growing. If there isn't a specific game production degree at your chosen institution, studying one of these other areas is useful. The more you can learn about how games are made, the more effective you will be as a producer. If you have a deep understanding of how to program a game, you will be better prepared to solve some of the technical issues your team will face. Oftentimes, degree programs will culminate in a final group project, where you can take on the producer functions to gain valuable experience.

There are other ways to improve your production skills and knowledge besides going to school. Some of these things include:

- **Attending conferences:** There are a lot of game conferences every year. The largest one is the Game Developers Conference (www.gdconf.com), held for one week each spring. Here, hundreds of speakers talk about all aspects of making games. Conferences are also a great place to network and meet fellow producers. They are always ready to swap techniques and war stories. Refer to the "Resources and Tools" appendix for a list of other conferences.

- **Studying the game industry:** Play games, so you are aware of the latest trends. Become familiar with common game development tools and technologies. Stay up to date with what's happening in the industry, including sales figures, hot topics, cultural shifts, and new platforms and technologies. Check the "Resources and Tools" appendix for a list of websites and other information.

- **Attending management training:** This includes both project management and people management classes. Check with your HR department if you are interested in external training as the company may pay for it if it's relevant to your job. Continuing education programs affiliated with universities may offer classes. There are also several companies that specialize in project management and leadership training. A quick Google search can be helpful in finding them.

- **Improving public speaking ability:** A producer is often talking in front of groups—whether it is at team meetings, in front of senior management for review, or while on a PR tour. Good public speakers exude confidence and leadership. If you are uncomfortable with talking in front of people, you can join a group like Toastmasters International (www.toastmasters.org) to meet other people and practice your public speaking.

2.3.2 Career Progression

Production is a career in which you can start out in an entry-level position and work your way up to a more senior production role. As you progress up the career ladder, you will figure out where your strengths are and choose a particular focus. You may also become skilled or knowledgeable enough in another aspect of game development and transition to a different role on the team, leaving the production role open for someone else.

The following are the basic stepping stones on a production career track. Keep in mind that companies may have different names and different requirements for getting promoted. It's best to check with your manager on what is needed to advance from one position to the next:

- **Production Assistant (PA):** This is an entry-level position. Little production experience is needed, just a willingness to learn, be helpful, and take on a wide variety of tasks as directed. The main focus of this role is to be an extra pair of hands for the production team: someone who can help schedule meetings, take notes, get status updates, organize playtests, and do whatever else is needed. In this role, you get exposed to different areas of game development, so it's a great learning experience. Your work tasks will shift daily as PAs are most effective when focused on short-term tasks and whatever is needed that day.

- **Associate Producer (AP):** This position has more responsibility and works closely with the producer on managing the day-to-day activities of the team. They may be tasked with producing specific parts of the game, such as the localizations or voiceover recordings. They usually have 1–3 years of production experience. They are mostly focused on what is needed that week or over the next few weeks, so they will have a set of regular responsibilities, such as running daily stand-ups, doing risk analysis, and setting up production pipelines. They may also manage PAs.

- **Producer:** This person usually manages an entire development team and has 3–8 years of experience. Their focus is on executing the plan. If the team is especially large, several producers may split responsibilities across it. For example, one producer might be responsible for all the art content, another might be responsible for design content, and a third might be focused on technical content. They look weeks and months ahead on the project. If the project schedule is organized into sprints, producers focus on the next 2–3 sprints. They are responsible for keeping the team on track, solving problems, ensuring the work hits the quality bar, and facilitating the production pipeline. They also anticipate, define, and mitigate risks. They will manage and mentor APs and PAs.

- **Senior Producer:** The responsibilities for this role vary depending on the studio. Usually, it is a more forward-looking and strategic role that is focused on leading the production team, pulling together the high-level plan and strategies for development, launching the game, improving processes, and mentoring producers and leads. The person also works with departments outside the development team to manage the entire development and release cycle for the game. The senior producer needs to anticipate problems before they happen and get mitigation strategies in place. They likely have at least 8–12 years of experience.

- **Executive Producer (EP):** Responsibilities for this role also vary. Some EPs are focused on managing the multi-year development and release plan for a game franchise, like Call of Duty. They determine the strategies for growing and maintaining the franchise, such as when sequels are released; what new content, in the way of characters and stories, is created; and what new technologies are integrated into the game (such as VR or AR). They may manage multiple products within the franchise. Other EPs might oversee the process of game development and focus on broader development tasks, such as establishing employee training programs, evaluating external vendors, improving processes, determining the needs of the project, and mentoring other producers.

2.3.3 Types of Producers

While a producer's main function is to manage the development team in order to deliver the game on time, on budget, and to a specific quality bar, there are specializations within this role. Generally, these types of roles are more likely to appear on larger teams, which is where a specialized role is more useful. Here's a brief overview of the types of production roles you might encounter:

- **Generalist:** A generalist will work on whatever is needed from a production standpoint, including improving process, managing engineers, or interfacing with publishing.

- **Technical Producer:** If a producer has prior experience as an engineer, they may specialize in technical production. This means they are skilled at working with engineers to scope out project features and can discuss the technical merits of various solutions. They are also good at explaining technical concepts to non-technical people.
- **Art Producer:** An art producer might have previous experience as an artist. As with Technical Producers, they are trained in the discipline they are managing. Art producers are able to work with artists to scope out features, discuss the merits of one approach or another when creating art assets, and help define an art pipeline that is effective.
- **Creative Producer:** This person may have a design background and is especially skilled at working with the various designers on the project.
- **Publishing Producer:** This role focuses on managing the publishing aspects of the project. Sometimes, the person come from a business background and is well-suited to managing the marketing, PR, CS, and other publishing needs of the game.
- **LiveOps Producer:** This person is responsible for maintaining the health of the game after it is released. This position is critical for an online multi-player game because once the game is released, it needs to be actively managed 24/7 to make sure that players can access it and aren't experiencing any game-breaking issues, and that new content is released to keep the game fresh and interesting. The LiveOps producer is responsible for responding quickly to any live issues that impact the player's experience and reviewing the data and analytics to determine what new features and content to add or what types of in-game events will resonant with the players.

2.4 Function of Publisher

The developer and the publisher have a symbiotic relationship. The developer provides a game, and the publisher markets and distributes the game. The publisher is highly invested in the success of the game, especially if they have also provided financing. One way to think of this relationship is as an amusement park; the developer provides the specific games and amusements, while the publisher manages the amusement park (parking, entrance fee, restaurants, restrooms, etc.). They both have a deep investment in the game's success but are supporting it in different ways. The publisher will expect a percentage of the game sales as payment for the services and support offered. This percentage could be 30% or higher, so it may be tempting to forgo working with a publisher in order to avoid this fee. However, a good publisher has a huge impact on the game's success, and the fee more than makes up for itself if the game is able to find a large audience. Don't underestimate the value of a publisher. In addition to financing, there are many other ways in which they support the launch of the game.

2.4.1 Financing

Financing options were discussed in more depth in Chapter 1, "Game Industry Overview." Publishers want to finance games that contribute to the bottom line. If a publisher has internal development teams, they will work with these teams to determine what games to make. The publisher wants to make games that fit within their release calendar and that are going to make a profit. Sequels to successful games are sure bets in a publisher's eyes, so if they have an internal development team who creates a successful game, the publisher finances sequels and updates to this game in the hopes of turning it into a profitable franchise. Sometimes, a publisher might be willing to finance something riskier with an internal team in order to test the waters for a new type of game genre or a new intellectual property (IP). When a publisher finances an internal development team, it can take some of the financial pressure off the team. The team knows they are getting a regular paycheck, and if a milestone slips, it is less likely to have financial implications for them.

If a publisher works with external developers, they still want to finance something that makes money, but they are more open to listening to developer pitches in the hopes of finding an unexpected hit. In cases where the publisher funds an external developer, financial arrangements are focused on milestone payments. The developer and the publisher will negotiate on how much money is needed to make the game and structure a payment plan around when key milestones for the game will be completed. They will also negotiate the royalty rate that the developer receives for each copy of the game sold. After the game is launched, the developer's profits will first be used to pay back the publisher, and then, the developer will start receiving royalty payments.

2.4.2 Distribution

Distribution methods were also covered in more depth in Chapter 1, "Game Industry Overview." Partnering with a publisher makes getting distribution for your game easier. An established publisher is already connected with the major distribution platforms and can support the developer in getting a game launched on a particular platform. Some digital storefronts won't work directly with independent developers and require a publisher to be part of the process. A publisher will also pick up any fees related to getting a game distributed, including creating boxed product and shipping it to retail stores. These costs can add up, and having a publisher foot the bill for them is extremely helpful. If you are an independent developer, the publisher makes up for these costs in how the milestone payments and royalty fees are structured.

2.4.3 Marketing and Public Relations (PR)

One of the biggest responsibilities of a publisher is to get people excited about playing the game, which is done through marketing and PR efforts. Marketing usually focuses on sales and advertising, and PR usually focuses on managing the public image of the game or company. In this era of social media, the lines between the two are becoming more blurred. In order to create a marketing and PR campaign, the publishers must be directly involved with the development team. This helps the publisher to better understand the game; what features are important; and how the story, setting, and characters are used in the game, which, in turn, helps them to build the best marketing and PR campaign. This also means that they may make suggestions about the game in order to make it easier to market. For example, they may want to partner with a license to raise brand awareness or use a voiceover to capitalize on a celebrity's popularity. PR works hand in hand with marketing to promote the game. Chapter 19, "Getting the Word Out," discusses this in more detail.

2.4.4 Production Support

Production support is another benefit offered by a publisher. This can be helpful if there are multiple things to coordinate with the release and launch of the game. The publisher may also pay for localization and testing efforts, and as part of the package, they may assign a producer from the publishing team to manage these efforts. As discussed earlier, a publishing producer will also manage all the pieces that go into publishing a game. They work directly with their counterparts on the development team to coordinate all the bits and pieces of developing and publishing the game.

2.4.5 Product Management

Product management is gaining in importance with game publishers. A product manager is someone who focuses on growing the game's success within the marketplace. They work with the development team and the publisher to define the game's feature release road map within the context of sales forecasts, launch strategies, target audiences, key competitors, and other market factors. Their goal is to look at the game as a whole to determine how to successfully launch it, grow its audience, and keep it viable with additional content during its life cycle.

Before launch, they will research comparable games that have already been released to help determine what minimum features might be critical for launch or what new features could be added to give the game a differentiating factor. After launch, they will review data and analytics to determine which game content the players are most engaged with and use this information to help the teams define what content updates to create and release.

Not every game will have a dedicated product manager. Product managers usually work on games that are part of a franchise or a new IP that has the potential to turn into a franchise. They are usually affiliated with the marketing and publishing departments, and don't necessarily work directly with the team on day-to-day development work. Their role is focused more on strategy and what tactics can be used to execute the strategy.

2.4.6 Live Operations

Live Operations (LiveOps) is a critical function for any online game that is available 24/7. Publishers may have an entire department devoted to LiveOps for a single game. This includes having teams available who can address networking issues, fix game-breaking bugs, release new updates, determine what new content is created, and generally actively manage the health of the game so that it is always available as well as giving players new content to enjoy. Sustaining a LiveOps team can be expensive, especially since it needs to be staffed around the clock. Large publishers are able to provide this type of support by setting up LiveOps teams in various offices around the world in what is known as a follow-the-sun model—as one team ends their workday, a team in another location is beginning theirs. More information on LiveOps is discussed in Chapter 20, "Releasing to Players."

2.4.7 Community Management

Community managers are responsible for the health of the community that forms around a game. At a high level, community management is responsible for creating, growing, listening, and managing the community. They do this by attracting new people or re-engaging inactive members through outreach efforts, such as surveys and promotions. They give active members content to engage with: for example, blog posts and news updates. As part of interacting with the community, they also listen and respond to feedback. Based on this feedback, they work with the development and publishing teams to improve the game, and then let the community know how their feedback was used to make the game better. As the community gets larger, there may be a whole team of community managers—one may focus exclusively on Facebook, while another focuses on forums, and so on. Their goal is to be responsive to the community to demonstrate that the company cares about them and what they think about the game. Richard Millington's book *Buzzing Communities* (2012) provides a good overview of how to build and manage communities.

2.4.8 Customer Support (CS)

Like community management, CS directly interfaces with people who play the game. Their role is to resolve complaints, provide technical assistance, and listen to player feedback. They may also be responsible for enforcing player behavior guidelines: for example, if someone is violating the game's code of conduct, a CS agent may apply a temporary ban to the player and communicate the reason why. If the player receives multiple violations, the CS agent is empowered to permanently ban them according to the guidelines. CS also processes refunds and provides assistance to players, as needed.

2.5 Publishing Your Game

Now that you have a better understanding of what publishers do, you want to consider your publishing options. As discussed in Chapter 1, "Game Industry Overview," there are many distribution options available

to independent developers who want to self-publish their game.
To clarify, distribution is merely making the game available for people to purchase. You can distribute a game fairly easily on digital storefronts without putting a lot of publishing effort behind it. However, if you choose to go this route, people won't know that your game is available, and therefore, it won't gain traction in the market. You'll want to weigh the pros and cons of self-publishing versus partnering with an established publisher.

2.5.1 Self-Publishing

If you are an independent developer, self-publishing is something to consider. Its main benefit is that you don't have to give away a percentage of game revenue to a publishing partner, and another is that you have greater control over when the game is published, how much you will charge, when updates are released, how the game is marketed, and so forth. If the game is a niche title that appeals to a small audience with a specific need, self-publishing might be a good option. Some publishers may not be interested in a niche title because of the specialized audience, so they may find the financial return not worth the time and money required to invest on their side.

One of the disadvantages of self-publishing is that, on top of the time, money, and effort you are investing in developing the game, you now need to put additional time, effort, and money into publishing it. This is a huge amount of work for a single team, and it is more difficult if you don't have experience in marketing, sales, advertising, PR, CS, and community management.

You may also find it difficult to get published on hardware platforms, like consoles or VR systems. Companies, such as Microsoft and Sony, who manage the distribution of games on their proprietary platforms prefer to work with established publishers. They know that experienced publishers already have a pipeline in place to market and distribute the game successfully. New developers who are trying to self-publish are not proven entities and thus will require more time and support from the platform holders. This is not to say that small developers can't publish successfully on these platforms, but it is harder to become a certified publisher on these platforms without a prior track record of success.

2.5.2 Publishing Partner

A publishing partner is an attractive option if you want the financial and other support that these partners offer. However, finding the right publisher will take time and effort. It's also possible that you can pitch your game to several publishers and not get any offers to partner with them. Your approach to finding a publisher needs to be methodical and focused on presenting your game and your company as something worthwhile in which to invest.

So, what are publishers looking for in a game? The publisher's motivations are mainly financial—they want to find a game that will make them money. They base their decision on whether they think the game is going to be profitable. Some of the criteria they use to judge this are:

- **Return on Investment (ROI):** A publisher will do what's called due diligence on any game before they fully commit to investing in it. They will do a market analysis to compare the sales figures of comparable games (called comps) with the projected sales figure of the game being pitched to them. This, along with the estimated development costs, is factored into an ROI formula to determine whether there will be a high or low ROI.
- **State of Game:** If the game is in some state of completion, this will also be a factor. If the game is almost complete, and only publishing support is needed, the publisher can invest less, which will boost their ROI. It also gives the publisher an opportunity to play the game and make their own determination about the quality and how well it will do in the market. A partially completed game shows that the developer has some financial stake in the game, which is more attractive to publishers. They are more likely to partner with people who have also made a significant investment.
- **Reputation:** Don't underestimate the value of the developer's reputation. If a developer is well-established as one who makes successful games, a publisher is more likely to provide funding, even if the game is in the concept phase. First-time developers will find it very difficult to procure significant funding from a publisher, even if they have an amazing demo. First-time developers still need to prove themselves and show that they can follow through and make a complete game.

2.5.3 The Publishing Relationship

If you work with a publisher, the relationship needs to be actively managed and maintained. The publisher needs to be informed of the game's progress against the agreed-upon milestones, and the developer needs to know that financial and other supports are available when needed.

If the developer doesn't provide regular status updates and builds of the game, the publisher may perceive this in a negative light. They may think that the developer isn't making progress and pull funding, or, in cases where the developer owns the IP, they may assign the project to another developer. The publisher also needs to provide feedback at appropriate points in the process, usually around milestone deliveries, to ensure that both the developer and the publisher are in alignment on what the game is going to be. Sometimes, a publisher may request a major change after the game is done, so the developer needs to scope out how much this change will cost and ask the publisher to provide the additional funds.

The developer and publisher relationship can be very complex since both parties have a high investment in the game's outcome. But they are also viewing the game from a different perspective and thus have a different set of priorities they are judging against. These different priorities can sometimes lead to major disagreements about decisions made for the game, so time needs to be spent talking through the decisions, weighing the various outcomes, and agreeing on which decisions are the best path forward.

A publisher will assign a producer to work directly with the developer and represent the publisher's interests on the project. As discussed earlier, the developer and the publisher producer will work closely on the game. In order for this production relationship to be effective, the developer and the publisher producer will want to define their areas of responsibilities on the project. Usually, the publisher producer coordinates sales, marketing, PR, community management, and sometimes localization efforts. Meanwhile, the developer producer will manage the day-to-day development of the game. Once the game is launched, a Live Producer may be thrown into the mix as well.

One important role of the publishing producer is reviewing the milestone deliverables to determine if they are at an acceptable level of quality or if they still need more work. Oftentimes, milestone acceptance is tied directly to releasing another funding payment. If the developer consistently misses milestone deadlines or delivers poor-quality work, the publisher may choose to pull funding and assign the project to another developer. In some cases, the project could be canceled outright. Chapter 4, "Laying the Groundwork," discusses milestone deliverables and aligning expectations in more detail.

2.6 Conclusion

A strong developer and publisher relationship is good for everyone. The development team, comprising artists, designers, engineers, and testers, is counting on the fact that the game will see the light of day and be enjoyed by players. They have to work closely with the producer to make the game a reality. In turn, the producer plays an integral function in ensuring that the developers are communicating with each other, and the publisher is communicating effectively with the developer. If any of these three entities, developer, producer, or publisher, is out of alignment with the others, it will impact the quality and timeliness of the project. A contractual agreement is useful in making sure that all the parties are aligned on expectations. Chapter 3, "Legal Overview," provides general information on the legal aspects that a producer should be aware of, including publishing contracts and protecting IP.

Legal Overview

3.1 Introduction

Working with an attorney to better understand legal issues in regard to intellectual property (IP), contracts, and licenses is strongly encouraged. There is a lot of legal information available on the internet which can provide some type of basic understanding of the legal issues a producer and development team should be aware of, but this is not a substitute for working with a lawyer. This chapter presents a basic overview of some things to know as you start creating IP and entering into contract negotiations with publishers and other partners. A producer is likely to be directly involved with the contract process by providing descriptions and schedules for milestones or by negotiating the terms of a licensing agreement. Be sure to work with a lawyer and fully understand any contracts, licenses, or IP issues before agreeing or signing anything. This chapter is

Learn more about IP rights from these websites.

- U.S. Copyright office: https://copyright.gov
- United States Patent and Trademark Office: www.uspto.gov

based on IP rights in the United States; if you are in another country, you will want to consult appropriate resources.

3.2 IP Rights

Ideas and creative expression are protected by law in the form of IP rights in the same way that tangible property can be bought or sold. However, because IP is not tangible, it must be expressed in a way that can be defined and thus protected. This includes all the components and tangible aspects of the game experience—story, art, music, and code. Ideas for game mechanics (such as Match 3 items and first-person shooting) are not protected by IP rights. However, once the game mechanics are made tangible as part of a playable game with art, code, and audio, the expression of the mechanic can be protected. This is why creating games within a similar genre (like first-person shooter or platform jumper) is not a violation of IP. There is a larger discussion to be had on how game clones have an impact on the quality of games in the industry, but these clones are not necessarily violating IP rights unless the games in question are actually using assets from another game. The cloning conversation is beyond the scope of this book, but it is important to be aware of.

Legally valid types of IP include copyrights, trademarks, trade secrets, and patents. Producers should understand how these work, particularly if developing an independent game. As you are searching for your ideal publishing partner, IP rights and who owns them will be a common conversation. A publisher is probably going to ask for the game's copyright to be conveyed to the publisher as part of the publishing deal. This will allow the publisher to reproduce the product and create derivative products.

A well-known independent developer is in a better position to negotiate with the potential publisher and keep the copyrights to the work.

Furthermore, development teams should be careful not to accidentally infringe upon trademarks or copyrights by including protected assets in the game. For instance, Coca-Cola® vending machines and Crayola® crayons cannot be used in games without obtaining permission from the companies that own these licenses. It's possible to negotiate a product placement deal that will allow the use of copyrighted or trademarked products, and such agreements can be beneficial to all involved parties. This is discussed in the section on licenses, later in this chapter.

3.2.1 Copyrights

A copyright protects the expression of an idea in a tangible format, such as a book or sculpture. However, the idea itself is not protected. A game idea cannot be copyrighted unless it's expressed in a tangible form, such as computer code. As soon as an idea is made tangible, copyright protection is in effect; it's not necessary to register a work with a copyright office. However, copyrights are governed by federal law, and in order to gain all the legal benefits of copyright enforcement in court, one must register the copyright.

A game publisher will take a game more seriously if the studio has already secured copyrights and can legally turn these over to the publisher. An indie studio must have all members of the development team agree to turn the copyright over to a single person or common company. This will help them to avoid legal complications later down the line. You can learn more about U.S. copyrights at copyright.gov.

3.2.2 Trademarks

Trade and service marks are also known as trademarks, which are governed by federal laws. These are symbols, words, or devices that identify and distinguish a particular good from others. For example, the shape of a Coca-Cola bottle is a trademark which differentiates it from other soft drinks. A trademark will keep others from employing a similar mark but will not keep them from creating and selling similar goods. A clothing store may feature a wide variety of denim jeans, but trademarks are used to identify individual brands.

In order to distinguish between goods, trademarks must be distinctive; the more distinctive they are, the stronger the trademark, the easier it is to enforce. Trademark strength is described by five terms: from weakest to strongest, generic, descriptive, suggestive, arbitrary, and fanciful.

Generic marks use common terms, such as "Coffee" or "Game," which makes these marks weak and nondistinctive. Thus, they are not protectable as trademarks.

Descriptive marks, such as "low fat" for foods that are low in fat, describe the purpose or function of an item. Generally, these marks are not protected unless they become very closely associated with a specific good through marketing, such as "Holiday Inn®."

Suggestive marks suggest the function of an item without actually describing it: for example, "Prismacolor®" colored pencils and "Memorex™" tape recorders. Suggestive marks are considered distinguishing and are protected as marks.

Arbitrary marks don't actually relate to the good in question; they're common words, symbols, and devices that appear to have been chosen arbitrarily: for example, Apple® computers. These marks are inherently distinctive and don't require a secondary meaning.

Fanciful marks are the strongest type and are easily enforceable; these are created specifically for use as trademarks. Examples include "Kodak®" and "Xerox®."

Trademarks must be registered with the United States Patent and Trademark Office (USPTO). Prior to registration, a company should be hired to perform a full trademark search. This ensures that a mark hasn't already been claimed by someone else. Once the applications have been submitted, the office can decide if the mark is unique and then register it.

3.2.3 Patents

A patent prevents others from making, using, or selling an invention for a fixed period of time (currently, 20 years). Once the term has expired, the patented invention becomes public domain, and anyone can make, use, or sell it. To obtain a patent, the inventor must document everything about the invention via descriptions and diagrams. All of this material must then be registered with the USPTO (www.uspto.gov). The invention must be new, tangible (it's not possible to patent an idea), and involve an inventive step and a useful application. Software patents include operating systems, compilers, graphics systems, and file systems.

3.2.4 Trade Secrets

Trade secrets are pieces of information that give a company a competitive edge. They're kept hidden from the public, especially competitors. Companies spend time and money to create these methods, techniques, and formulas, such as the secret formula for Coca-Cola. In turn, trade secrets bring value to the company. Trade secrets are protected by state laws but only if the information is kept secret and can't be obtained lawfully by others.

As discussed earlier, trademarks and copyrights will not cover game concepts or ideas. Instead, these ideas must be protected as trade secrets and kept confidential. This is why employee confidentiality is crucial and nondisclosure agreements (NDAs) are used. Prior to sharing your game idea with anyone, have the person you are telling sign an NDA. It is much harder to legally pursue someone who revealed a trade secret if they haven't signed an NDA.

3.2.5 Nondisclosure Agreements (NDAs)

NDAs allow you or a company to protect confidential information and trade secrets. They enable concepts to be treated as trade secrets by stating that conversations about them with another party must be kept secret. If the concept is discussed with someone who has not signed an NDA, then the concept is no longer considered a trade secret; instead, it is regarded as public domain.

The common types of NDAs are unilateral and mutual. Use a unilateral NDA when you are discussing a project with someone outside the game industry (e.g., independent investors). Since they don't have trade secrets to protect, and you do, this NDA will keep anything you say to them confidential and protected.

When people in the game industry talk about ideas with each other, a mutual NDA is used. For example, if a publisher and an independent game developer are discussing concepts, a mutual NDA will protect both parties. This is useful when a publisher is sending out a Request for Proposals (RFP); the publishers will want to discuss revenue goals and other things related to the RFP, and the developers might want to discuss projects they are currently working on so they can show the publisher demos. Be mindful if you are an independent developer working for hire on a project; it is not likely that your client will want you to tell anyone about the game, unless they explicitly give you permission or release you from an NDA you signed. For example, if you are working on a game for Publisher A and talking to Publisher B about doing a game for them, even if you signed a mutual NDA with Publisher B, you are still bound by the NDA you signed with Publisher A and thus can't talk about the work you are doing for Publisher A with Publisher B. A good practice is to just not disclose any confidential information unless you have received written permission from all interested parties.

Because publishers hear hundreds of game ideas a year, they may not want to sign an NDA with an external game developer. If they sign the NDA and hear a pitch for a game that turns out to be similar to one they're already working on, this could create legal complications for the publisher later on, when the game is released. Of course, this creates a dilemma for developers who are pitching ideas, so you will need to carefully consider which publishers you are talking to and if you are comfortable pitching a game without an NDA in place.

3.3 Types of Agreements

In addition to protecting your IP, there are also a set of agreements to be aware of when developing games and working with publishers. To reiterate, you will want a lawyer to review what you are doing to best determine what types of agreements you will need in place. Agreements basically outline a set of requirements and expectations between you or your company and another party. Some agreements you are likely to come across are development contracts, work-for-hire agreements, employment agreements, end user license agreements (EULAs), and terms of service (TOS).

3.3.1 Development Contracts

A development contract outlines the expectations and responsibilities for both the developer and the publisher, including financial terms, project concept, asset deliverables and advance payment milestone schedules, IP ownership, marketing plans, and distribution plans. If an internal developer is working on a game, there is no need for a development contract since the game is already being funded by the publisher, and all work is protected by NDAs and employment agreements. As you can imagine, these contracts are quite long and take a few rounds of negotiation before everyone is ready to sign.

One of the most important elements of a development contract is the financial terms, which includes when the publisher is going to make advance payments for funding the development, what the royalty structure is like, and when the developer will start receiving royalty payments. Be aware that a development contract is usually made between a publisher and an independent developer, where the developer has a stake in the financial success of the game. The developer will have a royalty percentage of game sales and thus will make more money if the game sells more copies. During development, the publisher will expect the developer to deliver milestones on the agreed-upon schedule before making the next advance payment (which funds development). It is in the developer's best interest to deliver the expected milestones on time so that they get the expected funding for their next milestone. The publisher will have a specific set of expectations for each milestone and will likely evaluate what was delivered against what was defined in the contract to determine if the milestone can be considered complete. Chapter 4 discusses how to define milestones in more detail.

Another aspect of the development contract is who owns the IP. If the publisher will take ownership of the IP, the contract will outline the transfer of IP rights from the developer to the publisher; this includes code, characters, textures, story, and concepts. The contract may also stipulate that the developer relinquishes all rights to any proprietary tools that were created during the development process, such as scripting tools, texture editors, or software plug-ins. If the game's subject matter is licensed (e.g., if the game is based on a movie), then the contract will include guidelines for how the developer can use the license. The contract may also cover other issues, such as:

- Who is responsible for QA testing?
- Who is responsible for localization?
- Who will handle publicity, marketing, and distribution?
- Who owns the ancillary rights for turning the IP into a movie, book, TV show, etc.?
- How will disputes between the parties be arbitrated?

See the sidebar from Jay Powell for more information on development contracts.

JAY POWELL, CEO, THE POWELL GROUP

There are two primary types of development contracts. One is a work-for-hire agreement, where a publisher owns an IP and is contracting a team to develop a new game. The other is a licensing agreement, where the developer is offering their game to a publisher for either development funding or marketing and distribution support.

A work-for-hire contract should contain:

- The explanation of rights (who owns what, who owns the IP, who owns the engine, and who owns the code);
- Timeline for delivery;
- Detailed approval process;
- Payment details, including deliverables;
- Development details (which can range from a feature list to a full design document);
- Allowance and plans for live operations of the game after it is launched;
- Royalty rate, recoupment details (e.g., royalty report), and payment terms.

A licensing contract should contain:

- Rights to sell: exclusive or nonexclusive; physical, digital, or both; territories; platforms; and languages;
- Price and payment details for:
    - Detailed milestone deliverables;
    - Any third-party software licenses;
    - What expenses will be deducted from Net Receipts;
    - What qualifies as an expense and who pays for it.
- Terms for how long the agreement is in place;
- Clarification on if the publisher has first right of refusal for new projects from the team;
- Plan for localizing the game;
- Details on how patches and new content will be addressed;
- Explanation of acceptance procedures;
- A deadline for the publisher to ship the game before the publisher incurs penalties;
- Information on marketing responsibilities:
    - Who is responsible for marketing?
    - What is the marketing plan?
    - Who handles outreach to influencers, websites, and other media?
    - How much time is the developer obligated to spend in interviews, streams, or travel to shows?

BEN SMITH, SR. PRODUCER (PARTNER DEVELOPMENT), DEFINING MILESTONES

I can only really speak for the publisher I worked for, and there was some flexibility as to how to define interim milestones in the middle of the project. But at each end, there were set gates that we absolutely had to nail. The first was the "vertical slice" prototype. The vertical slice is intended to be a playable demo for the game, honed towards demonstrating whatever the most important mechanics were for the moment-to-moment gameplay of a product. Nailing a vertical slice obviously allows the team to lock down the core of the product and answer as many key questions as possible. What is the player doing moment to moment? How does it feel? Is it fun? Can we build another X hours of this, given what it took to build this "15–20" minutes? What didn't work, and what needs to change? What else do we need to prove, and how do we build that stuff next? And so on. I'd argue that if you don't end up with a great vertical slice, you're never going to make a great game (certainly not in the time frame you have in your schedule). It's that important. Now, on the other end of the development spectrum were the other key milestones: alpha, beta, and final. From our perspective, alpha was supposed to be "feature complete." There could still be placeholder art or text or user interface (UI) elements, but everything HAD TO work in that built. (Narrator: It never did.) After alpha, beta was the first "shippable candidate"—in other words, the build wasn't just feature complete, it was asset locked. (Narrator: We never allocated enough time between alpha and beta to achieve this.) The last milestone we set was "final," as in this build can head to first party or off to gold master. Now, the first final candidate never actually was because there would always be a showstopper bug or two (or ten) to be fixed, but that was the goal. How you define those interim milestones I glossed over is obviously going to vary based on the type of game you're building. Whatever they are, they need to prove that you're on-track to complete the game on schedule (X% of levels, assets, whatever, done).

3.3.2 Work-for-Hire Agreements

Work-for-hire agreements are needed if you are hiring an external vendor to create assets for your game. The work-for-hire agreement transfers all rights for the assets the vendor created to the person who hired the vendor. If a work-for-hire agreement is not in place, then the vendor retains ownership over the assets and any of the IP he or she created. This means that you are not legally allowed to use these vendor-created assets in the game without permission from the vendor. For example, if you hire an external vendor to compose original music for the game, you can put a work-for-hire agreement in place so that you are considered the owner of the music from a legal standpoint, and you can do whatever you wish with it. All rights are transferred to you, and you have the legal ability to turn around and license this music to other people. In this scenario, if a work-for-hire agreement isn't in place, the composer owns all the rights to the music and can license it to you for a fee. If you are working with a well-known composer, this might be the arrangement agreed upon. If the vendor retains ownership of the assets, he or she doesn't necessarily have to grant you exclusive rights; he or she might opt to license them to other game studios.

If a work-for-hire agreement is put in place prior to the creation of these assets, then all of these complications can be avoided. Under a work-for-hire agreement, all rights to the assets are transferred to the person hiring the contractor, and the hiring party is considered the work's creator.

A work-for-hire can only exist in two situations. The first covers any work created by employees that is within the scope of their employment. For example, any code written by a programmer on your development team is work-for-hire. The employer, not the programmer, owns the rights to the work. If one is working with part-time employees, the situation can be complicated, and a lawyer should be consulted.

The second situation occurs when you hire a vendor to create something for the game (code, music, art, design), and you want to retain ownership of it. In this situation, the agreement must be drafted and finalized before any work begins. Works covered under this type of scenario must belong to one of the categories of commissioned work detailed in the Copyright Act: a translation, an instruction text, a test, answers for a test, an atlas, a contribution to a collective work, a compilation, supplementary material, or a contribution to a movie or other audiovisual work. For example, a magazine article falls into the category of a contribution to a collective work, so it could be a work-for-hire. A novel, on the other hand, doesn't fall into any of the previously mentioned categories, so it cannot be a work-for-hire. For more information on work-for-hire agreements, please consult the U.S. Copyright Office circular entitled "Works Made for Hire."

3.3.3 Employment Agreements

The employee-consultant agreement ensures that the company owns everything the developers work on; this makes an independent studio more attractive to potential publishers because it means that the studio has the authority to sell the IP rights to a publisher. In essence, the employee-consultant agreement means that every developer on the team has signed over his or her IP rights to the company. Each agreement is unique, but all of them cover certain points:

- **IP ownership:** Which IPs belong to the company? Which IPs belong to the employee? This also covers the transfer of all ownership of designated IPs to the company.
- **Employee resignations:** Employees who quit prior to the completion of the game will need to follow certain guidelines, such as documenting their work fully or agreeing not to poach other employees.

The company will need to decide how restrictive the language should be. Typically, these agreements are written by attorneys.

3.3.4 End User License Agreement (EULA)

The core purpose of the EULA is to eliminate the resale and rental of a game. Technically, the EULA grants the end user a license to use the game software. With PC games, the end result is that the end user is not buying the software, so they are not allowed to resell it. Because of the way in which console games were initially categorized for IP rights, they are allowed to be resold and traded at stores.

The EULA also gives the company more flexibility in terms of how it controls and distributes the game, and limits the company's liability with the end user. The company uses the EULA to outline the legal ways in which the user can use the software and can prohibit them from conducting illegal activities with it, such as hacking, reverse engineering, or other unwanted behaviors.

A EULA also sets the expectations for bugs and other defects in the game. Since the game will never be 100% bug free, the EULA indicates that the game software is presented "As Is," which means that the player cannot hold the company responsible for things like lost data or loss of sales due to issues or bugs with the game. Typically, the publisher will provide a standard EULA if the game is eligible.

3.3.5 Terms of Service (TOS)

TOS are agreements that define what behavior is expected from players while they are playing the game, especially for online games. This is where rules of behavior and what is acceptable are more explicitly outlined. As with the EULA, the player must agree to the TOS before playing the game. The types of offenses covered in the TOS include things such as:

- Cyberbullying and hate speech;
- Hacking;
- Cheating;
- Gambling;
- Trading game objects for real-world money;
- Disruptive game behavior (e.g., stream-sniping);
- Any other unwanted player behaviors.

Violating the TOS comes with consequences; in many cases, players can be temporarily or permanently banned from the game.

3.4 Working with Licensors

Pairing a well-known TV or movie license, such as Star Trek or Star Wars, with a game is quite common. Publishers like to do this because they can appeal to audience members who are already fans of the brand and are therefore likely to invest in the game. Licenses also bring more awareness to the game and can generate more PR and marketing, which translate into higher sales. In some cases, the game benefits from the marketing and PR activities for the movie or TV show on which it is based.

Oftentimes, publishers will take a game that doesn't have an established IP and pair it with a license to broaden the game's appeal. For example, if you have an action-role-playing game, people are more likely to purchase one based on Star Wars, which promises space travel, unusual settings, interesting aliens, and their favorite Star Wars characters, rather than one that features an unknown setting, characters, and story line.

Typically, producers are assigned to projects with attached licenses and are therefore not part of the negotiation to secure the rights to a license. A producer's focus is on the impact that licensing will have on production, especially the design, schedule, and asset creation.

If you are working with a licensor, it is possible that they will be involved in the game development process. The involvement may be minimal—for example, they may play the milestone builds and offer some feedback— or the involvement could be quite extensive—they may sit in on design meetings and have veto power over proposed game features.

It all depends on how the licensing deal is structured. At the very least, the licensor will be in charge of approving the game concept and key assets; this is because they want to maintain the license integrity. For example, if a game is based on a family-friendly cartoon, the game can't contain mature content that would cause it to get a mature age rating. The licensor will want the title to appeal to children and receive the appropriate rating. They will provide a brand bible during preproduction that defines what can or can't be done with licensed characters and settings. This may include information about the appearance of key characters and actions taken in the game.

When working with licensors, you will need to add time to the schedule for approvals. The approval process should be outlined in the licensing agreement and accounted for in the schedule. It's important for the licensor to understand the approval process and schedule so they don't slow down the game development process by taking a longer time than planned for approvals. Maintain a good relationship with the licensing contact so that concepts and assets are approved in a timely fashion.

Add a timeline for licensor approvals into the schedule, and be sure to review this timeline with the licensor on a regular basis. It is important for them to understand how delaying an approval can cause a delay in launching the game. If the game's producer is proactive about delivering everything that's needed to the licensor in a timely fashion, then a positive working relationship is more likely.

3.5 Conclusion

While you are not expected to be a legal expert on all the various legalities of making a game, it is important to be aware of when a lawyer is needed and why. This chapter presented a brief overview, and you are certainly encouraged to talk with a lawyer for further information.

PART 2
Creating the Prototype

The information in Part 1 provides a foundation for understanding the business of the game industry and presents some key choices to be made as a game concept becomes a released game. Part 2 builds on this foundation by walking readers through the process of taking a concept and turning it into a playable prototype. In this section, you will learn how to define your goals, how to appeal to stakeholders, and your overall game development process. You will evaluate the game concept; determine its strengths and weaknesses; and get more specific on the key features, proposed audience, and revenue model. This section concludes with information on creating a prototype. The chapters are:

Getting Started;

Creating Concept;

Prototyping.

—

CHAPTER 4

Laying the Groundwork

4.1 Introduction

You have a general understanding of the game industry and an idea for a game; now what? How can you turn this idea into something tangible and get people on board to help finance, create, and publish it? As with any new business, you need to start laying the groundwork for success by defining your goals and who the stakeholders are. This is also a good time to consider how you want to structure your milestones and what type of development process you want to use.

Putting together this foundation will give you something to build on as you flesh out your game idea. The milestone framework provides a way to think about the different phases of game development and how your game fits into a process. This chapter provides information on how to lay the groundwork for the development of your idea. You don't want to rush into the concept stage without thinking through what the goals are, who the stakeholders are, what the expectations are, and what process to use to execute all of these things. If you are working with a publisher, they will help establish these goals, stakeholders, and processes. If you are an independent developer, you will have more freedom to choose. Regardless of who is involved in defining the foundation and laying the groundwork, the techniques for doing this are applicable in all instances.

4.2 What Are the Goals?

Before you start making the game, take some time to answer the following:

- What's your motivation?
- What need are you filling?
- What problem are you solving?

Answering these questions helps define the goal. For example, a student's goal may be to create something to showcase their skill at design, art, or engineering. In this example, the motivation is to find a job, the need is to have a game that shows game development skill, and the solution is to show employers the skill and capability used to make a game. If you are a small game studio, your motivation may be to bring in revenue to pay your employees, the need may be to provide publishers with game development services, and the problem may be solved by making a game that fills a spot on the publisher's release schedule.

Once you've answered these questions, you can define more specific goals by using the SMART method. The term "SMART" was first used by George T. Doran in the November 1981 issue of *Management Review*. This method has gained popularity since then and is used by many people. SMART goals are:

- **Specific:** The goal is clear and well-defined (e.g., I want to make a succulent-themed Battle Royale game), not vague (e.g., I want to make a game).
- **Measurable:** The success of the goal can be measured. This provides a way to track progress towards the goal. Some ways to measure are sales figures (e.g., the game will generate $1 million in revenue, or the game will sell 10,000 copies), the number of concurrent players online (e.g., the game will have at least 200,000 concurrent players online at any time), or a conversion percentage of free players to paid players (e.g., 2% of people who download and play the game for free will purchase something in the game).
- **Attainable:** Pick a goal you can actually accomplish. Do you have the team or expertise to build and launch the next multimillion-dollar franchise, or is something on a smaller scale more attainable? You want to pick something that is realistic but still a challenge to achieve. If the goal is too easy, it doesn't provide a lot of motivation. Remember: if you want to hit the target, you actually have to aim beyond it—so pick a goal that is outside your comfort zone but still within reach. You are more likely to hit the target and then position yourself to exceed the goal.
- **Relevant:** The goal needs to be focused and consistent with the direction in which you, your team, and the game industry are moving. For example,

trying to make a game for an outdated hardware platform doesn't make much sense. Making something for an established and current platform, or a new platform, is more feasible.

- **Time-Bound:** Pick a deadline for achieving the goal. Think of this as a stake in the ground that you are aiming for. You might finish ahead of schedule, in which case you can start on the next goal. You might find yourself blowing past the deadline, which means you need to reassess the parts of the goal to see if they need to change in order to meet it. You can also adjust the deadline as needed, based on new information (and yes, this will cause other parts of the goal to change).

Once the goals are formulated, write them down in proactive and positive language. Use active verbs, define specifics, and include tangible ways to measure success. For example:

- "Six months from today, our team is going to release a succulent-themed Battle Royale game for 150 people as an Early Access title that generates $100,000 in revenue in the first 3 months."
- **Specific:** Yes. Lots of details about what the game is and what the expectations are.
- **Measurable:** Yes. The game will be an Early Access title that supports 150 players and will meet a $100,000 revenue goal.
- **Attainable:** Yes. Assume the game has the capability to make this type of game. This is a well-understood genre with a twist on the theme and the number of players that can play together.
- **Relevant:** Yes, for now. Battle Royale games are popular, and players are looking for new variations on this genre. Succulents are popular.
- **Time-Bound:** Yes, and two deadlines are mentioned: 6 months to develop and 3 months to generate the desired revenue.

Another vector when defining goals are things to avoid or eliminate. For example, eliminating a console version because the development team is not a licensed console developer or avoiding publishing funding because the game will be self-funded. It's important to represent these limitations when stating the goals so that the team fully understands the parameters they are working within.

Once the goals are defined, publish them to the team and the stakeholders. Everyone needs to know what the goals are and how they align with the overall vision and game plan. Remember that goals don't have to be set in stone. They are defining a set of parameters to aim for, and as you embark on the journey to fulfill the goals, you may find that adjustments are needed along the way. This is fine; you can adjust the goals as needed, especially if new information impacts the success parameters of the goal. For example, what if you get less funding than required? Do you throw out the goal or recalibrate it? When making goal adjustments, involving your team and stakeholders in these discussions is imperative. You are all in it together and all held accountable.

Which brings up another key thing about goals—hold yourself, your team, and your stakeholders accountable for achieving success. If you are all aligned and clear on what the goal is, being accountable is much easier. Make sure that the individuals on the team understand how their work contributes to the overall goal and that the team as a whole understands the contribution of each individual. Taking time to ensure this depth of understanding also builds better camaraderie and a stronger team. Once everyone is clear on the expectations, do regular follow-ups to track progress and remove any roadblocks. If things get off track, help identify the issue and get a solution in place.

When holding yourself and others accountable for goals, you also need to be transparent in order to establish trust with the team, which, in turn, strengthens their commitment and accountability to the goals. What does being transparent mean? In essence, it means being honest and presenting the truth of the situation as you understand it, providing information and updates in a timely and accurate fashion, being open with information, and gracefully receiving criticism and feedback. Being transparent builds trust with people and shows them that they are in a position to collaborate and participate in decision-making.

4.3 Who Are the Stakeholders?

In this book, the term "stakeholder" is used loosely to describe the key group of people who have a vested interest in the success of the game, be it the players, the development team, senior management, or investors. They are involved in high-level and strategic decisions pertaining to the game, and they are not necessarily part of the day-to-day decision-making. For example, a group of stakeholders will have a large say in what game is being made, including input on genre, platform, and revenue model, but they won't be as involved in the game's day-to-day development. However, if key decisions must be made during development, for example, pivoting to a different platform or genre, the stakeholders should be involved in these decisions. Each team or company will have different definitions of who a stakeholder is. For example, one company may designate the producers and discipline leads as the primary stakeholders, while at a different company, the president may be the primary stakeholder involved in numerous decisions about the game, but they may not be involved in the day-to-day execution of these decisions.

Spend some time determining who the stakeholders are for your project. You may need to define different groups of stakeholders for different aspects of the game. For example, if you are planning to launch the game in China, one of your key stakeholders will be your Chinese publishing partner—they will want to vet all the game content and have a say in the revenue model and platform, and the game's distribution. If the game is a launch title on a new gaming platform, stakeholders will include the third-party platform holder (since they will have a vested interest in ensuring that the title is ready for the platform launch) and the technical director of the game (as he or she will be instrumental in overcoming any technical hurdles with launching the game on a new platform). When deciding on stakeholders, you want to analyze the perspective they are going to bring and how they relate to the other stakeholders so you can prioritize areas where their involvement is most relevant to the game. Understanding what issues they care most about and when they need to be consulted is critical to a smooth game development process. You want to make sure the necessary people are part of key decisions; otherwise, you may find yourself redoing work or facing delays because you didn't have the right group of stakeholders involved in the conversation.

4.3.1 Stakeholder Mapping

One way to determine who the stakeholders are and what they need is by creating a Stakeholder Matrix or Power-Interest grid. This is a common method for evaluating who the stakeholders are, how much influence they have, and how frequently they need to be updated on project status. Start by listing all the stakeholders on the game—this includes people who may have little power or interest in it. In game development, you will likely have stakeholders from the following places:

- Sr. Management;
- Publisher;
- International;
- Discipline Leads;
- Internal Teams;
- External Teams;
- Players.

If you have a group that would be considered a stakeholder (like the players), pick a specific person to represent that group's interest as a stakeholder.

Next, categorize each person based on how much decision-making power they have and their level of interest in regard to the game development process. Figure 4.1 outlines a basic framework for what actions a producer needs to take with each type.

You can see that each person will be placed into one of four grids:

- **Manage Closely (High Power/High Interest):** This group has high impact on the success or failure of the game. These people likely sign off on milestones, write checks, or play a key role at the company. They will require constant updates and should be included in the project as much as possible.
- **Keep Informed (Low Power/High Interest):** This group is likely where the bulk of the development team and the testing department will be categorized. They are highly invested in the project, but their power to make decisions is on the low end. They have the authority to make a

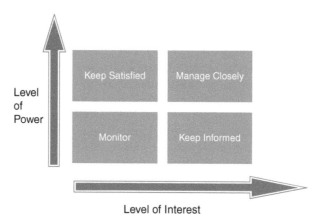

Level of Power

Keep Satisfied   Manage Closely

Monitor   Keep Informed

Level of Interest

FIGURE 4.1 Stakeholder mapping.

decision within their sphere of influence but likely don't have the power to completely derail the project. A weekly or monthly status report is useful for this group.

- **Keep Satisfied (High Power/Low Interest):** This might be where the players are categorized. They have power over the success or failure of the game after it is released but may not have avid interest in the game development process. If you are participating in a collaborative development effort with the community (or crowdfunded your game), you will want to give them enough information to be satisfied with the game's progress. Other people who fall into this category could be the software rating boards. A monthly status report is probably fine as long as there are no major issues. This group should be looped in on major issues when they arise.

- **Monitor (Low Power/Low Interest):** This group doesn't need regular updates, but keep an eye on them to see if their power or interest levels change. For example, the Live Operations team isn't going to be very interested in the game while it is in development, but once it is live, they will shift to a different quadrant (probably the "Keep Informed" group).

4.3.2 Stakeholder Communication Plan

Communicate with the stakeholders based on which quadrant they are in. Putting together a Stakeholder Communication Plan allows you to clarify who needs to weigh in on decisions. As the game gets bigger and more complex, more stakeholders will be involved. A communication plan is helpful when timely decisions must be made. The plan ensures that you have the right people in the room to make a decision and that once the decision is made, it is communicated out to the interested parties.

The plan can be structured around the individual stakeholders, or it can be built around different areas of the game. Figure 4.2 is an example of a Stakeholder Communication Plan for the individual stakeholders.

Stakeholder Name	Power	Areas of Interests	Main Goal	Contributions	Interactions	Frequency
President	High	Scope Change	Publishing a game that meets sales forecasts and player expectations	Key Decision Maker on Game Release, Approves Budget and Schedule Changes	Executive Producer, VPs	Monthly
Technical Director	High	Platform Tech Release Management	Creating game that is technically sound.	Key Decisions on Techologies Used for the game	Engineering Leads, Sr. Producer	Bi-Weekly

FIGURE 4.2 Stakeholder Communication Plan.

You can see that this pulls together the pertinent information about each stakeholder—what their levels of power/interest are, what their main goals are, what types of things they are most interested in, in what ways they contribute, and how frequently they should be given status updates. This is a living document and should be kept up to date as the game progresses, especially if a stakeholder changes power/interest levels, areas of interest, or goals.

Building a communication matrix around areas of the game is also useful as some stakeholders may be more invested in some areas of the game than others. So, you will have different groups of stakeholders needed for different issues. The matrix clearly defines who needs to be consulted for important decisions in any of these areas. Figure 4.3 is an example of this. You can see that each stakeholder has their Power-Interest result for each area, and the results are not always the same across the board for each person. For example, the president is a "Manage Closely" for any scope changes since these impact the cost, feature set, and schedule for the game, which, in turn, can affect projected revenue. The president is "Keep Satisfied" for Marketing and Road map Changes; he or she is influential in these areas but relies on the vice president of marketing to watch them closely. The president is "Keep Informed" for Localization, meaning that there is interest in this area, but the power is highest with the regional directors who determine what languages the game should be localized into. Finally, the president is marked as "Monitor" for Platform Technology since there is a reliance on the Technical Director to take an active Power and Interest in this area.

As you put together these stakeholder maps and communication plans, remember why you are doing this—you want to define who needs to be in the loop on which decisions, how often you need to provide updates, and what information should be included in the updates. Time spent doing this is a good investment, trust me. If it is done well, and people respond to it, you avoid situations where someone from outside the team disrupts

	Scope Change	Localization	Platform Tech	Roadmap Changes	China Launch	Release Management
President	Manage Closely	Keep Informed	Monitor	Keep Satisfied	Keep Satisfied	Monitor
Technical Director	Monitor	Monitor	Manage Closely	Keep Satisfied	Manage Closely	Keep Satisfied

FIGURE 4.3 Stakeholder status per area of the game.

the development process by asking a lot of questions, casting doubt on a decision, or asking for things to change (without clear reasons for this). These plans don't have to be complicated. How this information is organized is up to you; the key thing is to define the stakeholders, understand what they need, and then provide it.

4.4 Third-Party Considerations

If you plan to release the game on a console or mobile platform, or offer it as a digital download on a service such as Steam, there will be additional requirements from the third parties who manage these platforms. These include requirements such as how to display error messages in the game, restrictions on content, how to package the files for distribution, and so on. Other elements that have an impact are what revenue percentage the third party gets and their timelines for approving, packaging, and releasing the content.

If the game is published on a proprietary hardware platform, such as a console or mobile device, it must go through a third-party approval process. The processes for each company's platform are different, but they have common elements. First, the companies want to be involved in the game development from the beginning, including in reviewing and approving the game's concept. Second, they will have a set of technical requirements that must be adhered to that are specific to their platform. These requirements are defined by the appropriate platform holder and are focused on ensuring a consistent experience for the player in regard to how error messages are handled, how they connect and play with friends, how platform-specific terminology is used, and so on. If the game does not meet these requirements, it won't be approved for release. In some cases, you may be able to negotiate with the platform holder on how a requirement is implemented as sometimes, there are gray areas in the way in which the requirements are interpreted. Third, they will want to review, test, and approve the game before it is released. This could also include reviewing and approving alpha and beta versions of the game, so plan with these requirements in mind. The time frame for each round of approvals can be anywhere from 2 to 20 days. If the game fails in the final approval process (which happens quite frequently), it must be resubmitted, and the clock starts again.

Build the timelines and requirements into the game development plan to ensure that they are implemented and tested as part of the game. The platform holder will assign an account manager to work with you. They are an invaluable partner, and will help you navigate the requirements, submission, and approval processes. In order to get an assigned account manager, your development team or publisher must first be licensed to develop and release on that platform. The account manager may also provide feedback on the game or ask that you include a specific feature to show off some key functionality of the platform. More information on the requirements and approval timelines can be found on the developer websites for each platform. See the sidebar for information.

In the event that the game is released on a disc, which is becoming less common, the platform manufacturer will also need to replicate the disc, package it, and distribute it to stores. This process can take anywhere from 15 to 30 days, and this is on top of the time it takes to get it approved. So, if the plan is for the game to be on store shelves November 1, count backward from the ship date to get a better understanding of when the game actually needs to be done. Here's a high-level example timeline for a console game that will ship on disc:

- **November 1:** Launch Day!
- **October 5:** Disc replication and distribution begins.
- **October 4:** Game approved for replication.
- **September 4:** Game code submitted for approval.

In this example, game development concludes on September 4 for a game that ships in early November. This also assumes that the game goes through the approval process with minimal issues and doesn't need to be resubmitted. The reality is that the game will likely fail at some point in the submission process, so it's a good idea to include some additional time in the schedule (I'd suggest submitting the game in mid-August for a November launch on disc).

This schedule can be shortened by a month if the game is going to be digitally distributed. In this case, the replication and distribution can be removed from the timeline, but the code would still need to be submitted around October 1 to get approved and set up for digital distribution. The main purpose of this example is to illustrate how much impact third parties can have on the game development process and timeline. Third parties should be added to the stakeholder map and communication plan to ensure that the submission and approval process goes as smoothly as possible.

DEVELOPER WEBSITES

Android Developers: https://developer.android.com/distribute/console/
Apple Developers: https://developer.apple.com/
Epic Games Store: www.epicgames.com/store/en-US/about
Humble Bundle Developers: www.humblebundle.com/developer
Microsoft Developers: www.xbox.com/en-US/developers
Nintendo Developers: https://developer.nintendo.com/
Sony Developers: https://partners.playstation.net/
Steam: https://partner.steamgames.com/doc/home

PC games usually don't have such extensive requirements or need to go through an approval process. Generally, if you want to publish a PC game, it is pretty easy to do this without involving a third-party, even if you are distributing on Steam. Publishers distribute PC games directly to the consumer through either digital downloads hosted on a publisher-owned website or by duplicating, packaging, and distributing game discs themselves. If the PC game is going to be hosted on Steam, there are some requirements and processes to follow, but they are less involved and time intensive.

DANIEL TAYLOR, SR. PRODUCER, PSYONIX. DEFINING MILESTONES

Just a few examples of things to look out for when defining milestones

- Think beyond the time it takes to make the features/content: Be on constant lookout for hidden work, such as integration. This is where every department says they're done on time, but the feature does not work in the playtest. It's different for every engine and team, but in my experience, you're probably 3 weeks behind schedule now (as first, you need to get the feature working well enough for QA to test it, and they will then tell you that there are 20 critical bugs with it, which you'll need to also fix). Plan for feature integration after everyone has built their part.
- Be on the lookout for scaling and load testing. As games are moving more online, just because a feature works in the test environment doesn't mean it's going to work at scale. Did you schedule time to write load tests?
- If you're working with a licensed product, the licensor will drag their heels with approvals and constantly ask for changes. In your agreements, note how many revisions they get, and if they don't reply by X number of days, it's automatically approved. Otherwise, don't accept deals with hard dates.

4.5 Milestones

Now that you have an understanding of who the stakeholders are and what types of third-party involvement to expect, begin thinking about key milestones for the game. Your stakeholders want to know when they can play the game and assess progress since the last milestone. There are a few common milestones used in game development that provide a good starting point for building a development plan.

Milestones are useful because they provide the development benchmarks for tracking progress against quantifiable goals—some example goals are having 100% of user interface (UI) screens wireframed, 20% of the UI grayboxed and functioning in game, 10% of the UI screens styled by artists, and 10% final and ready for testing. Milestones tied to specific deadlines are commonly used in publishing contracts, and the developer is expected to deliver a completed milestone before the next payment is released.

Consider milestones a baseline for what is expected at that point in the development process.

Ideally, the team has defined a set of tangible deliverables that are realistic and doable in the given time frame. There will be cases when you are ahead of schedule based on what is expected in the milestone, and times when the milestone isn't 100% complete. If a milestone isn't 100% complete, the stakeholders and development team can assess where it missed the mark and recalibrate. This creates a natural decision point for reducing scope, pivoting to a different feature, or changing the projected release date. If a delivery doesn't meet the bar, work with the team to explain why, and detail what the plan is for getting things back on track.

Milestones are going to be defined differently at each company. What some companies consider an "Alpha," others may consider a "Beta." This book presents definitions of common milestones, but, as with anything, work together with your team and stakeholders to define the milestones your game will be measured against.

CHUCK HOOVER, GENERAL MANAGER, FACEBOOK REALITY LABS PITTSBURGH. DEFINING MILESTONES

One of the best tactics I've seen for defining milestones is to keep them simple. It's tempting to break them into detailed descriptions of the state of the build or a list of user stories. I've found that milestone definitions that become too granular can have two negative impacts. First, they can inhibit bottom-up development as the path becomes fixed, and the teams' freedom to solve a problem in a new way can get boxed in. And second, excessively detailed milestones are just difficult for a team to remember.

A good test to that end is: can each and every person on your team repeat the next milestone date and goal by heart without looking at any documentation? Do they know where to look to find that information for all subsequent milestones? If the answer to both of these is yes, then you are a long way towards having well-defined milestones.

As for tracking progress, one of the better tricks that we learned over the years was to be deliberate on what we define as "done" for each goal of a milestone. We ended up shifting away from the word "done" to the word "shippable" to help clarify what completion meant (not simply that your part was complete or that it met the definition but that we could ship the experience with a feature or bit of content when it reached "shippable.") That, coupled with a simple and visible set of goals, made almost any system for tracking progress more efficient and effective.

4.5.1 Prototype

Since the UX and gameplay experience are the key to a successful game, the Prototype build, sometimes referred to as a First Playable, is focused on demonstrating the core gameplay mechanics. The Prototype may have placeholder art, animation, and audio. Some of the technical challenges may not be solved, but someone can play the game and get an idea of the experience. Complete a Prototype as early in the development process as possible, and then continue iterating on this version. Chapter 6, "Prototyping," discusses this in more detail.

4.5.2 Vertical Slice

The Vertical Slice, sometimes known as a Beautiful Corner, builds on the Prototype. The purpose of the Vertical Slice is to provide a representation of what the final gameplay experience will be like for players. This means that the core mechanics and systems are implemented, along with a representation of what the art, animation, and audio will be like in the final game. This could be just one area of the game (i.e., a "beautiful corner") and may only contain a few minutes of gameplay, but it is able to clearly demonstrate the holistic gameplay experience and the final look and feel of the game. Publishers are extremely interested in seeing a vertical slice sooner rather than later since it is pivotal in determining if funding is unlocked for the full development of the game.

4.5.3 Alpha

The Alpha milestone has all the major game mechanics implemented, and placeholder art, animation, and audio for all content in the game, although there may be some areas in which the final art has been implemented (likely in the area used for the vertical slice). From an engineering perspective, the game runs on the correct hardware in debug mode, and major technical work is complete. There are a lot of bugs and rough edges in an Alpha. You want to be at this point about 50% through development. So, if you have a game that will take 24 months to develop, you want to set your goal for Alpha at the 12-month mark. If you have a game that takes 6 months to develop, you should plan to be in Alpha around the 3-month mark.

4.5.4 Beta

Beta typically means that all the engineering, art, audio, and design are complete, and only bug-fixing remains. At this point, you really shouldn't add new features or content and should instead stay focused on fixing bugs. If someone is insistent on getting in a last-minute feature change in the Beta, it's prudent to assess whether this feature can be included in a future game update instead. More information on change requests and how to handle them is discussed later on in this chapter. A game in beta might also be released as an Early Access title. If you do this, be clear with the players about what issues to expect with the game. The game should be at Beta around 75%–85% through development.

4.5.5 Minimum Viable Product (MVP)

The definition of minimum viable product (MVP) varies widely. In this book, I will define it as the first version of the game that can be officially launched. The game is content and code complete, and all the bugs have been fixed. However, the feature set and amount of content might be quite small, as the developers have the intent of adding more features and content with regular updates.

Pokémon GO is a good example of a game that followed this strategy. The first version of the game was released with the basic functionality for catching Pokémon and engaging in gym battles. The publisher released updates almost weekly to address UX issues and bugs that the players were experiencing. They added a new feature called Pokémon Appraisal almost 2 months after the initial release, and after that, new features were added regularly. With this strategy, the publisher was able to launch the game sooner, find out what players liked and didn't like, and figure out which features and content should be released next. For a better understanding of the Pokémon GO feature rollout, you can view the full list of Pokémon GO updates on a fan-created Wiki: http://pokemongo.wikia.com/wiki/List_of_game_updates. The MVP strategy seems to work well with free-to-play games since players are more forgiving of glitches, sparse content, and features if the game is free. The MVP is also sometimes released as an Early Access build.

4.5.6 Release

Release and MVP are very similar in that they both focus on versions of the game that are code and content complete, and any necessary bugs have been addressed by this time. The main difference is that an MVP is a limited set of features and gameplay, with a plan for when future features will be ready for release.

A release is a more robust game that has all the intended features and functionality. There may be plans to release an update in the future, but the game as it stands is feature-rich polished and hopefully doesn't have any major bugs. Games that retail at $60 are likely to focus on a full release rather than an MVP. At this point, the development process is 100% complete, and the team is not actively fixing bugs, adding features, or anything else. The game is ready to go, and the team is ready to take a break!

If this is a console or mobile title, the release version must be submitted to the appropriate platform holder for approval before it can be officially released. The platform holder may find a few issues that need to be addressed by the development team, which means that the team will need to fix them and resubmit the game for approval.

4.5.7 Post-Release

A post-release milestone contains content and feature updates for a game that's already been released. The players will download the additional content, and it will be available in the game the next time they launch it. The team won't want to define the specific content too far in advance as they will be reviewing player feedback to determine what content players would like to see in future updates. From a development standpoint, make sure the game is structured in a way that allows for additional content to be added. If you don't plan ahead for this during game development, it is difficult to go back and retrofit this ability onto a game that has already been released.

When you do make additional content updates, the development process will include the same milestones discussed in this chapter (i.e., it is best to treat content updates like any other game development project).

4.5.8 Milestone Plan

As with the Stakeholder Communication Plan, it is extremely useful to document what the milestone expectations are. The milestone plan is a good way to align expectations with your stakeholders. Work with the team to determine the milestone goals for each area of the game. See Figure 4.4 for an example of this.

4.6 Aligning Expectations

Aligning expectations between all the project stakeholders is a challenge, especially if people have different opinions on the goals and how to execute them. As a producer, expect to spend a fair amount of time explaining the vision, goals, and expectations for the game in order to get people on board with them.

Aligning goals ensures that everyone shares the same vision for the game, meaning that people understand the goals of the game, who the target audience is, what the revenue model is, how this contributes to the business goals of the publisher, and so on. Essentially, the development and publishing teams need to have a shared understanding of why the game is being made, what's being made, and how to determine when it is ready to release. This is hard to do, especially with a large team. Both the development team and the publisher need to be on board with the same vision and have the same expectations for how it will be realized.

How can you keep vision and expectations aligned? The most important thing is to keep everyone informed when critical decisions are made or when plans change. In addition, explain why particular decisions and choices were made. Having context for these decisions helps the team and stakeholders get realigned more quickly.

Making key decisions without input and then dictating them to the team or stakeholders is not wise. This type of behavior seeds mistrust and builds resentment in the team. Engaging in conversation and debate with the appropriate people when making choices about the game is critical to success. If you work with your team to define the game plan, you must also work with them to maintain or change it. The development team wants to hear about these changes from the decision-makers sooner rather than later. Strong, clear, and open communication is key to establishing a shared vision with the team.

One tangible way in which to share the vision and progress of the game is setting aside time to do internal demos of the latest version of the game or for the team to playtest it together. Point out what new elements were

	Prototype	Vertical Slice	Alpha	Beta	Release
Engineering	Basic functionality for a key game play loop is functioning.	Basic functionality for a few key features are in to demostrate very basic game play.	Key game play functionaltiy is in for all game features. Features work as designed, but may be adjusted and changed based on feedback. Game runs on target hardware platform.	Code complete, only bug fixing from this point forward.	Full code freeze. During this phase only crash bugs can be fixed. Critical bugs can be fixed with approval.
Art	Art assets are in the prototype, but they are placeholder and not representative of the final game.	Two to three key art assets are created and viewable in the build. The assets demostrate the look and feel of the final version of the game.	Assets are 40 - 50% final, with placeholder assets for the rest of the game.	All art assets are final and working in game. Only major bug-fixes from this point forward.	Full art freeze. No art fixes, unless it is to fix a crash bug.
Design	Key game loop is defined and can be implemented by engineering.	Basic features are defined, key game play mechanics have basic documentation and a playable prototype if possible.	All design documentation is completed. Feature implementation is in progress. 40 - 50% of design production tasks are completed. Major areas of game are playable as designed.	All design assets are final and working in the game. Only major bug fixes from this point forward. Minor game play tweaks can be done, based on playtest feedback.	Full design freeze. No design fixes, unless it is to fix a crash bug.
UX	First pass of UX flows are designed and implemented into the prototype.	Intial UX testing done on the game. Development team can start iteration on UX experience for key game play mechanics.	Continued UX testing on features as they are added and iterated on in the game.	Final UX testing on the game. Final UX feedback and polish are implemented.	Full UX freeze. Nothing fixed unless a critical UX issue.
Audio	If time allows, placeholder sounds are available in the prototype. Minimal audio is needed at this stage, unless it is required to prove out a key gameplay loop.	The sound of the game is determined, including voiceover, music, sound effects. Samples are available to communicate the sound vision of the game.	40 - 50 % of sound effects are in a working. Voiceover design is in progress, placeholder VO files are recorded. Music in process of being composed.	All final sound assets are in and working in the game.	Full audio freeze. Nothing fixed unless a critical audio issue.
Localization	Start planning localization friendly pipeline.	Set up and test localization pipeline for translation, integration, and testing. Content checks done to ensure that appropriate content can be created for each territory.	Text is finalized and sent for translations. Translations are integrated into the game. Initial linguistic testing can begin.	Localization is complete, only bug fixes from this point forward.	International software ratings are finalized. Localized versions are approved by appropriate territories.
Production	Initial plan for creating and playtesting the prototype.	Basic game requirements are defined. Initial development plan, budget, schedule are completed. Initial financial forecasts are completed. Build pipeline is established.	Full production has begun. The game requirments and game plan are fully completed and approved If working with licenses, all licenses are secured and an approval process is in place.	Development team is done with tasks. Production starts bug triage and focuses on burning down bugs until there is a suitale release candidate.	Release pipeline is finalized. Release plan is in place. LiveOps, community mangement, and publishing are ready for release and post-release activities.
QA	Playtesting the prototype and providing feedback.	Write initial test plans and automation checks for the game. Focus on helping development team test core functionality as it is implemented in the game. Some functional testin begins on completed features.	Game is now playable a full game, although there are some rough edges and holes in some of the functionaltiy. Playtesting can begin. Can test against the alpha deliverables expected for this milestone.	All aspects of game can be fully tested and bugged. Some playtesting continues in order to design to put the final polish on the game.	Begin testing RC candidates. Run checks for third party technical requirements. Testing patching and live services pipelines.

FIGURE 4.4 Milestone plan.

added, and tell the team who contributed these elements to the game. Additionally, post key information about the game in the team rooms. This information should include concept art, mission summaries, control schemes, and anything else that helps communicate what the game is.

4.6.1 Approval Process

Part of maintaining a shared vision and keeping expectations aligned is having a process in place for approvals. This is especially important when working with a publisher or an investor since they are paying for the development. They want to make sure their money is well spent and to be involved in key decisions about the game. If you establish a review and approval process with the publisher and stakeholders, you will avoid some headaches down the road. As discussed earlier in this chapter, there are a set of stakeholders that are actively managed, and an established approval process is one way to do this. Most likely, the publisher and stakeholders will want to see design documents, prototypes, progress on development, completed milestones, and so on. If they know there is a process in place through which they can review these things regularly and provide feedback, they are less likely to go to individual members of the development team to find out what's going on. Once stakeholders start going to individual team members, things can unwind quickly. The stakeholder may provide some feedback that the team member considers a change request and start altering their assigned work (without telling anyone) to accommodate this change. When this happens, the shared vision and expectations quickly begin to fall apart, and feature creeps starts becoming a problem.

The approval process differs based on the project size, how many people are involved, and how much information needs to be approved. Any process, not just approvals, should include these three elements:

- **Keep it simple:** Eliminate any unnecessary steps, and don't create bottlenecks by involving anyone extraneous to the process. For example, it would take weeks to get something approved if everyone on the team needed to sign off. Instead, focus on the key stakeholders for each area of the game. This doesn't mean you can't get feedback from others; in fact, you should do that. It just means that their feedback is not required to move on to the next phase for something.
- **Define and publish:** A process that is clear to everyone works better. If the process is published (by posting on the wall, on a team wiki, etc.), people will have a better understanding of how things work and the reasons behind each step. People involved in the process will also have a better understanding of their obligations. It's a bonus if you are able to actually track and display progress in real time as it is very effective for people to actually see progress being made.
- **Track it:** Assign one person to manage and track any process. Having a single point of contact streamlines the flow of information. This person is responsible for making sure everything is routed through the process and that any follow-ups are completed. They will also be able to collate

all the feedback into a single set of information to ensure that the team understands which feedback needs action and which feedback can be considered suggestions.

4.6.2 Change Requests

Change is inevitable, especially when making games. During the concept phase, the game idea may seem great in theory. However, once you make a prototype, you will realize that changes are needed to make the game better. As you show the prototype to different people, you will also get feedback from them on how to improve the game. Luckily, the prototype phase is the ideal time to make changes and explore ideas, features, and functionality. You are actively asking for feedback and making changes, and you haven't locked down the game's functionality and feature set. However, once the prototype phase is complete, work starts on the full game, and a development plan is being followed, making changes is more costly and time consuming. In addition, stakeholders are likely to request feature changes during development, which can have a knock-on effect on other features in the game. In order to best navigate these unplanned changes, put a good change request process in place.

As in the approval process, the best time to get something in place for this is as soon as possible. If you set the expectation with the stakeholders that there is a process to follow when asking for changes, it is much easier to plan around unexpected requests. While some people may not respect or use the process, it is far better to have something in place so there is some semblance of control, instead of nothing, which results in chaos. The change request process provides checks and balances during development so you can make good decisions on which changes to implement and when as well as which changes to put on the back burner.

The change request process is pretty straightforward. When someone requests a change, he or she fills out a form. The form includes the following:

- Description of request;
- Reason for request;
- Impact if the feature is not added;
- Recommended alternatives;
- Analysis of how this feature affects the project schedule, resources, and quality;
- What existing feature can potentially be removed to accommodate this request;
- Who needs to be notified of the potential change.

Ideally, the person making the request can answer all the questions or knows who they should contact in order to get the relevant information. The purpose is to ensure that the person asking for the change has a full understanding of what they are asking for and how it impacts the project. It also allows them to have a say in what work should be deprioritized in order to implement this request. In reality, the process is not this smooth, and in many cases, the change must be accommodated, along with all the other things that were already planned for. A good producer knows to include some time in the schedule for unknown work, but it is still good practice to thoroughly investigate, discuss, and understand any requested changes.

The producer reviews the change request with the team and ensures that the correct people have been consulted for information on how this request impacts the current development plan. Next, the producer can discuss the request with the stakeholders to see where it should be slotted into the development road map or discuss which features should be deprioritized to make room for the new request. When a final decision is made, everyone needs to be notified, and any planning documents should be updated.

DANIEL TAYLOR, SR. PRODUCER PSYONIX. ESTABLISHING A NEW PROCESS

The processes I've had the most success with are changing something, trying to solve too many things, and boiling it down to something simple.

One example is implementing monthly goals. I joined a team that had about eight different sprints happening at the same time, all using different sprint dates (with shared resources). At this point, we took all the timelines, stacked them on top of each other, highlighted what was expected at the end of each month, and tracked all goals by month. Some of the questions the team asked me were:

- When is our work due? Everything on the list is due at the end of the month.
- What if we don't finish it? Why do you think it can't be done on time? Let's explore that.
- What if it's still not done? It'll roll into next month, and we'll reduce the scope of other work.
- What if people take advantage of this system and just let their work be late? I'll be tracking everything everyone is doing and making sure it's being reviewed.

It's easy stuff if you keep it simple.

The most helpful thing I've found when trying to implement a new process is making sure you're comfortable with the idea that what you are championing won't end up being your idea (at all). What I've always sought to do is make my idea someone else's idea (now it's our idea). We take our idea and get other people on board, and now it's the group's idea. Keep running with this logic until it's implemented, and no one remembers where it came from. When selling a new process, sell it as temporary, and if it doesn't work for X amount of time, revert to the current way or decide as a group whether we want to evolve the new idea to something that better suits our style once we've tried it.

4.7 Project Management

One of the most effective ways through which to track all the all necessary work on the project is to utilize a project management process. Game developers tend to shy away from using any type of formal process and often jump right into making the game. They can feel that the process stifles creativity and removes the ability to add a cool thing to the game that wasn't planned, or that following it takes too much time. As a producer, I disagree with all of this. In fact, I believe that having a process makes it easier to be creative and add cool things to the game. It takes a lot of time at the beginning to set up and implement, but once it is in place, it becomes a useful and consistent way for people to know what to expect and how to get something done.

There are many useful project management books that provide detailed information on creating project plans and how to work with your team; most of these techniques and processes are applicable to game development, although modifications are often necessary to accommodate the sometimes chaotic nature of game development. *Project Planning, Scheduling & Control, Third Edition* (2001), by James Lewis, is recommended reading because it provides practical and easy-to-understand information about managing projects.

Because many game developers are not trained in project management, no common terminology or method is used from project to project. This makes it difficult for teams to understand how their tasks fit into the development process and impact the work of others. For example, a designer cannot script a level until the artist has built it, and an artist cannot complete character animations until the rigging is done. It is important for the team to be aware of these dependencies so they can schedule their work accordingly. When the work is not properly scheduled, the critical path becomes overloaded, and bottlenecks develop in the workflow, putting the game schedule at risk. Using a project management process alleviates some of these issues. The process also ensures that the team is working together to plan out what's needed, instead of just being handed a list of work with specific deadlines.

When team members see that the game production is under control, they are more confident in the game's success. A formal process allows the team to clearly see tangible progress, which motivates them to move forward in their work. For example, Scrum uses burn-down charts to show the progress the team is making. These charts allow teams to see when they are ahead of schedule, behind schedule, and right on schedule. If they are behind schedule, they can see this sooner rather than later and correct the timing before it becomes a problem that puts the project at risk.

Another benefit of using project management methods is that project metrics can be generated on how long it takes to do a task, and this information can be used when estimating the time it will take to complete similar tasks on future projects. Overall, this allows the producer and the team to generate more accurate task estimates.

The more accurate these estimates are, the easier it is for a team to plan the production cycle, decide which features and assets can be implemented, and determine more confidently when the game will be finished. For example, if an artist accurately tracks how long it takes to create a character model, this information is used to estimate this same set of work for another release.

The producer and leads greatly benefit from using a formal process. When a standard process is in place, it is easier to bring in new team members and get them quickly up to speed on the game's development progress. New people joining the team can get to work right away instead of having to spend a few days figuring out what they are supposed to be doing. Additionally, the producer and leads can spend their time actually managing the game development process, instead of putting out fires. Because you know exactly where the project is at any given time, no huge surprises should sneak up on you.

4.7.1 The Iron Triangle

A common saying among project managers is "The choices are good, fast, and cheap—you can only pick two." While the expression is tongue-in-cheek, the meaning behind it is very relevant to game development. If you want something fast and cheap, it won't be good. If you want it good and fast, it's not cheap, and if you want it good and cheap, it's not fast. Therein lies a conundrum for game developers since they typically want it all.

Figure 4.5 illustrates what's known as the "iron triangle" or triple constraints of project management: Budget, Schedule, and Scope. When getting started on your game development journey, it is wise to structure your milestones and plans with this triangle in mind so you have more control over the constraints these factors put on the game. Note that Quality is ultimately what is impacted when one or more of these elements change. If all of these factors are constantly changing during the development cycle, the project is never stable and is always at risk. One of the producer's biggest challenges while managing the game development process is striking a balance between the schedule, resources, features, and quality. As stated throughout

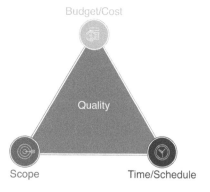

FIGURE 4.5 Project management constraints.

this book, all development teams are different and never have the exact same processes in place or risks to mitigate, but the producer's ultimate goal is still releasing a quality game on time and on (or under) budget. If the producer carefully controls the balance between the schedule, budget, and staffing, there is a much higher chance that this can be done. Other chapters in this book provide more information on how to plan for and control these variables; Chapter 7 goes into more detail on Schedules, and Chapter 8 goes into more detail on Budgets.

If you want to learn more about project management and how to be effective, there are lots of training opportunities and certification programs. Two of the most well-known certifications are Project Management Professional (PMP)® and Certified Scrum Master (CSM).

MATT IMMERMAN, PRODUCER, PROJECT MANAGEMENT.

I think the methodology you use is going to be highly dependent on the type of project you are working on and your team. I have generally found that, regardless of the type of project, I have a master schedule or road map done in Waterfall. Waterfall is great for that 1,000-ft view of a project, mapping out dependencies across disciplines, making sure there aren't huge gaps in people's workflows, figuring out deployment, and figuring out how much work can be parallelized. In my experience, it is generally less helpful and useful to the developers' day-to-day experience. To remedy this, the method I use most often, and have had the most success with, is a marriage of Waterfall and Scrum. I utilize Waterfall for all the things mentioned above and then distill that out into a typical Scrum workflow for the day-to-day work of developers, which includes establishing sprints, tasking, and prioritization. I always try to make all schedules and documentation available to the developers. Because they are so focused on their sprint tasks, it's good to give them the ability to see that 1,000-ft view so they understand how their tasks fit into the bigger picture and how we are tracking towards milestones.

4.7.2 Project Management Professional (PMP)

Project Management Institute (PMI) is an international organization that fosters the discipline of project management across all types of industries. It keeps track of current trends and recommended methods for project management, acts as a central repository for resources, and provides networking opportunities with other project managers. It offer three types of certifications, the most common one being the PMP.

PMI has designated a specific set of requirements that you need to fulfill in order to obtain a PMP. The requirements are fairly rigorous and include having up to 7,500 hours of project management experience, 35 hours of specific project management education, and a passing grade on the PMP certification test. After obtaining a PMP, a person must maintain active status by earning at least 60 professional development units (PDUs) over a 3-year period.

PMI also maintains *A Guide to the Project Management Body of Knowledge* (PMBOK® Guide) 2013, which is the main reference of the PMI standards for the project management process. It also lists relevant books, journals, and conferences that are related to the discipline of project management. It is updated every 3 to 4 years. The PMBOK is a general guide to the processes and methods endorsed by PMI, and it does not necessarily contain the details of all the project management knowledge that is available to PMPs.

Their website, www.pmi.org, has information on project management best practices and provides information on how to become a certified PMP. If you want to learn more about the basics of project management, this is a good place to start.

CHUCK HOOVER, GENERAL MANAGER, FACEBOOK REALITY LABS PITTSBURGH

Project Management Methods

Lots of them can be effective, but I would caution anyone against placing too much priority on a single method. Knowing Scrum, Kanban, Lean, etc. is fantastic as you can do a quick best-fit analysis and have options for discussion about what's going to be valuable. That said, I see a lot of people latch onto a method and become zealots around it. Methods are all made up; someone just like you worked out a method and wrote it down...that doesn't mean it's any more useful for your team than what you can create. Learn from what others have tried, borrow the best of them, but don't dogmatically stick to any of it. The best person to develop the method for your team is you.

In my experience, the most effective teams have methods that:

- Have thoughtful iteration baked in; testing and adjusting is paramount.
- Are developed with the team, for the team, not just by the leads or producer.
- Are hyper-defined. You can have a flexible method while still defining your process fully. You should know every aspect of how your process should work, so you can understand how to change it when it breaks down.
- Are transparent and simple to use. Methods that reduce the reliance on custom software or rigid tools allow your process to be more flexible and less dictated by the tool.

4.7.3 Certified Scrum Master (CSM)

Agile development is a set of methodologies that are focused on making a product via a process of iteration and feedback. Agile development emphasizes building an initial prototype of the game that contains very basic functionality and then iterating on this until the game is completed. Scrum is one of several agile methodologies to choose from. It is a management-focused methodology that is flexible enough to be used in a wide variety of game development environments. It is relatively easy to implement because it requires no formal training, only a commitment by the team to use the process. The basics of Scrum involve creating subsets of self-directed teams within the larger project team, which are headed up by a "Scrum Master," who is empowered to remove any impediments that affect the team's progress. The teams are cross-functional (artists, designers, and engineers) and small (normally 5–10 people). Teams work together to complete a set of tasks that will result in a tangible deliverable at the end of a set period of time. These set periods of time are called sprints and are usually 1 month in duration. The sprint is the building block for the game's progress because, at the end of every sprint, there is a tangible and playable game deliverable. The next sprint builds upon the previous sprint in an iterative process. For more details on Scrum, please refer to the books *Agile Software Development with Scrum* (2001) by Ken Schwaber and Mike Beedle, and *Agile Game Development with Scrum* (2010) by Clinton Keith.

A CSM has been trained in how to implement and manage Scrum on a project. The Scrum Alliance is the managing body for CSMs. Their website, www.scrumalliance.org/, contains information on becoming a CSM. This is less rigorous than becoming a PMP—you attend a 2-day training course and then take the certification exam. You will need to get re-certified every few years. CSM training doesn't provide you with a full set of project management tools; instead, it focuses on how to organize and set up a scrum team, which is very light on process and requirements. There is value in getting certified both as PMP (so you have a large box of tools to dip into for any type of project challenge) and as CSM (which is attractive to game development teams because it is light on process and very flexible with feature implementation).

RECOMMENDED READING

Rapid Development: Taming Wild Software Schedules (1996) by Steve McConnell outlines several different software development methodologies and discusses how to use them effectively. The author is a recognized expert in his field and is an evangelist for improving software practices in all industries. Even though this was written in 1996, the techniques and expert advice he offers are still extremely relevant to game development.

4.8 Conclusion

This chapter presents a lot of information on things to be mindful of when building the foundation for developing your game. There are a lot of pieces to coordinate, and you will spend a fair amount of time talking with different people about goals, milestones, and expectations. As you gather information, you will work with the stakeholders to define these things to ensure that everyone is on the same page and is on board with making the game. Once you have things more clearly defined, you also want to start thinking about how you will manage and organize all of these pieces; this is where good process and project management come into play. This chapter merely provides an overview of many of these topics, which will be explored more fully in later chapters. But, by this point in the process, you should have a good foundation to start working in earnest on fleshing out your game concept.

CHAPTER 5

Creating Concept

5.1 Introduction

You've spent time laying the groundwork for your game by gathering a group of stakeholders, thinking about expectations and milestones, and determining what type of development pipeline works for the game. Now it's time to start digging into the game itself and defining what it is and how to execute on this. Begin the process with a broad concept—usually a question you want to answer: for example, "What about a racing game where players ride around on dinosaurs?" As this concept is developed, additional ideas are generated to flesh out the concept and establish a vision that the stakeholders and team can align around. Over time, the characters and world are defined; the gameplay mechanics, genre, and key features are fleshed out; and the hardware platform is chosen. All these things are needed to create a full-concept treatment for the game.

During the concept stage, the team will probably include a producer, lead designer, lead engineer, and lead artist. This team takes the initial game concept, and, over course of a few weeks, evolves it into the game's core design. The producer's job in this phase is typically to manage the collaborative process, ensuring that the design is thoroughly documented. The lead designer or creative director will make sure that the game's elements support the initial concept. In some cases, a person in this group may have a hybrid role: for example, engineer and designer. In this case, the person will be responsible for representing both the technical and the design aspects of the game, and there may be conflicts in these areas that will be difficult for a single person to resolve. For example, the engineer portion may insist on using a specific technology, and the design portion may want to include a cool feature that isn't possible (yet) with the technology. If the same person has to think through both problems and make a recommendation, it will be more difficult. This is why it is important to have a team working together to talk through some of these issues. However, it is important that each person participating in the concept definition process has an understanding of their roles and responsibilities so that they can work most effectively together. Chapter 11 goes into more detail on this and why it is important.

This chapter provides an overview of how to flesh out a broad concept into a concept document, mainly from a production perspective. There are a lot of useful design books that go into more detail from a design perspective on how to do this. Two game design books that I highly recommend are Jesse Schell's *The Art of Game Design: A Book of Lenses, Second Edition* (2014) and Tracy Fullerton's *Game Design Workshop: A Playcentric Approach to Creating Innovative Games, Fourth Edition* (2018).

5.2 Brainstorming

Brainstorming sessions can be helpful at different times in the development process in generating new design ideas; out-of-the-box solutions for problems; or names for game characters, settings, or objectives. If you have the luxury of doing an original concept, you may want to start with a brainstorming session to generate a lot of different ideas to pick from. During a brainstorming session, the team generates a large number of ideas that pertain to a specific aspect, such as setting, character, or gameplay mechanics.

If managed properly, the brainstorming session can be a fun team-building exercise; everyone can talk about what makes games fun. If not managed properly, the meeting can result in frustration and wasted time. In order to get the best results from brainstorming, prepare ahead of time for a successful outcome. Generally, a useful brainstorming session accomplishes these goals:

- **The session's focus was maintained** and people didn't veer off onto other topics. If this did happen, the moderator was quickly able to redirect and focus the meeting.
- **Participants listened to each other:** If people are talking over each other, interrupting, or criticizing ideas, this quickly makes the session devolve into chaos and an unsatisfactory, useless meeting.
- **Many new ideas were generated:** Since the goal of brainstorming is to generate ideas, this is one of the most important indicators of success.

In order to get these results, the person running the brainstorming session must prepare beforehand and make sure others have prepared as well. Here are some guidelines for good sessions:

- **Every brainstorming session must have a focused purpose:** It might be to think of names for the main character or to come up with different kinds of environments that the player will encounter. Everyone present should know what the goal is. If you don't narrow the focus, the information generated during the session won't be as useful and is likely to be all over the map.
- **Have a moderator:** The role of the moderator is to run the session. They take notes, refocus the session when needed, and keep track of time. Everyone participating should be aware of the moderator's role and what the purpose of the meeting is.
- **Carefully select attendees:** Too many participants can cause a brainstorming session to drag on. It might be better to have several smaller brainstorms about different elements of the game. Also, it's best to have participants who know something about the subject matter. For example, a session about graphics and art direction will be comprised mainly of artists and a few programmers.
- **Expect everyone to prepare for the session:** Tell everyone what the focus of the session is so they can think about the topic and do research into technology, competitors' games, recent innovations in user interface (UI) design, or what-have-you. Having this information on hand will make the session more useful to all involved.

During the actual session, put some basic rules in place to make people more comfortable volunteering their ideas to a group:

- **No criticism:** Participants are not allowed to start picking ideas apart. The goal is to generate concepts, not eliminate them (that part comes later). If people start down the road of "that idea won't work because…," then the moderator needs to speak up and refocus the session on generating ideas.
- **No discussion:** The goal is to create ideas, not evaluate them and discuss them in detail. If a brainstorming session gets bogged down in conversation about the merits of an individual idea, then it will be a less productive session, and there will be less time to generate other great ideas.
- **No lulls:** Have a plan for any pauses in the brainstorming session; when ideas stop flowing, ask thought-provoking questions to get the brainstorm started back up again. For example, "What are our competitors doing on their games?" "What could we do to avoid a particular recurring problem in our game?"

After the session, group similar ideas together, prioritize them, and then write up a report of the session's results. The meeting notes should be shared with participants within the next day or so. The reason for this is twofold: First, you want participants to see what the results are and understand that their participation wasn't a waste of time; second, you want to generate action items from this session that people will follow up on.

Assign the highest-priority action items to specific members of the development team. For example, the session might have uncovered a cool design feature, but research needs to be done into what technology is required to support it.

Each person should have clearly defined action items for research and follow-up. These action items should take no more than a couple of days. Be prepared to have a lot of brainstorming sessions while you are fleshing out the game concept.

BRIAN SOWERS, ONE METHOD MONKEY LLC, SUCCESSFUL BRAINSTORMING

I find that open-ended brainstorming sessions at the start of a project tend to be useless. I've sat in on a lot of these meetings, and it always goes the same way—a ton of ideas are generated, and then a few high-level decision-makers go into a room and come out with… something completely different.

The best brainstorming sessions are focused and narrow-minded: They hammer on an individual feature or idea. They have clear takeaways and are driving towards decisions.

One little trick I picked up from a journalist—we took a bunch of index cards with tape on the back, wrote down ideas, and threw them up on a wall. As ideas seemed more or less promising, we would move them on or off the wall. We would group cards that worked well together and constantly juggle cards to different places as ideas clicked together. This gave the brainstorming some structure, and actual decisions were made in real time.

5.3 Initial Concept

As you start narrowing down ideas from the brainstorm sessions, you will hone in on the initial concept and start expanding on it. From a production standpoint, you want to guide your team to think about the goals, initial hook, core game loop, genre, platform, and target audience because all of these things will impact the initial concept. Some of these elements will evolve as you get further into development, but you want to have a solid foundation to start from (ideally on paper). The concept should be vetted before too much time, money, and effort are put into making the game.

5.3.1 Goals

Think about what the overall goal of making the game is by answering these questions:

- What are you making?
- Who are you making it for?

These questions are exactly what UX is about. By answering them and formulating them into a mission statement, you can create a litmus test for new ideas; if a new idea meshes well with the overall goals, it's probably a good fit for the game, but if the new idea clashes with the goals, it's worth reconsidering. Work with the team and stakeholders to define the mission statement and then publish it so that everyone can refer to it throughout development.

5.3.2 The Hook

The hook is a strong, attention-grabbing goal for the game. It becomes the basis for all game decisions and will be the core of the game's eventual marketing campaign. It's often presented as a question—"What if zombies lived in outer space?" "What if people could ride dinosaurs?"—with your game concept providing an answer. The hook is short, to the point, and gets people excited about learning more about the game.

5.3.3 Core Game Loop

The core game loop is the main set of actions that the player does in the game. These key actions form the framework of the gameplay mechanics: for example, running, aiming, shooting, gathering, building, or defending. The loop is the backbone of the game and can't be altered or removed without fundamentally impacting the game experience. For example, the game loop of Fortnite is harvest→ build→ defend: the player harvests items in the game world (or finds weapons), uses these items to build cover, and finally defends themselves with the cover or weapons they've acquired. The loop starts again when the player runs out of weapons or building materials. The story, setting, and characters add more depth to the game loop in order to provide surprise, challenge, and a sense of progression for the player.

5.3.4 Genre

A game's genre ties into the gameplay loop and refers to the type of challenges encountered during play. This categorization helps developers, publishers, and players understand what kind of game is being created. For example, in a first-person shooter (FPS), the player sees through the eyes of the character and is positioned behind the weapon used to shoot things in the game world. Classic FPSs include Doom® and Half-Life®. Other game genres include fighting, sports, simulations, role-playing, strategy, and third-person shooters.

Genre affects a game's design. Here's an example of how it shapes a fictional game idea about zombies in outer space:

- **Real-time strategy:** This is a top-down view game that features an army of zombies fighting against waves of invading aliens. The player would manage resources, build defenses, and direct a battle plan.

- **Fighting game:** If it were a two-player fighting game, there would be several zombie or alien characters to choose from. They would battle against each other in one-on-one combat in a third-person view. The game might feature combination moves, finishing moves, and unlockable characters.
- **Role-playing game:** As an open-world role-playing game (RPG), this concept would allow the player to take on the role of a zombie or an alien, and then level up their character with strength, weapons, and other characteristics while completing missions.

5.3.5 Platform

Platform refers to the hardware the game uses. The basic platforms are PC, console, mobile, and VR; an overview of these is discussed in Chapter 1. When fleshing out the game concept, consider which platform the game is on and make sure the concept and core game loop are tailored to the platform. In some cases, the game's core mechanics will be similar across all the platforms, with the main changes occurring in controller inputs (mouse/keyboard vs controller vs touch screen) and quality of graphics (the highest resolution is possible on PC, with consoles and mobile operating with less graphical processing power). If a game is released on multiple platforms, consider which design elements are best suited to each.

If you can only release the game on a single platform, think about how to incorporate the strengths of the platform into the concept. For example, a more in-depth game, like an MMO, works better on a PC since the mouse and keyboard setup allows for more complicated UI menus and keyboard controls. On console, a third-person action game works well with the controller, and you can simplify the in-game menus so that the player can quickly switch between different items or activities. On mobile, the touch screen makes it more difficult to have games that require accuracy or complicated menus.

5.3.6 Target Audience

The target audience for each platform will also impact the game concept. For example, PC players will likely spend hours in a single gameplay session, whereas mobile players will spend minutes. This is because PC players tend to set aside time for gaming, which is done in the comfort of their home. Mobile players tend to grab a few minutes of gaming in between errands or while standing in lines. Spending time defining who the target audience is will help determine which platform should be the primary one and which should be the secondary one.

Delving into the details of defining a target audience is beyond the scope of this book. There are several marketing resources available online that discuss the target audience in more detail and how to define it. In general, think about the demographics of your target customer (age, gender, income, education, occupation, kids, etc.) and their psychographics or personal characteristics (values, hobbies, interests, lifestyle, etc.). The more specific, the better. After gathering this information, writing personas is very helpful. A persona is a fictional description of a specific person who embodies one of the target audiences for your game. For example:

> Irene is a 27-year-old single woman living in Pittsburgh. She is a college graduate and is the assistant manager at a local bank branch. She lives comfortably in a one-bedroom apartment and enjoys playing action RPG games on her Xbox One (5 hours a week). She is planning to go abroad for a hiking and camping vacation this summer. She enjoys dining out at least twice a week with friends.

Getting specific with these personas helps you think through what features and innovations are needed in order to appeal to your intended audience. The processes of the marketing, art, and design teams building up the personas is more important than the persona itself as personas will evolve as the team gets deeper into the game design.

5.3.7 Revenue Model

Chapter 1 goes into more detail on the various types of revenue models that can be integrated into a game. The chosen revenue model will also have a direct impact on the core gameplay mechanics. For example, if the game will be free-to-play, the core mechanics may be built around the concept of spending money in order to progress more quickly in the game. For a subscription-based game, there needs to be a plan in place to continually release content on a monthly basis in order to encourage players to keep their subscriptions current. Think about how the revenue model will impact the game concept, and remember that the target audience will also tie into which revenue model you use. For example, hard-core gamers spend more money on games per year than mass market gamers. Hard-core gamers are willing to purchase a game for a one-time fee as long as the reviews are good, and the game is quality. Mass market players are more likely to try a game that is free-to-play.

5.4 Competitive Analysis

Competitive analysis is a study of games that are similar in style or genre to the game that you're making. This includes games that have already been released, and games that will be released in the future, especially ones shipping at the same time as your game. The analysis includes information about the competing games' features, pricing, platform, distribution model, and launch date. For games that have already released, you will want to include sales figures and average review ratings. You can gather some competitive data from a variety of places; see the sidebar for a few recommended resources.

If you're pitching a game to a publisher, the competitive analysis is proof that you've performed due diligence. It demonstrates knowledge of the market and shows that you're trying to differentiate your game from the competition. It can also show that your game concept fits into what the market wants and provides data to forecast revenue based on how similar games performed.

RESOURCES FOR COMPETITIVE ANALYSIS

- Entertainment Software Association: www.theesa.com/
- Game Rankings: www.gamerankings.com
- Metacritic: www.metacritic.com
- Newzoo: newzoo.com/

5.5 SWOT Analysis

In addition to a competitive analysis of other games, you will also want to conduct a SWOT analysis that analyzes your game's strengths, weaknesses, opportunities, and threats. The SWOT analysis identifies the viability of the game's concept, market opportunities, and anything that might jeopardize its success. Once you've done this, think about how to exploit or neutralize these elements, as needed. In order to get the most out of this analysis, make sure you understand what is needed for each element in the analysis:

- **Strengths:** These are positive influences under your control. For example, securing the license to the most popular animated movie of the year is a strength. The game is guaranteed to benefit from marketing tie-ins to the movie, and it should have international appeal.
- **Weaknesses:** These are negative influences under your control. Developing a game in direct competition with a market leader when you have no new differentiating features to set your game apart is a weakness. If there are no differentiating features, it will be difficult for this game to stand out and appeal to the target audience.
- **Opportunities:** These are positive influences outside your control. An opportunity is when a major competitor's launch date is pushed out several months at the last minute, meaning your game will have more visibility when it launches earlier. You had no direct control over this, but it is a huge opportunity for the game, and you should prepare to exploit it.
- **Threats:** These are negative influences outside your control. If you are working on an MMO, but on your release day, a major competitor releases a massive new expansion pack, it's a threat. It's going to have a negative impact on your sales, but the decision wasn't yours.

To get you started, Figure 5.1 lists some topics to consider when doing the SWOT analysis.

Figure 5.2 shows an example of a SWOT analysis form. In addition to filling out the form, it is important to include information on how to exploit the strengths and opportunities, and neutralize threats or weaknesses. Use this information to ensure the game features, revenue model, distribution method, and other business decisions are going to enhance the game's

STRENGTHS	WEAKNESSES
Core player actions	Inexperienced team
Innovative game features	No USPs
Unique selling points	No innovation
Production values	Platform choice
Licensed IP	Poor company reputation
Pricing/Revenue model	Financial issues
Appeal to International Markets	Tight schedule
Bundling with hardware or software	Low team morale
Team experience	Weak leadership
OPPORTUNITIES	THREATS
Lifestyle and market trends	Political influences
Technical innovations	Competitor's strengths
Competitors' weakness	Competitor's release dates
Niche target markets	Waning market demand
Partnerships	Loss of key staff
Middleware trends	Loss of financial backing
Release dates	Technical innovations

FIGURE 5.1 Topics for SWOT analysis.

INTERNAL FACTORS				
	Strengths	How to Exploit	Weaknesses	How to neutralize
1			1	
2			2	
3			3	
4			4	
5			5	

EXTERNAL FACTORS				
	Opportunities	How to exploit	Threats	How to neutralize
1			1	
2			2	
3			3	
4			4	
5			5	

FIGURE 5.2 Example of SWOT analysis.

success. This analysis is created during the concept phase and updated throughout the development process. Make sure the team and the stakeholders also understand this analysis as this will impact which features they choose to prioritize over others.

The SWOT analysis is finished, and the high-level game concept has been defined with the following information:

- Goal;
- Hook;
- Core game loop;
- Genre;
- Platform;
- Target Audience;
- Revenue model.

Now you can summarize all the information into a one-page concept brief and present it to the stakeholders. Gather their feedback and make adjustments as needed until they feel comfortable signing off. Getting stakeholder buy-in at this early stage positions the team to more effectively flesh out the concept into a full-concept treatment.

5.6 Concept Treatment

After the stakeholders approve the initial direction, the core team develops a more robust concept treatment. The concept treatment includes all the things presented in the concept overview and then provides the player experience, characters, controls, setting, story, art style, audio design, and technology needs in more detail. As a document, the treatment is likely to be 20–50 pages, depending on the complexity of the game and the amount of concept art included.

5.6.1 Player Experience

Start by thinking about the first five minutes of the player's experience: "What actions are they doing in the game, what are the challenges and rewards, and how steep is the learning curve?" As with personas, it can be very helpful to write 1–2 pages that describe in detail the player experience when they first start the game. This is a useful way to communicate the game to the stakeholders. When writing about the player experience, plan to include the following elements:

- Player challenges, such as end-level bosses and puzzles;
- Player rewards, such as points, extra weapons, or special items;
- Learning curve, which is how fast the player can learn the basics and start having a fun experience;
- Control scheme, which is how the player uses the controller or keyboard;
- Player actions, usually described as verbs, such as running, jumping, and casting spells;
- Social aspect, which is how players will connect and play with their friends.

Though this is not a comprehensive list of gaming systems, it's a first step towards finding out which game systems are needed and how they will all work together.

5.6.2 The Three C's

The three C's refer to Characters, Controls, and Camera. These elements focus on the relationship between the player and the things they interact with in the game. For example, "How does the player's character react in the game world when the player presses the 'action' button, and what content is displayed on the screen?" There are several design books that discuss

Characters, Controls, and Camera in more detail, so this section will just provide a high-level overview of how to think about these elements when creating a concept.

The character avatar is controlled by the player and interacts with NPCs encountered during the game. Consider how much control the player has in creating the avatar. In some cases, this character will be created by the designer with little input from the player—Mario and Kirby are examples; both are characters that have a specific appearance, personality, and actions that are fully controlled by the game designer. In other cases, a player may have more control over the appearance, clothing, personality, and choices of their character avatar, as in World of Warcraft.

For NPCs, think about how they will be used in the game. Will they be a player sidekick or an authority figure? Are they used to give quests and rewards to the player? Are they just there to bring life to the world and not have any impact on the gameplay? Will the NPCs change in any way based on the player choices? What are the relationships of the NPCs to the player's avatar?

The controls are the main way in which the player interacts with the game. Think about how control schemes will be laid out for different platforms. As discussed earlier, PC and console games will have different controller layouts, and now is a good time to think about how the control scheme will be designed. This is also a good foundation for implementing the initial control scheme into a prototype. For this section, a picture is worth a thousand words, so consider including an image of the type of control with callouts of the various player actions. A simple game prototype with playable controls provides a better understanding of how well the control scheme conveys the experience you want the player to have.

The camera's main function is to display the scene to the player. Sometimes, the player will have direct control of the camera. For example, an FPS often uses a dual input scheme in which character movement is controlled by one input, and camera movement is controlled by the other. In this instance, the player has very specific control over what they see on the screen. Other times, the camera is controlled by the game and will move based on what interactions the player is having. For example, you might be playing a third-person game where the camera moves programmatically to a particular viewpoint on the map. If the programmed camera movements are done well, they will feel like a natural part of the game, and the player will be able to see all the important things on the screen. In some cases, the camera motion isn't as well-designed, and there are blind spots on the screen that the player can't see. This has a negative impact on the player's enjoyment of the game.

5.6.3 Accessibility

Designing your game to be accessible to all types of players is critical, so you want to start planning for it in the concept phase. Accessibility means designing an experience that all players can enjoy, even those that may have some type of physical or mental limitation. Some examples include designing controls that can be remapped or are compatible with different input devices, choosing color schemes and values that make it easier for color-blind players to distinguish everything on the screen, or adding subtitles when characters are talking. One of the best sources of information on accessible game design is the Game Accessibility Guidelines website: http://gameaccessibilityguidelines.com/. Familiarize yourself with these guidelines, and follow them when designing the player interactions in the game.

5.6.4 Setting and Story

A game's setting is the fictional world in which the action takes place; this includes the time period, genre, and location. Setting has an impact on the look and feel of the game, and affects the environment, objects, location, and character designs.

For concept treatment, include details on the setting, such as history, government, religion, and anything else that evokes the setting. Concept art is also very helpful.

Story helps immerse the player in the game and can imbue the action with greater emotional power. During the concept phase, it's not necessary to flesh out all the details of the story. Instead, focus on creating a 2- to 3-paragraph story synopsis that integrates the setting, gameplay, characters, and key events into a cohesive whole.

5.6.5 Concept Art

Concept art is an excellent tool for communicating the game's vision and art style because it can be appreciated by all of the stakeholders. Everyone is looking at the same image and can see how the game will look before any art assets are created. Remember that concept art can take days or weeks to produce, so allot for this when planning out the time needed for creating the concept treatment.

5.6.6 Audio Design

Audio helps to immerse the player in the game world, so you want to think about the audio design when writing the concept treatment. This should include some information on the sound effects, music, and voiceover, and how they will be used to enhance the game setting and player experience. Things to consider from an audio perspective are:

- What will make each character's voice unique?
- What is each character's role in the game, and how can voiceover emphasize this?
- What kind of music best fits the look and mood of the game?
- When will the player hear music? In the UI? During gameplay? During cinematic scenes?
- Will the sound effects be realistic or more stylized?

5.6.7 Technology

As the concept treatment is developed, the lead engineer can start evaluating the technology needs for the project. This means reviewing what the technical challenges will be and then figuring out which game engine will best suit the project needs. There are a few engines available, such as Unity and Unreal, that provide out-of-the-box solutions and tools. The developer or publisher may also have proprietary technology that can be used to make the game. Include a brief overview of the technology needs in the concept treatment so that the stakeholders are aware of any additional technology licensing costs and the types of technical risks that are likely to occur during game development.

5.7 Assessing Risks

Once an initial version of the concept treatment is finished, sit down with the team, and do a risk assessment. Risks are potential problems, such as a key member of the team leaving before the project is finished or an external vendor missing a final deadline for a deliverable, or not finishing the graphics pipeline in time for the team to start production. Assessing these risks is an ongoing process and should continue through the project's entire development cycle. Once you've identified the risks, prioritize them, and then create a mitigation strategy for each one.

Every risk is different. Some risks may have a high likelihood of occurrence, but a low impact; others may have a high impact, but a low chance of actually happening.

Steve McConnell's book *Rapid Development Taming Wild Software Schedules* (1996) contains an excellent chapter on risk management and is recommended reading for anyone who wants to learn more about this. As he points out, a project utilizing risk management is not as frantic because there's no need for the producer to run around putting out fires. Instead, the team can focus on finishing the game because risks have been identified, and mitigation strategies have been developed. His approach is divided into risk assessment and risk control.

During risk assessment, the team must

- Make a list of risks that could have an adverse effect on the project.
- Determine the likelihood of each risk actually happening.
- Prioritize the highest-impact risks first.

Many risks can impact your game's ship date, quality, feature list, and/or cost. During the risk assessment phase, identify as many of these as possible, and prioritize them. The biggest risks are ones that are likely to actually happen and will have a huge impact if they do. For example, if you are working with a licensor, they will want to have final approval before the game is launched. There is a chance that the licensor will not give approval in a timely fashion, and if this happens, the launch could be delayed until approval is given. Late approvals have a high likelihood of occurring (based on my experience) and

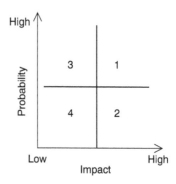

FIGURE 5.3 Risk classification grid.

will have a huge impact on the game's development timeline. Because this risk is called out, a mitigation strategy can be put in place. For example, work with the licensor early in development to create an approval process that has checks and balances in place.

Figure 5.3 is a basic classification grid for four levels of risk. Additional risk levels can be added if deemed necessary. Categories 1 and 2 include critical risks, and strategies must be put in place to deal with them if they actually happen.

After the team identifies the risks, they need to create a plan to control the risks by:

- Developing a management plan, which helps the team neutralize or eliminate critical risks. The plan for each risk should be consistent with the plan for the overall project;
- Putting the risk-resolution plan into effect;
- Tracking the resolution of known risks.

The team will continue to use the same process of risk assessment and control to identify and manage any new risks encountered during development. While the producer takes point on driving the risk management process, risk assessment and mitigation is the responsibility of the entire team.

5.8 Conclusion

The concept is the foundation the game is built on. Spend time early in the process to vet the concept and make adjustments where needed. Once the stakeholders have approved the initial concept, the team can develop it into a full concept treatment. Time invested in writing documentation and preparing concept art is well-spent because it is much cheaper to put something down on paper and make changes. Once you start translating the design document and concept art into a prototype, making fundamental changes becomes more expensive and complicated. Chapter 6 explains how to translate the concept treatment into a prototype.

Prototyping

6.1 Introduction

Now that you've spent some time brainstorming and vetting your concept, you want to prototype it to see if it is viable and worth exploring more fully. Prototyping is an invaluable tool in understanding what the game experience will be like for the player. You may come up with what seems to be a fantastic concept on paper but is terrible when translated into a playable game. If you prototype the key game mechanics before you embark on a full production cycle, you can save yourself a lot of time and money before discovering that the game isn't fun. Or you can use prototyping over a period of time to improve the key components of the gameplay until you have something fun that is worth developing into a full game. This chapter explores how to prototype effectively.

6.2 Why Prototype?

People may be very confident about their game idea and want to rush right into making it. They may resist starting with a prototype because it takes time, and they may be wary of the prototyping revealing the weaknesses of the concept. But prototyping should be an expected part of the development process. By spending time early in the development process, you can uncover key problems and fix them before they become bigger issues down the line. The benefits of the prototype are numerous, and its value to the finished game is well worth the investment.

The cost of making a prototype can be quite low when compared to that of developing a full game. You only need 2 or 3 people who, between them, can design and engineer the prototype. Give them a set deadline for creating something for review, and then let them loose to see what they can accomplish. This method is much cheaper than tasking out an entire development team with the code, art, and design for a full-blown feature.

Prototypes are also invaluable when comparing and contrasting ideas. You will find that game developers can be very opinionated about how to best implement an idea or feature. They can argue with each other about it and never come to a satisfactory solution, and the feature will end up being done haphazardly, with each person trying to implement what they feel most strongly about. Prototyping is a way to settle these disagreements sooner and more thoughtfully. A prototype can reveal the strengths and weaknesses of a concept or particular gameplay feature and lead to thoughtful discussions about how to make the best version possible. If people disagree on an approach, they can prototype both ways, present to a neutral group for feedback, and get better data on which decisions to make.

Getting early feedback is also a huge benefit. If the prototype proves the basic idea, the team can show it to other people (or potential players) and get useful feedback on how to refine the game mechanic for an even better experience. Some developers will upload early versions of their prototypes for people to download and provide feedback on. Minecraft and Stardew Valley are examples of games on which the creator sought feedback early and often in the development process.

If you need to communicate an idea to a group of people, a prototype is invaluable. A working prototype is the fastest way to explain what your game is about and why it will be fun. A solid prototype can evolve into a demo that you can show to potential investors as part of your game pitch (more on that in Chapter 9, "Pitching Your Game").

Another nice thing about prototypes is that they can be done at any time in the development process. Usually, a lot of prototyping occurs at the beginning of the process during the concept phase. However, the team may decide to prototype new features later on in the process, even when they are close to shipping the game. A quick prototype can help the team decide if a new feature fits. They may decide that it is worth having two people spend a few days testing out a new feature that could have a huge impact. For example, if you are trying to settle on a good control scheme for the game, you might be struck with inspiration late in the process as to how the controller should function. You can prototype the controller layouts pretty easily and then do some UX testing with the various options in order to determine which layout is ideal. Multiple prototypes can be in production at any time—focus on what is needed and the quickest way to get it done.

Prototyping is a tool that anyone can use, even if they are not skilled programmers. Because a prototype is a tool to help people understand how something works, people can repurpose an existing game to demonstrate their idea. A lot of game engines come with editing tools and art assets that are good for creating prototypes. Someone can spend a day learning the basics of the editing tool and probably create a somewhat useful prototype to start communicating their idea. Pen and paper prototypes can also be effective. There is more information later in this chapter about analog and digital prototypes.

Finally, don't limit prototypes to just testing out gameplay mechanics. Prototypes can also be used to test out new content creation pipelines, different art techniques and styles, or anything else that is not well-defined that needs to be communicated to people. For example, you could put together a prototype of how the localization pipeline works with placeholder assets. The prototyped pipeline can provide a good understanding of the issues that occur when extracting text for translation and then integrating it back into the game.

6.3 What Are Your Goals?

By understanding the prototype's goals, you can ensure that it is focused on the right thing. Is the goal to prove the fun factor of a game feature, to demonstrate a variant on an existing feature, to investigate a new idea, or to find an alternative approach? These goals inform how much time and effort should go into creating the prototype, and help decide if an analog or digital prototype is necessary. Here are some different ways in which you can focus your prototype:

- **Exploratory:** Sometimes referred to as a throw-away prototype. This is focused on answering questions about ideas or on testing a new feature or design and will not be reused in the final game. These types of prototypes should be made as quickly and cheaply as possible, especially since they won't be part of the final game. Convincing people that a prototype can just be thrown away is hard, especially when resources and timelines are constrained. But building a game on top of an exploratory prototype is similar to building a house on a sand foundation. You can do it, but it will eventually collapse in on itself.
- **Experimental:** This type of prototype refers to something that is validating a system that is already in place. For example, if you have a localization pipeline set up, you can create an experimental prototype with placeholder assets to test the flow of the pipeline. You can make adjustments as needed. Another example of an experimental prototype is adjusting the character statistical values in the game. You can create an experimental prototype to test out how various statistic impact the gameplay. In this case, the game system is already defined, you are just experimenting with the numbers.

- **Iterative:** This is probably the type of prototype that comes to mind when making games. It is made with the intent to evolve it into something that ships as the final game. Iterative prototypes are more expensive and time-consuming to make since the foundation has to be strong and the technical architecture has to be built so that it can be expanded to support more features and systems. While these are more expensive to make, in theory, you will save money later in the development cycle since you don't have to create the game from scratch. As with an exploratory prototype, an iterative prototype begins by answering a question. As more information is learned, more answers can be added to the prototype.
- **Vertical Slice:** This is somewhat of a hybrid in that it demonstrates the gameplay mechanics but also has been polished and refined to reflect what the final game experience is, including art, audio, and UX. Oftentimes, a vertical slice is a section of the game that showcases the key objectives and actions that players experience. Vertical slices are useful to show at publishing pitches (more on that in Chapter 9, "Pitching Your Game"). They also allow you to gather requirements and timelines for what it will take to create the full game. You can track how long it took to create things for the vertical slice and use this information to improve your estimates on how long things will take for the final game.

Once the goal is defined, and you have an idea of how much time and money you can spend, your next choice is whether you will make an analog or a digital prototype. Analog prototypes can be made with pen and paper, repurposed board games, dice, decks of cards, or any number of other things. Find what works best for your needs. Analog prototypes can be made by anyone since no specialized programming skills are needed. Analog prototypes can be useful in testing how statistics balance against each other. For example, if you want to test the random number generation of a certain set of statistics, you can set up a spreadsheet to calculate this via formulas, or you can use good old-fashioned dice to see what the results are.

Digital prototypes are what come to mind more frequently in the context of game development. They may take more time, especially if learning a new technology or if art needs to be created. The time invested is well-spent, though, as a digital prototype creates a better testing experience by presenting a dynamic and playable game. In some cases, the ability to configure different values can be added to the functionality, which allows more flexibility in testing different scenarios. For example, if you wanted to test out a new sports mechanic, the prototype could allow players to easily configure the size of the playing field, the number of players on the field, or the duration of the match timer.

When making a digital prototype, keep your goals in mind and focus on what's important. Oftentimes, if you are focusing first on the gameplay mechanics, you don't need to include great art to demonstrate the gameplay. Once you are satisfied with how this version of the prototype works, you might want to add in some better art to further refine your prototype.

You also don't need to create the initial prototype on the target platform. You might create a PC prototype for a console game and just plug a controller into your PC for testing purposes. However, don't get stuck in a position where you start building the final game on a prototype that isn't architecturally sound.

When prototyping, there's a drive to ignore visuals in favor of systems, but you don't get a good feel for a mechanic without at least approaching the actual aesthetics around it. The best prototypes look at a system holistically—sound, art, and mechanics.

I worked on a game where the central hub scene was a growing tree with birds living in and around it, and we constantly played with how the birds would behave. Working on it was a slog—everything was gray and boring, and nothing I implemented was interesting. I would've happily axed the whole feature. Then, our artist dropped assets in, and everything came alive. It was a real "aha" moment where the game as a whole clicked, and the work went from boring to exciting.

The vast majority of prototypes can be knocked out in less than a week. Some take longer—more experimental concepts can require a lot of iteration before you get at the heart of them—but most are things you can put together quickly and iterate on a bit before making a judgment call.

I throw prototypes away the moment I stop being interested in the mechanic. Sometimes, this is the first attempt, when it clearly screams, "This isn't going to work." Sometimes, it's a bit later, after I've iterated a few times, but the idea isn't meshing the way I thought.

I was working on a prototype for a game about giant monsters destroying a city. I had pitched the idea, and in my head, there was a lot of room for creative gameplay. The only problem was that after the initial prototype, the basic moment-to-moment gameplay was kind of terrible. It took me about a week of iteration to scrap that entire project.

6.4 Who Is the Audience?

The audience for the prototype also has an impact on your approach. If the prototype is going to be consumed by fellow developers, you don't need to spend as much time making art assets and polishing it. You can just present a rough prototype without quality art, animation, or audio and explain to your fellow developer what you hope to accomplish. Nine times out of ten, the developer will understand the purpose of the prototype, be able to play it, and provide useful feedback. When you set the context and goals for the prototype ahead of time, and let people know what type of feedback you need, the prototype process is more useful. For example, you may decide to prototype a new sports game mechanic and want to get feedback on the controller interaction, but instead of including fully animated characters, the prototype features cylinders that move around the field. Without context, the developers may focus on the movement of the cylinders and wonder why they look so terrible, and provide feedback on that aspect, instead of on the controller interaction.

Don't underestimate the power of a prototype to get the team excited about an idea. If they have a good understanding of the game from a prototype, they can share this enthusiasm outside the team and create positive momentum for the game.

If your audience is comprised of executives or publishers, you want to present a more robust and polished prototype, something more along the lines of a vertical slice. Executives and publishers will have a better reaction and clearer understanding of the game if the prototype looks and plays closer to the final game. The risk of showing them something that is in progress or contains a lot of placeholder assets is that either they will have a bunch of feedback on the unfinished parts of the game that ultimately isn't as useful, or they will see how much work is left to do and feel they have more latitude in asking for changes. You don't want to find yourself in the position of defending the game design and artistic choices simply because you showed a prototype too soon to a group that expects something closer to the final version of the game.

Players or potential players are another group that may have access to a prototype. If your game is in Early Access, it may be tempting to release an unpolished prototype for this purpose. However, even though the game is in Early Access, and the expectation for its quality is lower, you still want to present your players with a fun and playable version of the game. They should be able to interact with it and make progress, and there should be limited times where it crashes or has bugs. If you want players to give you feedback on a rough prototype of something, be very clear in any release notes about the state of the game and what type of feedback you desire.

6.5 Feedback and Iteration

Once the prototype is ready for feedback, decide what feedback is needed, how it is gathered and organized, and how it will be implemented in the next iteration. If you don't have a plan for gathering, reviewing, and using feedback, the whole prototype process is not very useful. Feedback is as important as creating the prototype in the first place.

If you have a UX team, they should also be heavily involved in this process. Prior to doing formal UX testing, work with the UX designer and researcher to do Rapid Iterative Testing and Evaluation (RITES). This is where early versions of the prototype are evaluated by the UX department for usability and engagement. They can make suggestions early in the prototyping process that will improve the quality of the final UX experience.

When soliciting feedback on your prototype, make sure you are showing it to the right audience and asking the right questions. As discussed earlier in this chapter, there are different types of audiences and their feedback will have a different impact on the game. Start by setting goals for what you want to find out. Do you want feedback on the usability of a particular user interface (UI) screen, or do you want to learn how the balance changes affected the difficulty of the game? Be clear about what you are testing and ask appropriate questions without defaulting to "selling" the prototype since this will make the feedback biased. Try to present the prototype as neutrally as possible, and create an open forum for discussion where the reviewer can talk about both the positives and the negatives of their experience.

You can add some light structure to the feedback session in order to make the most of the time and ensure that all the feedback is collected so it can be reviewed later. Start by setting the context of the prototype and stating the goal of the feedback being solicited. Once the reviewer understands the context, they can tailor their feedback appropriately. Next, ask the following questions:

- **What do you like about this, and why?** This is where the user provides their positive evaluation of the prototype. Understanding why they like it is important because it provides more data on what feedback should be implemented in the next iteration. It also will let you know if the prototype did a good job of communicating the goals.
- **What do you wish this had, and why?** This is a useful way to solicit more critical feedback without dwelling on the negative aspect. This gives the user a context for framing what they don't like about the prototype and a way to better articulate why, which means you won't get useless critical feedback like "This sucks." Focusing on what was wished for also helps the feedback session to remain positive. Again, the why is very important as the user's reasons for why they like or don't like something could run counter to the goals of the prototype. Understanding the why helps prevent feedback that isn't relevant from being implemented.
- **What if the prototype could do X, and why?** This opens up the conversation to discuss suggestions and new ideas. You might get inspiration from someone's suggestion. When having this discussion, treat it like a brainstorm session, and don't censor or shoot down ideas during the conversation. Instead, gather the feedback and synthesize it later. Once you have all the feedback, you can then start deciding what works and what doesn't work.

If people take the time to give feedback, they will want to know how it is used, so set up a way in which to organize and process the feedback. People are less enthusiastic about giving feedback if they believe that nothing is done with it, which can have a negative impact on team morale. A spreadsheet is probably the easiest thing to start with, and it is easy to sort the feedback to find common themes.

As the amount of feedback increases, you may want to use something like Trello or JIRA to organize and categorize it. The key thing is to make sure the feedback is collected, reviewed, synthesized, and implemented. For feedback that is not implemented, it is good practice to circle back to the people who provided it and explain why it was not used. This demonstrates that you seriously considered their opinion, and they will be more willing to provide feedback in the future.

During the prototype phase, it can be easy to get too attached to an idea, especially if it's your own. Make sure that everyone participating in the feedback loop has an open mind about both the positive and the negative feedback. It all needs to be evaluated against the stated goals in order to make the best use of it. People need to remove personal feelings from the evaluation so good decisions can be made. UX testing is useful for getting valuable data, which can offset the subjectivity of people's opinions. Chapter 15, "UX," goes into more detail on how to incorporate UX into your development process.

Both of these websites offer tools and methods for prototyping and gathering feedback:

- Design Thinking Bootleg, https://dschool.stanford.edu/resources/design-thinking-bootleg, is a set of tools and methods developed by the d.School at Stanford.
- Design Kit www.designkit.org, provides lessons and tools for human-centered design, developed by IDEO.org.

6.6 Conclusion

Making a prototype is a critical part of creating a game because it lets you test ideas and get input from other people before a lot of time and money are spent. When creating prototypes, be clear about what the purpose is and that the right questions are being asked and answered. Work with your team to use prototypes early and often, listen to their feedback, and make sure you follow up with people on how the feedback was used. In addition to proving out game features, a prototype is useful in estimating a budget and schedule for a full game because the effort involved in making it informs what effort is needed to make a full game.

PART 3
Establishing Requirements

Once a concept has been defined and fleshed out a bit, either by creating a prototype or by writing a design document, its requirements need to be established. The requirements outline in more detail the estimated effort required for making the game. This includes creating a budget and schedule. If you are planning to pitch your game for external funding, the estimated budget and schedule is an important part of the pitch. Investors need to understand costs and time frames so they can figure out if the return on investment is worth their effort. This part provides an overview on how to create budgets and schedules and then pull together all the information you've generated thus far into a compelling game pitch. The chapters are:

Budget;

Schedule;

Pitching.

CHAPTER 7

Schedule

7.1 Introduction

Schedules are synonymous with producers. In fact, some people think that creating and tracking a schedule is a producer's primary function! Hopefully, this book shows that this is not the case, but schedules are an important part of the production process. A schedule provides a lot of information that is useful to everyone on the team. It details what needs to be done, how much time the work takes, and who will be doing the work, and, as an added bonus, it shows the order of when the work is done.

This chapter presents a general overview of key things to consider when making a schedule and walks you through the process of creating a sample schedule. Remember that a schedule is just a tool that helps guide and track progress, and creating one that is 100% accurate is not realistic. The schedule is a close approximation of what is needed, and it must be updated and revised as new information is uncovered about the work.

7.2 Why Schedules Are Important

In my experience, development team members are suspicious of schedules. They view the schedule as something that dictates work, establishes inflexible deadlines, and isn't accurate, and thus, it is not useful to them. Sometimes, it is hard to argue against these points, especially if the schedule is outdated, has incorrect information, and didn't seek estimates and input from the team when it was created.

Game development schedules are also frustrating to create and track because changes in features, priorities, and scope of work are common occurrences. Defining and scheduling the "fun factor" for games is challenging, so the schedule has to be flexible enough for the team to experiment with and iterate on some of the key game features. The team may spend time and energy going down one feature path only to find that it is not going to work, so they scrap that set of work and start down a new path. This is a reality of game development and should be accounted for when scheduling. This approach doesn't mean that schedules aren't important. In fact, I'd argue that this makes a schedule even more important since it is a tracking tool that measures progress against the development goals. If a baseline schedule is tracked and updated, understanding when the development cycle is way off schedule is easier.

Create a useful schedule early on in the development process. A baseline schedule is a good starting point for the team to use in understanding the time and effort needed to make the game. If you don't know where you are going, and you don't have it defined in a schedule, figuring out how close you are to the destination is impossible. In short, the schedule is a road map. It may map out the quickest and most direct route, but you could be delayed by car trouble and need to make adjustments. The schedule may map out a more scenic journey that allows you to explore more features, but as time runs out for getting to the final destination, you may need to cut out some stops (aka features) along the way.

Involving the team in creating the schedule is critical. Hopefully, you have a core team you can collaborate with. If the team isn't involved, they won't have ownership of the work and may resent being held accountable for deadlines they didn't commit to. The producer shouldn't create the schedule in a vacuum and then expect the team to deliver on it; the team will feel micromanaged and backed into a corner, and morale will suffer as a result. The team wants to work together to achieve the development goals and collaborate on detailing the work that is reflected in the schedule. The team is also the best source for vetting the specific set of work that is needed, along with the priorities and risks associated with it.

Finally, remember that the schedule is dependent on the budget and team size. If you have a small team, it may take longer to accomplish a defined set of work. You can try to accelerate the schedule by adding more people to the team or by spending money to outsource some of the work. Be advised that there is a time cost associated with adding new people to the team—so be sure to account for those overhead costs when creating the schedule. For example, if you decide to bring on two more animators to reduce the timeline of the animation schedule, you will want to schedule in time to onboard them to the team and get them ramped up on the tools and development pipeline, and build time into the art director's schedule to review and approve the work of two more artists. In some cases, adding more people to the team will actually increase the schedule because of the overhead costs.

7.3 Creating a Schedule

Creating a schedule takes time, especially when parts of the game are not yet final. The time is spent gathering information from a variety of sources— the project stakeholders, the team, other departments, and sometimes outsourcing vendors. As more information is gathered, more detail can be added to the schedule, which increases its usefulness as a project management and tracking tool.

As you can see in the sidebar, there are a wide variety of project management software packages available for creating schedules. The best one to use depends on your needs. Do you need something that the whole team can use? Do you need to track a large number of assets through an art production pipeline? Are you tracking the actual time spent on each task? Do you just need to track the work being done in a sprint? The best thing to do is take a look at what software is available, use the trial version, have your team use it, and then decide what works best. At minimum, you will want to be able to define a piece of work, assign someone to do it, assign a duration or deadline, and indicate any dependencies between tasks.

Find something that you and your team will find easy to use. If people aren't using the software to update the status of their work, the schedule quickly becomes outdated and useless. Assigning one person to track and update the schedule is invaluable. They can talk directly with the team about progress, update the project management software, and generally be the go-to person when it comes to answering questions about the status of the schedule. This can be quite time-consuming, so be sure that someone has a few hours a day that they can devote to this (even better if this person is also the one tracking the budget).

PROJECT MANAGEMENT SOFTWARE

There are a wide variety of project management software packages available. There is no single one that is perfect for tracking game development, so it's hard to limit this to one recommendation. In my career, I've investigated quite a few project management software packages, and the following is a list of some of the more useful ones. Each of these has slightly different features and functionality, so you will want to demo them and figure out what will work best for your project management process. It's also useful to talk to fellow producers and project managers to better understand what they use.

Asana: https://asana.com/
Basecamp: https://basecamp.com/
Confluence: www.atlassian.com/software/confluence
Hack Plan: https://hacknplan.com/
Hansoft: www.perforce.com/products/hansoft
JIRA: www.atlassian.com/software/jira
Microsoft Project: https://products.office.com/en-us/project/project-and-portfolio-management-software
Monday: https://monday.com/
Pivotal Tracker: www.pivotaltracker.com/
Project Manager: www.projectmanager.com/
Shotgun: www.shotgunsoftware.com/
Smartsheet: www.smartsheet.com/
Trello: https://trello.com/

If using one of these project management programs seems like overkill or gets too complicated, you can always fall back to using Google Sheets to set up a tracking system that is simple to use and accessible to your team: Google Sheets: www.google.com/sheets/about/

Create an initial schedule that maps out the key milestones and goals. As you get closer to a key milestone, you will work with the team to flesh out the required work in more detail. Each production team will have a different way of tracking and scheduling work, so the purpose of this chapter is just to review the basics for creating a useful schedule. As you get more experienced with creating and tracking schedules, you will get better at estimating, understanding all the work that needs to be tracked, and dealing with any task or schedule changes that inevitably occur.

Don't expect to create an accurate schedule that maps things out months or years in advance; at best, you can schedule key milestones or goals to hit along the way, and then flesh out the specifics as you get closer to each one. For example, if the game needs to ship before Thanksgiving, you can work backward from the ship date to define a set of key deadlines:

- **Launch:** One week before Thanksgiving.
- **Third-Party Submission:** One month before launch.
- **Release Candidate:** Two weeks before third-party submission.
- **Beta:** One month before release candidate.
- And so on…

After you set the goals and milestones, take some time to define the exit criteria, which are predefined conditions that must be fulfilled before a set of work is deemed complete. Working with your team to determine the exit criteria for each of the development goals is useful because it forces you to spend time really considering what work needs to be done. Exit criteria also reduce ambiguity about whether a milestone is complete and whether it makes sense to move to the next phase. These criteria also make it easy to communicate to the team what the goals are and what success looks like.

Exit criteria are tangible things and very easy to define. For example, the exit criteria for a release candidate might be:

- All Priority 1 features are complete and playable;
- All Priority 1 and 2 bugs are fixed;
- Publishing and development have reviewed and approved the game for submission;
- All necessary submission materials and documents are complete.

Start creating an initial schedule by listing major goals and exit criteria. Remember to account for work being done by the various departments, including production, art, engineering, design, audio, localization, QA, external vendors, and marketing. Include approvals in this schedule as well since not having the appropriate approvals can cause schedule delays. As development progresses, more information and exit criteria can be added to the schedule.

After putting a high-level list of goals and deliverables together, you may be able to fill in some estimated dates or timelines. If you have a targeted ship date, you can start counting backward to roughly determine when the other goals should be completed. Again, this is not an exact science, so don't try to make it perfect. It's more important to think through all the pieces that are needed and understand the scope of work involved than it is to have accurate estimates down to the day. Figure 7.1 is an example of one way to start breaking down this information.

While the initial schedule provides a good framework for the development process, there is a need to create a more detailed schedule that outlines specific tasks, who is doing the work, and time estimates. This information helps the team to figure out the scope of the project as a whole, and you may be able to make some decisions early on about how much content needs to be created. For example, are you going to launch with 5, 10, or 20 game levels? The number will depend on how long it takes to make a level and how many people are needed. After making a detailed schedule, you may find that eight levels at launch is the most realistic goal based on the information you have. You may opt to create a more detailed schedule based around milestones or sprints; work with your team to decide what makes the most sense. In order to best determine all the little things to do, it is helpful to break down these large deliverables and tasks into smaller ones.

7.4 Work Breakdown Structures

Work breakdown structures (WBSs) are useful for breaking down large tasks into smaller ones. By breaking down a large task into specific, incremental tasks, you will gain a better understanding of all the work that is needed to create a specific section of the game. This will take some time, and people may be resistant at first, but it is worth the time spent since all involved will have a much clearer picture of the work that is needed to complete a

Game Project Name	Estimated Date	Notes
Languages: English, German, French, Italian, Spanish		
Production		
Concept Phase Completed		
Requirements Phase Completed		
Initial Game Plan Completed		
First Playable		
Alpha		
Code Freeze		
Beta		
Pre-Cert Submission to Microsoft		
Code Release Candidate		
Certification Submission to Microsoft		
Approvals		
Concept Approval		
Requirements Approval		
Game Plan Approval		
License Approval		
Console Manufacturer Approval		
Design		
Deliverables Completed for Concept Phase		
Deliverables Completed for Requirements Phase		
Detailed Documentation Completed for Game Features		
Character and Story Documents Completed		
Voiceover Scripts Completed		
Mission and Scenarios Designed		
Mission Prototypes Scripted		
Playtesting		
Final Missions Scripted		
Art		
Deliverables Completed for Concept Phase		
Deliverables Completed for Requirements Phase		
Prototypes Completed		
First Playable Level Completed		
Special Effects Completed		
UI Completed		
Cinematics Completed		
Engineering		
Deliverables Completed for Concept Phase		
Deliverables Completed for Requirements Phase		
Art and Design Tools Completed		
Production Pipeline Completed		
Engineering Prototypes Completed		
All Major Game Play Features Implemented		
Code Freeze		
Audio		
Sound Designs Completed		
Sound Prototypes Complete		
Placeholder VO Recorded		
Final VO Recorded		
Final Music Implemented in Game		
Localization		
Determine Localization Needs		
Organize Assets for Translation		
Integrate Assets		
Functionality Testing		
Linguistic Testing		
QA		
Test Plan Completed		
First Playable Testing Completed		
Alpha Testing Completed		
Playtesting Completed		
1st Code Release Candidate to QA		
Code Release		
Cinematics (External Vendor)		
Deliver Initial Specs to Vendor		
Storyboard from Vendor		
Animatic from Vendor		
Rough Cut from Vendor		
Final Movie from Vendor (no sound)		
Movie to Sound Designer		
Final Movie Ready for Game		
Marketing		
Demo Build		
E3 Build		

FIGURE 7.1 Example of initial schedule.

game feature. When the team works together to break down the work like this, they also gain a better understanding of what each person's tasks and responsibilities are and how all the work relates to an individual's specific set of tasks. They will uncover dependencies between their works that they didn't realize existed.

Here is a sample of a WBS process for determining what tasks are necessary to create a shippable character:

1. The team meets to discuss all the work involved in creating a character from beginning to end. All areas need to be represented, including production, art, design, engineering, and QA.
2. The group discusses the character creation process and details all the tasks they can think of that are needed to create a character. These tasks should be clearly defined as an action that can be completed by a person. For example, "create initial character design," "create character concept art based on design," etc. The goal is to break the work down into tangible tasks that can be assigned.
3. The tasks are grouped together by department and placed in rough chronological order. Dependencies between tasks are not yet detailed. The main goal is to make a complete list of all the work needed; the dependencies will be noted later when the full schedule is created.
4. The appropriate person provides a time estimate for each of the tasks. The goal is to get a rough idea of how much time it takes to complete a character. The end result is a list of the work that is needed, along with estimated times. Figure 7.2 is an example of a WBS.

The WBS process works best for work that can be clearly defined and quantified. For example, the tasks for creating art assets such as characters, levels, and UI screens can be really well-defined with this process. Other types of work, such as creating a new game mode, are less easily defined since there may be some technical and design unknowns that need to be researched first. There may not be historical data to review for these unknowns, so the work is harder to break down and define.

7.5 Estimates

As you work with the team on estimates, you may encounter some resistance. Generally, estimates are inaccurate, and the team may argue that time spent estimating work is time wasted. They would rather jump in and start the work, then figure out what else is needed. The nice thing is that, in game development, there is flexibility on which approach to use. When I'm working with a team on estimates, I acknowledge their concerns about the estimation exercise, but I also explain to them that this exercise allows us to build some type of frame around the work, so we can get an approximation of how far out of the frame we are. Thus, presenting estimates is another tool with which to scope the work. It's hard to argue that attempting to scope the work

Art Tasks (Planet Utopia)	Duration
Create prototype	5 days
Implement prototype feedback	1 day
Block out intial level layout	20 days
Create placeholder textures	3 days
Fix first round of bugs	3 days
Create destructible objects	2 days
Add final textures	10 days
Create player reference map	.5 days
Create special effects	2 day
Optimize level for budget constraints	5 days
Polish map	5 days
Fix final round of bugs	3 days
Design Tasks (Planet Utopia)	**Duration**
Design initial level layout	2 days
Design initial mission scripting	2 days
Script prototype	.5 days
Playtest prototype scripting	.5 days
Implement prototype feedback	1 day
First pass of mission scripting	5 days
Review scripting	1 days
Script second pass	5 days
Verify all supporting files are tagged correctly	1 day
Create localization tags for in-game dialog	1 day
Polish scripting	3 days
Fix final round of bugs	2 days
Sound Tasks (Planet Utopia)	**Duration**
Create sound design	3 days
Implement sound design prototype	2 days
Implement prototype feedback	2 days
Complete first pass of sound implementation	3 days
Polish sound	2 days
Fix final round of bugs	1 day
QA Tasks (Planet Utopia)	**Duration**
Playtest prototype	1 day
Test geometry and terrain navigation	7 days
Check textures	2 days
Test initial scripting	1 day
Test second pass scripting	1 day
Final test all level geometry and textures	5 days
Final test for mission scripting	1 day
Approvals (Planet Utopia)	**Duration**
Approve initial layout	1 day
Approve initial art prototype	1 day
Approve initial design prototype	1 day
Approve sound design	1 day
Approve final level, scripting, and sound	1 day

FIGURE 7.2 Example of WBS.

is a bad idea, so when the team understands that estimates are not going to be used to lock them into a commitment and instead are being used to help them better parcel out the work, they are more willing to engage in creating estimates.

Keep the following things in mind when doing estimates:

- Estimates are a best guess utilizing current information, and they won't be accurate.
- Estimates should be revised as more information is gathered. Any changes in scope or schedule caused by changing estimates should be immediately communicated to the stakeholders.
- Involve the team in the process. This is critical as you want them to take ownership of the work and effort that is needed. Talk to them about why estimates and schedules are useful and will help them with their work.
- Estimates are a way to help quantify the work. If you can't define the work and the effort needed, you don't have anything to track progress against. If you can't track progress, you are driving blind and don't know how far off base things are in relation to the deadlines.
- Use historical data when you can to provide the estimates with more insight and accuracy. Historical data is especially useful when working with the team who generated the data to begin with.

If the team is adamant that something is impossible to estimate, investigate using time-boxing to get better information. A time-box is a fixed period of time that someone uses to complete a task. The task requirements, exit criteria, and start/end dates are defined. The requirements should be prioritized so that the most critical requirements are completed first. Work with the team to choose an appropriate amount of time for the exercise. In some cases, a few weeks is good, whereas in others, only a few days are needed. Once you've agreed upon the work to be done within the specified time period, the work begins. The individual or team doing the work begins and stops when either the work is completed, or the time-box deadline is met (whichever comes first). If the work is not completed within the time-box, review how much progress was made. Based on this, work with the team to determine if the work should continue, if the work done is good enough, or if the work should stop and be removed from the game. Cutting the work completely is a viable option if the effort already put into the feature indicates that it will take too long to implement on the given schedule. This method is useful for gaining control over features that seem to be constantly behind schedule.

For example, if an engineer estimates that it will take 1 month to implement a tool-tip system, agree on 1 month as the time-box. Communicate with the engineer on a regular basis to check progress. If it seems that progress is being made against the 1-month deadline, great! As the engineer progresses, he or she should gain a better understanding of the problem and be able to adjust the estimates as needed. At the end of the time-box, review the feature with the engineer. It may be that the system is implemented and good enough to ship; that it is implemented but needs another week of testing and polish; or that it is not complete, and the engineer is still unable to determine how much more time is needed. At this point, you may decide to cut this feature if there isn't time to continue work on it. Another possible outcome is to work with the engineer to define another goal and time-box for the tool-tip system, and check their progress again later. Repeat the time-box process until the feature is complete, or it is determined that the feature can't be done within the overall schedule.

7.6 Putting It All Together

Once you've put together a high-level schedule and broken down the work into specific tasks, you can start putting together an actual schedule. Remember that the schedule is a living document with the primary purpose of providing a baseline for tracking progress. With game development, it is difficult to work in absolutes because of the uncertainty in the design, technical, and art processes. Other industries, such as construction, have more certainty when it comes to building things, so a schedule is likely to be more accurate in regard to estimates and deadlines.

Once the tasks are defined, they can be added to a project schedule. This includes the dependencies between tasks and details specifically who will do the work. As the schedule is built, continually check in with people on the estimates and make adjustments, as needed. As more information is gathered about the work, it is natural for people to increase or decrease their estimates for a task; they will also uncover work that needs to be added to the schedule.

When putting tasks into a schedule, you may want to limit the task duration to 1–2 days, 3–5 days, or some other manageable increment of time. Limiting the number of days assigned to a task helps people to more specifically define the work needed to complete a larger feature.

For example, if a designer lists a task called "create UI wireframes for the game," and it is estimated that this will take 8 weeks of work, you probably want to work with them to break this down into more bite-sized chunks. Instead of approaching this as creating all the wireframes, you might detail the specific areas that need user interface (UI), or the individual screens, and then determine the work needed. This allows you to work with the designer to prioritize the parts of the UI that should be wireframed first and the ones that can wait, and keep the effort scoped appropriately. For a wireframe, you don't need art assets or concept art—so if the 8-week estimate includes art, you will discover this when breaking down the work and be able to keep the designer focused specifically on creating the wireframes. The art effort involved in the UI screens can be broken down and tasked out separately in the schedule.

If there is difficulty in determining how long a task will take, the person should work with their lead to make an educated estimate based on experience. Do not leave the duration for any task blank because this will not provide a true picture of the overall schedule. Accurately estimating tasks is very subjective, but your ability to do so improves with experience. It is good to build some extra time into the schedule to accommodate any work that takes longer than originally estimated. Some people like to add this extra time on a per-task basis, while some people prefer to just add extra time at the end of the schedule without allocating it to a specific task.

When durations are assigned to the schedule, add in time for sick days, holidays, and vacations. You cannot assume that everyone will be in the office every single workday. Also, do not schedule overtime. This is a bad practice and will quickly lead to an unhappy (and therefore unproductive) team. Instead, limit the scope of the project so that everything can be completed in a reasonable amount of time. In fact, all the task durations should be based on accomplishing about 5–6 hours of work during a normal 8-hour workday. The other 2–3 hours per day accounts for the time people spend checking email, going to meetings, and dealing with general non-task-related work.

Keep in mind that task dependencies and assigned resources can dramatically affect a schedule. For example, if it takes several days to get something approved, this could bring work to a standstill and, in turn, create a bottleneck. If someone is overloaded with too many tasks, he or she cannot maintain the expected pace, and this can also cause delays, especially if others are waiting for the work to be completed before they can begin their assigned tasks.

Figure 7.3 is the first iteration of a level creation schedule, based on the WBS depicted in Figure 7.2. This does not account for any dependencies between tasks or have any resources assigned. Based on this, creating a level would only take 15 days.

		Name	Duration	Start	Finish	Predecessors	Resource Names
1		Project Dropix Level Production	15 days	2/1/21 8:00 AM	2/19/21 5:00 PM		
2		⊟Art	15 days	2/1/21 8:00 AM	2/19/21 5:00 PM		
3		Create prototype	5 days	2/1/21 8:00 AM	2/5/21 5:00 PM		
4		Implement prototype feedback	1 day	2/1/21 8:00 AM	2/1/21 5:00 PM		
5		Create level geometry	15 days	2/1/21 8:00 AM	2/19/21 5:00 PM		
6		Add placeholder textures	3 days	2/1/21 8:00 AM	2/3/21 5:00 PM		
7		Fix first round of bugs	3 days	2/1/21 8:00 AM	2/3/21 5:00 PM		
8		Create destructible objects	2 days	2/1/21 8:00 AM	2/2/21 5:00 PM		
9		Add final textures	10 days	2/1/21 8:00 AM	2/12/21 5:00 PM		
10		Create player reference map	1 day	2/1/21 8:00 AM	2/1/21 5:00 PM		
11		Create special effects	3 days	2/1/21 8:00 AM	2/3/21 5:00 PM		
12		Optimize level for budget constraints	10 days	2/1/21 8:00 AM	2/12/21 5:00 PM		
13		Polish map	5 days	2/1/21 8:00 AM	2/5/21 5:00 PM		
14		Fix final round of bugs	5 days	2/1/21 8:00 AM	2/5/21 5:00 PM		
15		⊟Design	5 days	2/1/21 8:00 AM	2/5/21 5:00 PM		
16		Design initial level layout	2 days	2/1/21 8:00 AM	2/2/21 5:00 PM		
17		Design initial mission scripting	2 days	2/1/21 8:00 AM	2/2/21 5:00 PM		
18		Create initial prototype scripting	2 days	2/1/21 8:00 AM	2/2/21 5:00 PM		
19		Implement prototype feedback	2 days	2/1/21 8:00 AM	2/2/21 5:00 PM		
20		Script first pass of mission scripting	5 days	2/1/21 8:00 AM	2/5/21 5:00 PM		
21		Script first pass of multiplayer scripting	2 days	2/1/21 8:00 AM	2/2/21 5:00 PM		
22		Review scripting	1 day	2/1/21 8:00 AM	2/1/21 5:00 PM		
23		Script second pass	5 days	2/1/21 8:00 AM	2/5/21 5:00 PM		
24		Verify all supporting files are tagged correctly	1 day	2/1/21 8:00 AM	2/1/21 5:00 PM		
25		Create localization tags for in-game dialog	1 day	2/1/21 8:00 AM	2/1/21 5:00 PM		
26		Polish scripting	3 days	2/1/21 8:00 AM	2/3/21 5:00 PM		
27		Fix final round of bugs	2 days	2/1/21 8:00 AM	2/2/21 5:00 PM		
28		⊟Sound	3 days	2/1/21 8:00 AM	2/3/21 5:00 PM		
29		Create sound design	3 days	2/1/21 8:00 AM	2/3/21 5:00 PM		
30		Implement sound design prototype	2 days	2/1/21 8:00 AM	2/2/21 5:00 PM		
31		Implement feedback	2 days	2/1/21 8:00 AM	2/2/21 5:00 PM		
32		Complete first pass of sound implementation	3 days	2/1/21 8:00 AM	2/3/21 5:00 PM		
33		Polish sound	2 days	2/1/21 8:00 AM	2/2/21 5:00 PM		
34		Fix final round of bugs	1 day	2/1/21 8:00 AM	2/1/21 5:00 PM		
35		⊟QA	7 days	2/1/21 8:00 AM	2/9/21 5:00 PM		
36		Playtest prototype	1 day	2/1/21 8:00 AM	2/1/21 5:00 PM		
37		Test geometry and terrain navigation	7 days	2/1/21 8:00 AM	2/9/21 5:00 PM		
38		Check textures	2 days	2/1/21 8:00 AM	2/2/21 5:00 PM		
39		Test initial scripting	1 day	2/1/21 8:00 AM	2/1/21 5:00 PM		
40		Test second pass scripting	1 day	2/1/21 8:00 AM	2/1/21 5:00 PM		
41		Final test all level geometry and textures	5 days	2/1/21 8:00 AM	2/5/21 5:00 PM		
42		Final test for mission scripting	1 day	2/1/21 8:00 AM	2/1/21 5:00 PM		
43		⊟Approvals	2 days	2/1/21 8:00 AM	2/2/21 5:00 PM		
44		Approve initial layout	2 days	2/1/21 8:00 AM	2/2/21 5:00 PM		
45		Approve initial art prototype	2 days	2/1/21 8:00 AM	2/2/21 5:00 PM		
46		Approval initial design prototype	2 days	2/1/21 8:00 AM	2/2/21 5:00 PM		
47		Approve sound design	2 days	2/1/21 8:00 AM	2/2/21 5:00 PM		
48		Approve final level, scripting, and sound	2 days	2/1/21 8:00 AM	2/2/21 5:00 PM		

FIGURE 7.3 Level creation schedule, with no dependencies or resources assigned.

	⊕	Name	Duration	Start	Finish	Predecessors	Resource Names
1	🗓	⊟Planet Utopia Level Production	63 days	2/1/21 8:00 AM	4/28/21 5:00 PM		
2		⊟Art	63 days	2/1/21 8:00 AM	4/28/21 5:00 PM		
3		Create prototype	5 days	3/22/21 8:00 AM	3/26/21 5:00 PM		Artist 1
4		Implement prototype feedback	1 day	4/27/21 8:00 AM	4/27/21 5:00 PM		Artist 1
5		Create level geometry	15 days	2/1/21 8:00 AM	2/19/21 5:00 PM		Artist 1
6		Add placeholder textures	3 days	4/12/21 8:00 AM	4/14/21 5:00 PM		Artist 1
7		Fix first round of bugs	3 days	4/15/21 8:00 AM	4/19/21 5:00 PM		Artist 1
8		Create destructible objects	2 days	4/23/21 8:00 AM	4/26/21 5:00 PM		Artist 1
9		Add final textures	10 days	2/22/21 8:00 AM	3/5/21 5:00 PM		Artist 1
10		Create player reference map	1 day	4/28/21 8:00 AM	4/28/21 5:00 PM		Artist 1
11		Create special effects	3 days	4/20/21 8:00 AM	4/22/21 5:00 PM		Artist 1
12		Optimize level for budget constraints	10 days	3/8/21 8:00 AM	3/19/21 5:00 PM		Artist 1
13		Polish map	5 days	3/29/21 8:00 AM	4/2/21 5:00 PM		Artist 1
14		Fix final round of bugs	5 days	4/5/21 8:00 AM	4/9/21 5:00 PM		Artist 1
15		⊟Design	28 days	2/1/21 8:00 AM	3/10/21 5:00 PM		
16		Design initial level layout	2 days	2/18/21 8:00 AM	2/19/21 5:00 PM		Designer 1
17		Design initial mission scripting	2 days	2/22/21 8:00 AM	2/23/21 5:00 PM		Designer 1
18		Create initial prototype scripting	2 days	2/24/21 8:00 AM	2/25/21 5:00 PM		Designer 1
19		Implement prototype feedback	2 days	2/26/21 8:00 AM	3/1/21 5:00 PM		Designer 1
20		Script first pass of mission scripting	5 days	2/1/21 8:00 AM	2/5/21 5:00 PM		Designer 1
21		Script first pass of multiplayer scripting	2 days	3/2/21 8:00 AM	3/3/21 5:00 PM		Designer 1
22		Review scripting	1 day	3/8/21 8:00 AM	3/8/21 5:00 PM		Designer 1
23		Script second pass	5 days	2/8/21 8:00 AM	2/12/21 5:00 PM		Designer 1
24		Verify all supporting files are tagged correctly	1 day	3/9/21 8:00 AM	3/9/21 5:00 PM		Designer 1
25		Create localization tags for in-game dialog	1 day	3/10/21 8:00 AM	3/10/21 5:00 PM		Designer 1
26		Polish scripting	3 days	2/15/21 8:00 AM	2/17/21 5:00 PM		Designer 1
27		Fix final round of bugs	2 days	3/4/21 8:00 AM	3/5/21 5:00 PM		Designer 1
28		⊟Sound	13 days	2/1/21 8:00 AM	2/17/21 5:00 PM		
29		Create sound design	3 days	2/1/21 8:00 AM	2/3/21 5:00 PM		Sound Designer 1
30		Implement sound design prototype	2 days	2/9/21 8:00 AM	2/10/21 5:00 PM		Sound Designer 1
31		Implement feedback	2 days	2/11/21 8:00 AM	2/12/21 5:00 PM		Sound Designer 1
32		Complete first pass of sound implementation	3 days	2/4/21 8:00 AM	2/8/21 5:00 PM		Sound Designer 1
33		Polish sound	2 days	2/15/21 8:00 AM	2/16/21 5:00 PM		Sound Designer 1
34		Fix final round of bugs	1 day	2/17/21 8:00 AM	2/17/21 5:00 PM		Sound Designer 1
35		⊟QA	18 days	2/1/21 8:00 AM	2/24/21 5:00 PM		
36		Playtest prototype	1 day	2/19/21 8:00 AM	2/19/21 5:00 PM		Tester 1
37		Test geometry and terrain navigation	7 days	2/1/21 8:00 AM	2/9/21 5:00 PM		Tester 1
38		Check textures	2 days	2/17/21 8:00 AM	2/18/21 5:00 PM		Tester 1
39		Test initial scripting	1 day	2/22/21 8:00 AM	2/22/21 5:00 PM		Tester 1
40		Test second pass scripting	1 day	2/23/21 8:00 AM	2/23/21 5:00 PM		Tester 1
41		Final test all level geometry and textures	5 days	2/10/21 8:00 AM	2/16/21 5:00 PM		Tester 1
42		Final test for mission scripting	1 day	2/24/21 8:00 AM	2/24/21 5:00 PM		Tester 1
43		⊟Approvals	10 days	2/1/21 8:00 AM	2/12/21 5:00 PM		
44		Approve initial layout	2 days	2/1/21 8:00 AM	2/2/21 5:00 PM		Management
45		Approve initial art prototype	2 days	2/3/21 8:00 AM	2/4/21 5:00 PM		Management
46		Approval initial design prototype	2 days	2/5/21 8:00 AM	2/8/21 5:00 PM		Management
47		Approve sound design	2 days	2/9/21 8:00 AM	2/10/21 5:00 PM		Management
48		Approve final level, scripting, and sound	2 days	2/11/21 8:00 AM	2/12/21 5:00 PM		Management

FIGURE 7.4 Level creation schedule, with resources assigned.

Figure 7.4 is the same schedule, but with resources assigned. The amount of time needed to complete this work is 63 days. The time increased because there are a limited number of people who can do the work. If the art and design work are split between multiple designers and artists, the time to create this level can be reduced.

Figure 7.5 is a version of the schedule with just the dependencies defined and no resources assigned. This version is useful in understanding how all the pieces work together and where bottlenecks can occur in the pipeline. The total time needed to create this level is now 37 days because some tasks can't be started until others are completed. If tasks earlier in the pipeline take a long time to complete, it will block progress for tasks later in the pipeline. A schedule can help identify where these bottlenecks are, so they can be solved. In this case, several levels might be in development at one time, and someone can work on their tasks for Level A while waiting for the others to complete their work on Level B.

Figure 7.6 shows the schedule with both the resources and dependencies assigned. In this version, the level will take 41 days to complete. This takes into account the dependencies and how the resources are allocated. This schedule offers the most accurate timeline, based on all the known information. It also provides a good baseline for understanding where to add resources to shorten the timeline, places where there are bottlenecks, and something with which to measure progress.

	⊕	Name	Duration	Start	Finish	Predecessors	Resource Names
1	🗓	Project Utopia Level Production	37 days	2/1/21 8:00 AM	3/23/21 5:00 PM		
2		⊟ Art	35 days	2/3/21 8:00 AM	3/23/21 5:00 PM		
3		Create prototype	5 days	2/3/21 8:00 AM	2/9/21 5:00 PM	44	
4		Implement prototype feedback	1 day	2/3/21 8:00 AM	2/3/21 5:00 PM	45	
5		Create level geometry	15 days	2/4/21 8:00 AM	2/24/21 5:00 PM	4	
6		Add placeholder textures	3 days	2/25/21 8:00 AM	3/1/21 5:00 PM	5	
7		Fix first round of bugs	3 days	2/10/21 8:00 AM	2/12/21 5:00 PM	37	
8		Create destructible objects	2 days	2/15/21 8:00 AM	2/16/21 5:00 PM	7	
9		Add final textures	10 days	2/17/21 8:00 AM	3/2/21 5:00 PM	8	
10		Create player reference map	1 day	2/17/21 8:00 AM	2/17/21 5:00 PM	8	
11		Create special effects	3 days	2/17/21 8:00 AM	2/19/21 5:00 PM	8	
12		Optimize level for budget constraints	10 days	3/3/21 8:00 AM	3/16/21 5:00 PM	9;10;11	
13		Polish map	5 days	3/17/21 8:00 AM	3/23/21 5:00 PM	12	
14		Fix final round of bugs	5 days	2/8/21 8:00 AM	2/12/21 5:00 PM	41	
15		⊟ Design	32 days	2/1/21 8:00 AM	3/16/21 5:00 PM		
16		Design initial level layout	2 days	2/1/21 8:00 AM	2/2/21 5:00 PM		
17		Design initial mission scripting	2 days	2/1/21 8:00 AM	2/2/21 5:00 PM		
18		Create initial prototype scripting	2 days	2/4/21 8:00 AM	2/5/21 5:00 PM	17;4	
19		Implement prototype feedback	2 days	2/3/21 8:00 AM	2/4/21 5:00 PM	46;36	
20		Script first pass of mission scripting	5 days	2/25/21 8:00 AM	3/3/21 5:00 PM	5	
21		Script first pass of multiplayer scripting	2 days	2/25/21 8:00 AM	2/26/21 5:00 PM	5	
22		Review scripting	1 day	3/4/21 8:00 AM	3/4/21 5:00 PM	20;21	
23		Script second pass	5 days	3/5/21 8:00 AM	3/11/21 5:00 PM	22;39	
24		Verify all supporting files are tagged correc	1 day	2/1/21 8:00 AM	2/1/21 5:00 PM	12	
25		Create localization tags for in-game dialog	1 day	2/1/21 8:00 AM	2/1/21 5:00 PM	12	
26		Polish scripting	3 days	3/12/21 8:00 AM	3/16/21 5:00 PM	23;24;25	
27		Fix final round of bugs	2 days	2/2/21 8:00 AM	2/3/21 5:00 PM	42	
28		⊟ Sound	29 days	2/3/21 8:00 AM	3/15/21 5:00 PM		
29		Create sound design	3 days	2/3/21 8:00 AM	2/5/21 5:00 PM	45	
30		Implement sound design prototype	2 days	2/4/21 8:00 AM	2/5/21 5:00 PM	4	
31		Implement feedback	2 days	2/3/21 8:00 AM	2/4/21 5:00 PM	47	
32		Complete first pass of sound implementatic	3 days	3/5/21 8:00 AM	3/9/21 5:00 PM	22	
33		Polish sound	2 days	3/12/21 8:00 AM	3/15/21 5:00 PM	23	
34		Fix final round of bugs	1 day	3/15/21 8:00 AM	3/15/21 5:00 PM	40	
35		⊟ QA	30 days	2/1/21 8:00 AM	3/12/21 5:00 PM		
36		Playtest prototype	1 day	2/1/21 8:00 AM	2/1/21 5:00 PM		
37		Test geometry and terrain navigation	7 days	2/1/21 8:00 AM	2/9/21 5:00 PM		
38		Check textures	2 days	2/1/21 8:00 AM	2/2/21 5:00 PM	9	
39		Test initial scripting	1 day	2/1/21 8:00 AM	2/1/21 5:00 PM		
40		Test second pass scripting	1 day	3/12/21 8:00 AM	3/12/21 5:00 PM	23	
41		Final test all level geometry and textures	5 days	2/1/21 8:00 AM	2/5/21 5:00 PM		
42		Final test for mission scripting	1 day	2/1/21 8:00 AM	2/1/21 5:00 PM		
43		⊟ Approvals	34 days	2/1/21 8:00 AM	3/18/21 5:00 PM		
44		Approve initial layout	2 days	2/1/21 8:00 AM	2/2/21 5:00 PM		
45		Approve initial art prototype	2 days	2/1/21 8:00 AM	2/2/21 5:00 PM		
46		Approval initial design prototype	2 days	2/1/21 8:00 AM	2/2/21 5:00 PM		
47		Approve sound design	2 days	2/1/21 8:00 AM	2/2/21 5:00 PM		
48		Approve final level, scripting, and sound	2 days	3/17/21 8:00 AM	3/18/21 5:00 PM	12;26;33	

FIGURE 7.5 Level creation schedule, with dependencies assigned.

	⊕	Name	Duration	Start	Finish	Predecessors	Resource Names
1	🗓	Planet Utopia Level Production	41 days	2/1/21 8:00 AM	3/29/21 5:00 PM		
2		⊟ Art	39 days	2/3/21 8:00 AM	3/29/21 5:00 PM		
3		Create prototype	5 days	2/3/21 8:00 AM	2/9/21 5:00 PM	44	Artist 1
4		Implement prototype feedback	1 day	2/3/21 8:00 AM	2/3/21 5:00 PM	45	Artist 1
5		Create level geometry	15 days	2/4/21 8:00 AM	2/24/21 5:00 PM	4	Artist 1
6		Add placeholder textures	3 days	2/25/21 8:00 AM	3/1/21 5:00 PM	5	Artist 1
7		Fix first round of bugs	3 days	2/10/21 8:00 AM	2/12/21 5:00 PM	37	Artist 1
8		Create destructible objects	2 days	2/15/21 8:00 AM	2/16/21 5:00 PM	7	Artist 1
9		Add final textures	10 days	2/17/21 8:00 AM	3/2/21 5:00 PM	8	Artist 1
10		Create player reference map	1 day	3/8/21 8:00 AM	3/8/21 5:00 PM	8	Artist 1
11		Create special effects	3 days	3/3/21 8:00 AM	3/5/21 5:00 PM	8	Artist 1
12		Optimize level for budget constraints	10 days	3/9/21 8:00 AM	3/22/21 5:00 PM	9;10;11	Artist 1
13		Polish map	5 days	3/23/21 8:00 AM	3/29/21 5:00 PM	12	Artist 1
14		Fix final round of bugs	5 days	2/8/21 8:00 AM	2/12/21 5:00 PM	41	Artist 1
15		⊟ Design	34 days	2/1/21 8:00 AM	3/18/21 5:00 PM		
16		Design initial level layout	2 days	2/1/21 8:00 AM	2/2/21 5:00 PM		Designer 1
17		Design initial mission scripting	2 days	2/3/21 8:00 AM	2/4/21 5:00 PM		Designer 1
18		Create initial prototype scripting	2 days	2/5/21 8:00 AM	2/8/21 5:00 PM	17;4	Designer 1
19		Implement prototype feedback	2 days	2/3/21 8:00 AM	2/4/21 5:00 PM	46;36	Designer 1
20		Script first pass of mission scripting	5 days	2/25/21 8:00 AM	3/3/21 5:00 PM	5	Designer 1
21		Script first pass of multiplayer scripting	2 days	3/4/21 8:00 AM	3/5/21 5:00 PM	5	Designer 1
22		Review scripting	1 day	3/8/21 8:00 AM	3/8/21 5:00 PM	20;21	Designer 1
23		Script second pass	5 days	3/9/21 8:00 AM	3/15/21 5:00 PM	22;39	Designer 1
24		Verify all supporting files are tagged correctly	1 day	2/1/21 8:00 AM	2/1/21 5:00 PM	12	Designer 1
25		Create localization tags for in-game dialog	1 day	2/2/21 8:00 AM	2/2/21 5:00 PM	12	Designer 1
26		Polish scripting	3 days	3/16/21 8:00 AM	3/18/21 5:00 PM	23;24;25	Designer 1
27		Fix final round of bugs	2 days	2/9/21 8:00 AM	2/10/21 5:00 PM	42	Designer 1
28		⊟ Sound	34 days	2/3/21 8:00 AM	3/22/21 5:00 PM		
29		Create sound design	3 days	2/3/21 8:00 AM	2/5/21 5:00 PM	45	Sound Designer 1
30		Implement sound design prototype	2 days	2/4/21 8:00 AM	2/5/21 5:00 PM	4	Sound Designer 1
31		Implement feedback	2 days	2/9/21 8:00 AM	2/10/21 5:00 PM	47	Sound Designer 1
32		Complete first pass of sound implementation	3 days	3/9/21 8:00 AM	3/11/21 5:00 PM	22	Sound Designer 1
33		Polish sound	2 days	3/16/21 8:00 AM	3/17/21 5:00 PM	23	Sound Designer 1
34		Fix final round of bugs	1 day	3/22/21 8:00 AM	3/22/21 5:00 PM	40	Sound Designer 1
35		⊟ QA	32 days	2/1/21 8:00 AM	3/16/21 5:00 PM		
36		Playtest prototype	1 day	2/1/21 8:00 AM	2/1/21 5:00 PM		Tester 1
37		Test geometry and terrain navigation	7 days	2/1/21 8:00 AM	2/9/21 5:00 PM		Tester 1
38		Check textures	2 days	2/1/21 8:00 AM	2/2/21 5:00 PM	9	Tester 1
39		Test initial scripting	1 day	2/8/21 8:00 AM	2/8/21 5:00 PM		Tester 1
40		Test second pass scripting	1 day	3/16/21 8:00 AM	3/16/21 5:00 PM	23	Tester 1
41		Final test all level geometry and textures	5 days	2/1/21 8:00 AM	2/5/21 5:00 PM		Tester 1
42		Final test for mission scripting	1 day	2/8/21 8:00 AM	2/8/21 5:00 PM		Tester 1
43		⊟ Approvals	38 days	2/1/21 8:00 AM	3/24/21 5:00 PM		
44		Approve initial layout	2 days	2/1/21 8:00 AM	2/2/21 5:00 PM		Management
45		Approve initial art prototype	2 days	2/1/21 8:00 AM	2/2/21 5:00 PM		Management
46		Approval initial design prototype	2 days	2/1/21 8:00 AM	2/2/21 5:00 PM		Management
47		Approve sound design	2 days	2/5/21 8:00 AM	2/8/21 5:00 PM		Management
48		Approve final level, scripting, and sound	2 days	3/23/21 8:00 AM	3/24/21 5:00 PM	12;26;33	Management

FIGURE 7.6 Level creation schedule, with resources and dependencies assigned.

As these examples show, a schedule can vary widely depending on a variety of factors. This is why spending time and effort to define the tasks, understand the dependencies, and make educated estimates is worthwhile. A schedule is only as useful as the information it contains. Once a baseline schedule is established, don't let all the time and effort spent in creating it go to waste. The schedule must be tracked and updated, and it should be revised frequently to reflect any new data.

7.7 Tracking Tasks

Appoint a single person to be the keeper of the schedule. As with the budget, having one person in charge of tracking and updating is extremely helpful. This person will have the project-wide view of how things are progressing and is positioned to raise red flags sooner rather than later.

Keep the team updated on how things are progressing. This can be done in team meetings, with status emails, or by posting updates on a whiteboard (or all three). The key thing is for the team to receive regular updates and understand how their work fits into the whole of the project. If the team doesn't get updates, it's as if they aren't working with a schedule at all since they are not aware of what the goals are and how things are tracking towards them.

If team members are falling behind on tasks, they should let the schedule tracker know as soon as possible, even if they think they can catch up in time to meet the deadline. While people can make up for lost time, it is better to know about probable delays ahead of time so contingency plans can be made. The producer might be able to find someone on the team who can jump in and help, which makes someone's doing overtime less likely.

Schedule delays can be critical, so knowing about critical delays is even more important. For example, if the level scripting tool is not completed by the time the levels must be scripted, this puts a large part of the design schedule at risk. If you are aware of delays ahead of time, you have a better chance of coming up with a contingency plan that mitigates the schedule risk. For example, imagine that a milestone is coming up, and the game is expected to be feature complete with placeholder content. You find out a week ahead of time that Artist A thinks he might not complete his level. Because you know ahead of time, you can assign an extra resource to help him get back on track or alter the testing schedule so this map will be checked last in the testing cycle, thus buying the few extra days needed to complete the level.

In addition to tracking the work that was done, the schedule tracker should also inform the team about upcoming deadlines. This gives the team useful information on how much time is left to meet the deadline, so they can better determine if their work is going to be completed on time. The schedule tracker should also follow up with team members individually for updates and check progress. This is a good way to uncover additional work that needs to be tracked or work that is being blocked due to unfinished tasks. In my experience, talking with individuals on the team is very valuable for understanding the work that's been done and what risks need to be mitigated.

7.8 Conclusion

Creating a useful schedule requires a lot of effort and time from the team, and they may be reluctant to participate in such an exercise. As a producer, you should understand the value a schedule has and be able to communicate this to the team in a convincing manner. Once the team has committed to making a schedule, they can work together to create a set of goals for the project, and then break down all the work that will be needed to fulfill these goals. Remember that a schedule is not going to be 100% accurate. Now that you have an understanding of the schedule, it's time to delve into the basics of budgets—including why they are important and how to create them.

Figures 7.3–7.6 illustrate the relationship between tasks, resources, and dependencies. This series of figures is also meant to show you how to pull all the information you gathered into a formal schedule. As discussed earlier in this chapter, there may be different scheduling approaches or tools that work better for your team, and your schedule may not look like the example at all. However, it is helpful to understand these examples and the process behind creating this type of schedule.

CHAPTER 8

Budget

8.1 Introduction

Once a game concept is defined, costs are one of the next things to consider; this means making a budget. Budgets are necessary to determine how much a game costs to make, and they are a factor in determining how much profit it will generate. Ideally, the money spent to make the game will be recouped shortly after it is released, and any money made on top of this is considered profit. The producer is usually the person responsible for creating and managing the budget, and they use this, along with the schedule and resources, to ensure that all parts of game development fall within the project scope. Chapter 4, "Getting Started," talks in more detail about how budget, schedule, and resources work together to determine the scope and quality of the project.

This chapter provides a general overview of creating and tracking budgets but is by no means comprehensive. For more detailed information and training on how to create and utilize budgets, forecasts, and other financial components most effectively, check out the Federal Deposit Insurance Corporation (FDIC) Money Smart for Small Business Program (www.fdic.gov/consumers/consumer/moneysmart/business.html). This is an online course developed by the FDIC that provides information and training on budgeting and financing for small businesses. A lot of the information presented is directly applicable to managing the finances of a game development project. This program teaches users how to manage cash flow, make a budget, and keep records, and other useful skills.

8.2 Budgets

Is this a low-budget independent game, or is this a multi-million dollar budget for the next sequel in an AAA franchise? While the size of budget impacts the resources and schedules for the game, there are common elements that should be considered when creating budgets of any size. First and foremost, how much money is the game likely to make when it is released? This will have an impact on how much money investors are willing to spend. For example, if the game is projected to sell millions of copies and generate tens of million dollars in revenue, the budget is likely to be a lot larger than a game that is predicted to generate a few hundred thousand dollars in revenue. So, how do you determine what type of budget to make?

8.2.1 Financial Forecasts

One way to do this is to generate a financial forecast. These forecasts compare how much revenue the game is expected to generate against the estimated expenses needed to make the game. As you can imagine, the goal is for the game to generate profit. To determine how much revenue it will make, the publishers will use historical sales data. For example, if the last version of Blockbuster X sold 50 million copies, publishers will use this as a baseline for determining how many copies the sequel to Blockbuster X is likely to sell and use this number to forecast revenue. If there aren't prior versions of the game to compare against, publishers will use comparable games (aka "comps") with a similar genre, target audience, quality level, and so on to gather useful data for predicting revenue.

This data is then used in a financial forecasting model to determine the estimated profitability of a game. The information is laid out in a spreadsheet and usually forecasts the next 12–18 months. The sheet is set up so that variables can be changed, such as how many copies will be sold or the selling price, so that different financial scenarios can be tested. After reviewing different scenarios, the publisher might determine that selling the game at a lower price is likely to lead to it selling more copies, thus generating more profit than selling fewer copies at a higher price. The goal of this exercise is to determine the optimal balance between cost and profit.

8.2.2 Creating a Budget

When creating the budget, build in some flexibility to account for variances in estimates compared to actual costs. If the budget is too rigid and doesn't allow for overages in one area or underages in another, it is hard to work with the ebb and flow of the costs of game development. Think of the budget as a tool for managing the game costs and resources—it is useful for keeping things on track, but it is not always going to be accurate since it is based on estimates or doesn't account for unexpected costs. You also want to account for various scenarios in the budget. For example, you may not be able to hire the animator you want and resort to outsourcing animation (which could be more expensive).

Involve the right people when making the budget. Your team has key information on their project needs, so involve them in the budget process to ensure that these needs are reflected in the budget. If the team is involved, they have a better understanding of the budget constraints and are better equipped to work within them. Once the budget is complete, update it frequently. Track how much money was actually spent versus what was budgeted, and go back and revise future budget estimates based on any additional data. If you have a group of stakeholders to answer to, be sure to keep them in the loop on the budget as well, especially if you need to ask for more money. The people holding the purse strings are more inclined to provide more money if they have been updated about the budget all along rather than being blindsided by a request.

8.3 Cost Breakdowns

Remember, no two budgets are exactly the same, but there are general things to plan for, including people, hardware, software, and overhead expenses. The budget should also account for marketing and publishing costs as these can have a huge impact on the game's overall profitability. Feel free to create separate development and publishing budgets. The development budget is a necessary part of the game pitch to potential investors, and if you are able to get a publisher on board, they will budget for and foot the bill for any publishing costs. If you are self-publishing, you will want to include these costs in your initial budget, so you have all the necessary information to determine whether you should make the game.

Remember that the initial budget is based on estimated best guesses for each category, and you will need to utilize the information you've already generated about the game. A prototype can be a useful tool in determining the costs and effort needed to make the larger game. If you don't have a prototype, you will need to work with your project leads to come up with the best estimate for what work needs to be done, who needs to do it, and how much it is likely to cost. Again, understand that resources, budget, and schedule are all dependent on each other, so you can't make changes in one of these areas without them impacting the others.

Don't assume that cheapest is best as this will ultimately affect the quality of the game. For example, if you have 6 months to create a game that is good quality, hiring entry-level developers is not ideal. They will take longer and deliver lower quality than senior-level developers. More experienced developers will cost more money up-front, but they are more likely to deliver what is needed within the time frame. If you hire less-experienced developers, you may save money up-front but spend money that wasn't in the budget if they need longer to deliver the game at the desired quality. However, if you have several years to complete a game, you might want to hire some entry-level people and train them on the job so that they can be experienced team members for the next project.

Let's focus specifically on a development budget, with the understanding that you can use these same steps to generate a publishing budget when needed. Begin by compiling a list of the following major budget categories:

- **People:** Who is needed for art, engineering, design, testing, production, and UX? Your proposed schedule is a good source for this. This is likely your largest expense (unless you are a one-person show working below market cost).
- **Hardware:** People will need computers, mobile devices, or console development kits. How many servers are needed? What cables and networking supplies are needed?
- **Software:** This includes the basics, like Microsoft Office, and more specialized development software, like a game engine or 3D art creation program. Don't forget about bug tracking, source control, or any other software needs.
- **Licensing Fees:** If you are working with an established intellectual property (IP), you will likely pay some type of licensing fee.
- **Outsourcing:** How much are you going to need to spend on outsourcing art, engineering, testing, audio, etc.?
- **Overhead:** This includes rent for office space, insurance, benefits, office supplies, snacks, utilities, and shipping costs.
- **Travel:** Are you planning to demo your game at any conferences? Include estimates for airfare, hotel, and miscellaneous travel expenses.
- **Business Support:** If you are an independent developer, you probably want to set aside some money for a lawyer and a Certified Public Accountant.

Next, just as you did with the major tasks in the schedule, break the costs down into smaller line items. Use the schedule and prototype you made earlier to help you scope the personnel needs. Since personnel is likely the biggest portion of your budget, you'll want to spend some time breaking down these staffing costs and provide more specifics on who is needed, how many, and when. Figure 8.1 is an example of how to organize this information into a spreadsheet. This spreadsheet shows all the people that are needed and when they will roll on and off the project. If you are able to define with some clarity when people are needed, and when they aren't, your budget will be more accurate.

In Figure 8.1, the number of each type of personnel is indicated in the "Number" column, which is then multiplied by the "Monthly Rate" and "Number of Months" needed on a project. All of these costs are added

Art Personnel	Number	Monthly Rate	# of Months	Cost
Lead Artist	1	$8,000	24	$1,92,000
Concept Artist	1	$6,000	10	$60,000
World Builder	5	$6,000	12	$3,60,000
Object Artist	3	$6,000	8	$1,44,000
Animator	2	$6,000	8	$96,000
Design Personnel				
Lead Designer	1	$8,000	24	$1,92,000
Designer	4	$6,000	18	$4,32,000
Writer	1	$6,000	6	$36,000
Engineering Personnel				
Lead Engineer	1	$8,000	24	$1,92,000
Networking Engineer	2	$6,000	16	$1,92,000
Sound Engineer	1	$6,000	12	$72,000
Tools Engineer	3	$6,000	18	$3,24,000
AI Engineer	2	$6,000	12	$1,44,000
Production Personnel				
Producer	1	$8,000	24	$1,92,000
Associate Producer	1	$6,000	18	$1,08,000
QA Personnel				
Lead QA Analyst	1	$8,000	24	$1,92,000
Tester	6	$6,000	10	$3,60,000
GRAND TOTAL	**36**	**$1,12,000**	**268**	**$32,88,000**

Based on 24 month development cycle
Monthly rates are for example only, do not reflect actual rates

FIGURE 8.1 Personnel budget.

together for the "Total Project Cost" column, which allows you to see the total costs for each person at a glance.

You can also format your other project costs in this format to illustrate when you need to have hardware, software, office furniture, and other project variables in place. This is a good way to track fixed monthly costs, such as rent. Figure 8.2 shows a spreadsheet that tracks these costs.

Once the budget estimates are done and laid out in this format, the "monthly burn rate" can be calculated. The burn rate is how much money is spent each month on the project. Being aware of the burn rate is important, so you can always stay ahead of the necessary costs and keep game development going. Hopefully, there will be enough money in the bank to cover several months of work. You can also make adjustments to monthly costs to raise or lower the burn rate (which you may want to do if cash flow is going to be less or more than expected in a given month). A general rule of thumb for burn rate is that each person on the project costs about $10,000 a month. This includes salaries, necessary hardware/software, office expenses, and other overhead. If the team is comprised of six people, a high-level estimate of the monthly burn rate is $60,000. This rule of thumb is useful when scoping out the costs for an initial project in which there is limited data.

Once the budget is done, it can be plugged into the financial forecasts to see whether the game is projected to turn a profit. If the profit margin is slim, you

Hardware	Number	Rate	Cost
Computers	36	$3,000	$1,08,000
Console Development Kits	18	$10,000	$1,80,000
Graphics Cards	14	$300	$4,200
DVDs	200	$2	$400
Software			
Perforce	36	$750	$27,000
3DSMax	9	$4,000	$36,000
Photoshop	3	$600	$1,800
Visual C++	9	$3,000	$27,000
Licensing Fees			
Planet Utopia Licensing Fee	1	$1,00,000	$1,00,000
External Vendors			
Voiceover	1	$60,000	$60,000
Music	1	$20,000	$20,000
Cinematics	1	$1,00,000	$1,00,000
Localization	4	$30,000	$1,20,000
Food			
Snacks	12	$200	$2,400
Late Night Dinners	24	$200	$4,800
Shipping			
International Postage	1	$300	$300
FedEx	1	$500	$500
GRAND TOTAL			**$7,92,400**

Based on 24 month development cycle
Rates are for example only, do not reflect actual rates

FIGURE 8.2 Budget for other costs.

may want to revisit the budget to see where you can cut additional costs. This exercise is also useful if you are trying to decide whether you should release your title as Early Access. The money earned during Early Access can help the project stay funded until it is ready for final release.

8.4 Tracking a Budget

Once the budget is established, and money is being spent, start tracking against the budget. You should have some type of bookkeeping system in place, where you can track all expenses and compare the actual costs against the budgeted costs. If you are working at a large company, you may have the luxury of an accounting department that tracks costs and generates reports, which will aid in this process. At minimum, any budget expenditures should be recorded on a weekly or monthly basis. Once a month, review the monthly expenses to make sure they are in line with the budget. During this time, budget estimates for future months can be updated to account for any new information.

Appoint one person on the production team to be responsible for tracking the budget. Any expense request should go through them, and they should work closely with accounting to ensure that proper reports and audits are being done each month. In order to keep costs within budget, you want to be mindful of who is authorized to spend what. For example, if $100,000 is allocated in the budget for audio outsourcing, the senior audio director may have the authority to spend this money on the vendors and supplies that he or she feels are necessary without seeking approval. However, a junior audio assistant would not have the authority to make this type of financial decision without first reviewing and gaining approval from a more senior person or the producer.

Any expenditures will eventually go through the accounting department, and each department has a different process for approving and tracking expenses. Keep this in mind for time-sensitive requests. For example, if a software license needs to be purchased, the order will likely need to be routed through the accounting department, so the license fee can be paid. Only then will the person who needs the software gain access to it. The alternative is to have the person pay for the license fee out of pocket and then submit an expense report to accounting. Just be sure you understand the accounting policies before paying out of pocket for any expenses.

8.5 Mitigating Budget Overages

Like anything else on the project, the budget is not going to be exact, and there will be times when something is going over budget or when something that needs to be in the budget wasn't included. When this happens, don't panic. Start by assessing the current budget and the current actual expenses, and see which areas of the budget can be adjusted. You might find that you didn't spend nearly as much on travel as budgeted, so you can dip into the travel fund and reallocate some of that money into the budget for the new computers you need. You might be able to reduce the number of people working on a feature or save money by outsourcing; the key is to think about the project as a whole and where there is some flexibility in cost, time, or resources.

If the budget is tracked and audited on a regular basis, and this information is communicated to the stakeholders, you will be in a better position to ask for more money when needed. Ideally, budget overages should not be a huge surprise, and instead, potential overages will be identified with enough time to come up with a solution or mitigation strategy.

Budgets are also used to create profit and loss statements (also known as P&Ls). P&Ls are reports that summarize how much income a company generated versus how much money they spent in a given time period. These reports are useful once a game has launched to track the actual profit and/ or loss. It can also help determine when the game will reach the breakeven point (which is when just enough profit has been generated to cover the costs of the game).

8.6 Conclusion

The producer is expected to create and track the budget for a game. This requires planning ahead of time, making best estimates, and continuously tracking and updating the budget in real time. Be cost-conscious when needed so that there is money for the critical things on the project. Work with your publisher on funding and tracking your budget, and don't be afraid to let them know sooner rather than later that things are going over budget. If the budget was created with some flexibility, there are likely ways to work with the team and the publisher to get things back on track.

CHAPTER 9

Pitching Your Game

9.1 Introduction

By this point in the development process, you may be fortunate enough to already have funding and publishing support. If this is the case, pitching your game will be less critical. If you are still looking for partners, get ready to schedule some pitches! Pitching games is not an easy task because you must be able to successfully communicate the full-game experience for the player, even though the game is not completed—in fact, the game may only be in the concept phase and may have no tangible assets. The publisher or the investor must get a clear understanding from the pitch of whether the game will deliver on this proposed experience and be financially successful. As discussed in Chapter 1, "Game Industry Overview," there are quite a few options for developers to self-finance and self-publish their games. Be sure to investigate these options before going too far down the road of pitching to publishers and investors. You might save yourself some time since you will be able to focus on making the game instead of creating pitch documents, polishing prototypes, and trying to schedule pitch meetings.

9.2 Your Goals

Most game developers will be pitching to a potential publisher or investor. In some cases, as with publisher-owned developers, you might need to pitch the game internally to get a greenlight to move forward with full development. If you're in this situation, you still want to prepare the necessary pitch materials and practice your presentation skills, so you can put your best foot forward when representing the work that your team has done for the game.

You can use the SMART method discussed in Chapter 4 to define your goals and what is needed from a potential partner. Having a clear understanding of what you are asking for allows you to present the best pitch to your audience. Generally, you are likely to be looking for one of these situations:

- **100% funding and publishing support:** This is extremely rare, especially for an unproven team. Even if you have rock stars that worked on some of the biggest games for other companies, the investors and the publishers are more interested in what your specific team has accomplished together.
- **Publishing support:** You have the funding in place (either through crowdsourcing or through self-funding), and you are looking for a publisher who will help you launch the game. Partnering with a publisher will give you access to a proven marketing and distribution network that is funded by the publisher. You will need to pay some type of royalty for the publishing services, but the game is going to be exposed to a larger audience. Getting picked up by a publisher is challenging, but it is a more likely scenario if the game already has funding in place.
- **Partial Funding:** You may have different investors lined up to finance the game, with each one contributing a percentage of the necessary funding. In this scenario, you will pitch the game to different types of investors and will need to tailor the pitch accordingly. Crowdfunding requests would also fall into this category.

As you consider what you need from a partner, you also want to think about areas in which you are willing or unwilling to compromise. For example, are you willing to let the publisher attach one of their licenses to the game? Will you let the investors decide what key features should be part of the MVP? Will the publisher be allowed to request changes to the core gameplay or story? Once you bring outside entities into the game development process, there will be areas that they have feedback on and will want to change. Accept this as inevitable, and plan for it accordingly when doing your research on potential partners.

One thing that will definitely be discussed during the pitch process is who will retain ownership of the game's intellectual property (IP). If a developer has created an original IP and is looking for publisher support, there is a strong possibility that the publisher will want to gain control of the IP. This is especially true in cases where the game could potentially turn into a franchise. If the publisher owns the IP, they are able to create content and other games based on this IP without input or permission from the original developer. Be prepared for the IP conversation, and make sure your development team is aligned on who will retain the IP rights.

9.2.1 Request for Proposals

Request for Proposals (RFPs) are things publishers send out for projects they want to develop externally. These are usually projects based on licenses or smaller projects that they don't have the bandwidth to handle internally. Most publishers have a stable of developers who they regularly work with, so this group will get first crack at an RFP. However, you can improve your chances of getting on one of these preferred lists by doing some networking with publishers at conferences and other events. Be sure you have an intriguing elevator pitch that describes your development team and why they would be a good publishing partner. You can then follow up by requesting a meeting to present a more in-depth look at your team. Focusing on securing an RFP or work-for-hire game is one way in which game studios help fund their original game ideas. Steady work keeps cash flow going, and if you are able to designate a small team to continue working on the original game concept, this is a win-win situation.

The publisher's RFP will include details on the game concept, license, target platform, budget, revenue model, and desired schedule. The RFP will be sent to multiple teams so they can prepare a bid of how much money and time is needed to make this game. There is likely to be some back-and-forth discussion between the publisher and the team during this phase as the team will likely have a few questions and need some clarifications. The teams will each send back a proposed bid that includes price, schedule, and maybe some initial design work that describes key gameplay elements. Of course, the publisher is looking for the highest-quality work at the most reasonable price. They may not automatically choose the lowest bid because they have an understanding of the trade-offs that are needed in order to balance cost and time with quality.

At this point in the process, the publisher is not expecting a developer to provide a prototype that wouldn't be cost-effective for them to spend time on. Instead, the publisher is looking for a team that has the experience (and skill) to do the job that is needed. Developers can show their experience by referring to other games the team has made in the past.

Once the developer returns a bid, the publisher will review all of them and likely pick a few to go to the next round of due diligence. During this phase, the publisher is going to dig deeper into the developer's experience and abilities to make the game. Section 9.6 provides more details on what to expect during this vetting process.

Once this is done, the publisher will select one of the developers to do the work. Even if your team is not selected in this process, the publisher will likely add you to their preferred list of developers if they had a good experience with you throughout the process. You might be called upon in the future to bid on another RFP.

9.3 Your Audience

Consider the audience for your pitch, and tailor the presentation as needed. If you are pitching to a publisher, find out if they are more interested in signing the game or the game team. Sometimes, publishers are looking for strong developers to partner with, and the deciding factor is the quality of the team, with the game being pitched of secondary importance. In this instance, a publisher may ask the developer to work on a different game instead of the one pitched in order to make a deal.

Before pitching, research the publishers and past titles they've released. Try to talk with other developers who've partnered with this publisher. You want to get a full picture of what the publisher is looking for and understand if they will be a good partner for you. You are evaluating publishers, but at the same time, they are evaluating your team.

If you are doing a crowdfunding campaign, understanding your audience is critical. People who contribute to crowdfunding campaigns are likely looking for something different from a traditional publisher. Many successful crowdfunded games were not concepts that traditional publishers would have had a strong interest in publishing because the team was unproven, the IP or concept appealed to a niche audience, or the game seemed risky because it didn't relate to what was currently popular. These qualities can be advantageous when creating a crowdfunding campaign, so spend some time figuring out how to position your game to appeal to this type of audience.

Regardless of who the audience is, they will all want to see similar types of information in your pitch.

9.4 Preparing for the Pitch

When you are creating the pitch, focus on providing the basic information that your audience wants. This includes what the game is about, the market position, the experience of the team, and the plan for actually making the game. Ideally, you have a playable demo or gameplay trailer that can show representative gameplay.

Some developers may have a preferred format for pitches, which gives them consistent information on all the games that are pitched to them and allows them to make an apples-to-apples comparison when looking at the concept, team, and costs. This structured format also allows publishers to quickly determine what the next steps would be. There will be some variations in the pitches based on who the audience is, how far along the game is in development, and what is requested in the proposed partnership. There are several parts to a successful pitch; it's not just a demo or a one-sheet explaining the game concept.

At this point in the process, you should have generated most of the information needed for the pitch. If you haven't, refer to the following chapters for more information:

Each of these chapters contains information that can be utilized in some form in the pitch. The unique thing about a pitch is that it has to be a condensed version of everything that's been created for the game. You can't make an effective case for partnering up with your team by merely handing off a design document or prototype, and you don't have a lot of time to review the full game plan you've created. At best, you will have 60 minutes to pitch your game, but this may be as short as 15 minutes, so distilling the pertinent information is important for a successful pitch.

BEN SMITH, SR. PRODUCER (PARTNER DEVELOPMENT), GAME PITCH PROCESS

At least in the group I worked in, you could think of almost every pitch we viewed as being artisanal. Developers brought pitches to us in every imaginable state—some were pitching using only written assets; some had visual targets (what they intended the look of the game to be); and some, but fewer than you might think, had invested in building at least a slice of gameplay. Sometimes, we were being pitched by agents and a studio CEO; sometimes, we were being pitched by external studio leadership alone. Occasionally, studio leadership would bring a developer or two along to field questions we might ask. Since every pitch was different, it's hard to boil down what the process was like. I'll tell you what we wanted to see since it happened so rarely. What we really wanted to see was a running game. We wanted to get hands on. A game is about the experience, and anyone can talk about an idea, show a couple of cool pieces of art, and get you excited. What makes games different is how they feel. How they play. If you want to have a successful pitch, it probably means building as much of a "vertical slice" as you can afford and bringing that in. If you have a fully playable level, all the better. How you get to that is the real rub, of course, financially.

9.4.1 Elevator Pitch

Start with a strong elevator pitch that sparks interest in learning more about the game and development team. It should include:

- **Strong Opening:** A good way to hook the listener is to pose a solution to a problem or ask a question they want to hear an answer for. For example, what happens if 100 animals battle against each other to be the last one standing? The key is to find something intriguing enough to get them to listen further.
- **Who you are:** Provide information about yourself so the listener understands why you are qualified to make this pitch, and give an indication of your ability to follow through on this. For example, a pitch

from someone who was previously the lead designer for a large gaming franchise is going to seem more relevant.
- **High Concept:** Explain the concept, genre, setting, etc. of the game in 1–2 sentences.
- **Unique selling points (USPs):** Expand on the high concept by providing 2–3 things that sets your game apart from the competition. Provide an example or two if you have time.
- **Team Background:** Give an overview of why your team is qualified to make this game, including their background, interests, and motivations.

Pull all these things together into a 1- to 2-minute speech and practice, practice, practice. This is your go-to talking point if someone asks you what you're working on, which happens a lot at conferences and networking events. As you deliver the pitch, continue to refine it based on the feedback and reactions you get. Soon enough, it will hit the sweet spot where it frequently opens up opportunities to schedule a longer pitch meeting.

9.4.2 Executive Summary

The executive summary is usually one sheet that details information on the game and how it will be positioned in the market. Think of it as an expanded elevator pitch with additional information on the market opportunities for the game. It should include:

- **High Concept:** See the information above.
- **Key Features:** This explains key areas of the game: for example, the genre, gameplay mechanics, setting, and social features.
- **USPs:** Think of these as the bullets that will appear on the website or back of the box to sell the game to prospective players.
- **Revenue Model:** Is the game free-to-play, subscription based, one-time price, etc.? If there is something unique about the revenue model, include that information.
- **Market Position:** What are your game's competitors? Who is the target audience? How does the game address the market needs?
- **Team Background:** See the information above.
- **Images:** If you have screenshots or concept art, this is a great place to use them. A compelling image goes a long way in showing off the game and the ability of the development team.

Pull this together into a 1-page document and have a graphic designer do a professional-looking layout. If you can't fit it all onto a single sheet, you can put together a small slide deck with 3–5 slides that contains this information. Again, have a graphic designer format the deck so it looks professional and inviting. Either format is acceptable as long as it can be quickly reviewed and digested. The person looking at it will only spend a few minutes on it so don't make it too text heavy.

9.4.3 Demo

If a picture is worth a thousand words, then a playable demo is the equivalent of a novel. If you have something a potential partner can actually experience, it trumps any documentation, team experience, or concept art. Chapter 6 discusses making a prototype and why it's important, so hopefully, there is already something in development that can evolve into a more polished game demo. If you are working on a vertical slice, that can also be used for the pitch. Ideally, the game demo provides an experience of what the final gameplay will be like (essentially the same way a vertical slice functions). The demo should be polished and show off the core mechanics. Focus on something that looks and feels great to the player, rather than something that has hours of gameplay and content. The main purpose of the demo is to sell the experience of the game, and it only needs to be a few minutes long in order to do this.

Be aware of how the potential partner will interact with the demo. Will the demo be part of the face-to-face pitch, and if so, will it be a hands-on or a hands-off demo? A hands-on demo is preferable as this means that the potential partner can actually play and experience the demo firsthand. This is advisable only if you are highly confident that the player won't experience horrible bugs, get stuck in unfinished areas of the game, or otherwise have a less-than-ideal experience.

If the demo is more fragile, a hands-off demo is a better option. The potential partner still gets to see the demo firsthand, but you or someone from the development team is actually playing through the demo and showing off the strong points of the game. This method is also advised if you have a limited amount of time for the pitch as you can play through it much faster and make sure all the important areas are showcased.

Another option is to grant hands-on access to the demo after the pitch meeting. In this scenario, you will send people a version of the demo that they can download and install themselves. They will play it without anyone from the development team around to answer questions. You must have high confidence in the demo in order to go this route. The demo should be able to stand alone and clearly demonstrate why the game is amazing. As part of this, you will need to write detailed information about how to get the demo up and running, along with information on the game's control scheme, core mechanics, and any known issues.

If you are doing a crowdfunding campaign, a demo is pretty much required in order to have a successful campaign. People are more likely to fund a game that already has a playable demo because it shows that the developer has some level of capability in actually making a game. The demo can be part of the introduction video on your crowdfunding project page.

9.4.4 Trailer

If you have time and resources, preparing a gameplay trailer is also useful for your pitch presentation. It doesn't take the place of a playable demo, but it is a good backup plan if the demo doesn't work, or if you are not far enough along in development to have a compelling demo. The trailer can utilize concept art, gameplay cinematics, character models, and so on. You will want to find a talented editor who can bring the game to life with all these different elements (especially if gameplay capture is not an option). Like the demo, the trailer needs to sell the experience of the game and tap into the viewer's emotions.

In addition, a trailer is a useful way to show off the game if someone doesn't have time to play a demo. They can take a look at the trailer, get excited by the game, and easily show the trailer to other people and get them on board as well. The trailer is also useful for crowdfunding campaigns.

9.4.5 Developer Backgrounds

As mentioned previously in this chapter, include developer backgrounds in your pitch information. For the key people on the team, provide a biography that highlights their area of expertise, previous games they've worked on, and any other relevant experience. These bios will become part of the larger pitch deck you put together. If you have good references from other companies the team has worked with, these can be included as well. If they've worked on well-received games, you can also include aggregate review scores of these to further showcase the team's expertise.

Established developers with good reputations are usually able to set up pitch meetings. Newer developers need to demonstrate their credibility, but if you have a playable demo, this can help offset any questions about the team's credibility.

9.4.6 Market Research

All the market research you did when refining and fleshing out the game concept should be reflected in the pitch. Potential partners want to know that you understand the market and how your game fits into it. The market research is also used when highlighting the strengths of the game and mitigating any weaknesses. Marketing research includes:

- **Understanding of market conditions:** Is your game capitalizing on a new trend that is expected to have large growth over the next few years? Is it based on what is currently popular, and if so, will it come out in time to benefit, or will it miss the opportunity? What percentage of the market does the type of game you are making currently have?
- **Familiarity with the competition:** What are your game's competitors? What are their strengths and weaknesses? How does your game capitalize on these? What are the competitor's sales figures and review scores? How will your game compare in these areas?
- **How the revenue model functions:** How will the game make money? If it is free-to-play, what is the plan for microtransactions? What is the profit margin? Will this revenue model work in today's market?

- **How your USPs address a market need:** Will your game add something new to similar games in the genre? Are your USPs going to set you apart from your competitors? Why will players be interested in your game versus another game?
- **Understanding what the target audience:** Who are you trying to sell to—hardcore gamers, casual gamers, or somewhere in between? What is the ideal age range and socioeconomic background? What are the core interests of your target audience?

All this information and understanding needs to be distilled into the core elements for the pitch. If you need to include more detailed information, you can put it in a supporting document and provide it as part of any follow-ups with the potential partner.

9.4.7 Production Plan

As with the market research, you will need to distill the budget, schedule, and scope information you've put together for the production plan into something that can be used in the pitch. A high-level production plan shows that you understand the effort required to make the game.

For the pitch, the production plan presents a high-level budget. For example, if you are asking for full funding, you want to show the cost breakdown of where the money will be spent. Is it being spent wisely on things that are directly related to the game? Are you overspending in some areas and underspending in others? Do you have a realistic budget to make the game you pitched? If you are looking for partial funding, the partners want to know what areas of the game still need funding and where their investment will go. For the budget, you don't need to present a detailed cost breakdown, but if you feel comfortable doing this, feel free. You can present a high-level summary of costs that shows how much major areas of the game will cost, such as personnel, localization, testing, equipment, and marketing.

Are there other areas where you will need support from your partner? For example, who is going to handle the testing and localization? Is this something your team alone can handle, or will you need partner support? If you need support, how much will it cost, and how long will it take? The partner will want to know you have a good understanding of the effort you are asking them to undertake on behalf of the game.

Approach showing the schedule in the same manner, and focus on showing a high-level timeline and how the milestones map to this timeline. Include a very brief description of what each milestone will contain.

Finally, you want to include a high-level risk analysis and mitigation strategy. Chapter 5, "Creating Concept," provides information on how to do the risk analysis. As with the budget and schedule, you won't include the full-risk analysis in the pitch, but be prepared to adequately answer any questions the potential partner has about the risks. The risk analysis can also be included as a supporting document for any follow-ups the partner wants to do.

JAY POWELL, CEO, THE POWELL GROUP

Making Connections

You may need to do some lead generation to get some pitch meetings booked. Do research on publishers or investors you are interested in working with, and figure out who the best people to contact are. LinkedIn can be very helpful in finding this information. Craft an introduction email along with a follow-up email. Keep these brief and to the point. You do not want to send a partner an introduction email that is a page long. They'll look at it, see that it's a lot to read, and simply close it. Four sentences and an executive overview of your game should be enough. State who you are, what the opportunity for them is, and what the benefit to them will be. It is imperative that you always present the opportunity in such a way that they see the greater benefit to them from the partnership.

Using your introduction email, your first objective should be to establish contact, outline credibility, and determine interest. From there, you will want to have the partner ask for more information or set up a meeting. If you do not get a response to your first email, wait one week, and send the follow-up email you previously wrote. Do this twice for a total of three attempts to reach your contact. If you haven't received anything after the initial email and two follow-ups, then search for a different contact at the company, or deprioritize that partner for the short term. Don't waste time relentlessly trying to pursue a company that isn't connecting with you. The best partners are the ones that are enthusiastic and excited about the game.

9.5 Making the Pitch

Now that you've created all this information for the pitch, what's next? Spend some time creating professionally laid-out pitch documents; this extra effort makes your team seem more professional and polished. You will also use these documents quite a bit, so time and money invested in the layout is well worth it.

Put together the following documents:

- **Executive Summary:** As discussed earlier in this chapter, this is a one-page summary with key information about the game and market position. Use this document when cold calling potential partners for a pitch meeting. See the "Making Connections" sidebar for more information on how to make an initial connection with a potential partner. Your elevator pitch will also come in handy as an icebreaker when cold calling people.
- **15-Minute Pitch Deck:** If you are able to schedule a face-to-face pitch meeting, have a deck ready that gives a 15-minute overview of your game. Use this time wisely. This provides more in-depth information on things presented in the "Executive Summary." It also includes information on the budget, schedule, and other support needed from the partner. Figure 9.1 shows the ten slides that Jay Powell, CEO of The Powell Group,

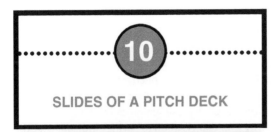

SLIDES OF A PITCH DECK

1 WHO ARE YOU?
Start simple. Show the logos for your company and team.

2 GAME OVERVIEW
Show the publisher the basics. Outline the genre, platform, target audience, monetization model, and have 3 to 6 features as bullet points.

3 UNIQUE SELLING POINTS
These are what make your game UNIQUE. "Post-Apocalyptic Setting" is a feature, it is not unique to your game.

4 STORY OR BACKGROUND OVERVIEW
Engage the publisher. Show them why the world you are creating is brlliant and alluring.

5 TRAILER OR GAMEPLAY VIDEO
A kickass trailer is always great but you can highlight the best of your game with a well produced gameplay video as well.

6 CONCEPT ART AND SCREENSHOTS
Publishers are visual, showcase your art team here. Make sure you highlight the UI in your screenshots.

7 SCHEDULE AND BUDGET
Break this down into monthly milestones with as much detail as possible for the deliverables each month.

8 COMPANY PROFILE
Summarize your past work as a company, your vision, and any recent successes.

9 EXPERIENCE OF TEAM LEADS
Who are the leads that wil be managing this game? Show their past work and highlights of their career.

10 CONTACT INFORMATION
Website and social media information for the company as well as email and phone number for your business lead.

www.powellgroupconsulting.com

FIGURE 9.1 Ten slides for a pitch deck.

recommends for a pitch presentation. If you are crowdfunding the game, the 15-minute pitch should probably be condensed to a 5- to 7-minute video and really focus on the USPs that a crowdfunded audience wants to support.

- **Full Pitch Presentation:** If the pitch meeting goes well, the partner is going to want more details on the game and to do some follow-up meetings. The full pitch presentation can go into more detail on the game concept, why your team is good to partner with, market position, and so on. At this point, they may ask questions or have feedback that you will want to incorporate into the pitch. If you are crowdfunding, this type of information should be included in your project summary. Look at other successful games on Kickstarter to see how they structured their project review.
- **Supporting Documents:** As part of the follow-up, you might want to provide a full budget and schedule, a full competitive analysis, or all the market research information you prepared for your game. This level of detail is only necessary if you are in serious talks with a potential partner.

Your goal in the pitch process is to narrow down the field of potential partners and find the one who is the best match. Hopefully, as they narrow down the field of potential game projects they will invest in, they will determine that you are also a match for them. As you embark on this process, be prepared for it to take time—you won't get a deal overnight. Several weeks may go by in which you do not hear anything from your potential partners, and once you've both decided to move forward to the next steps, there will be times when you are waiting for something to happen.

Invest time in practicing your pitch presentation. You should know the information backward and forward, and be able to present it without the deck. Be confident, enthusiastic, and energetic throughout the process. There will be frustration and rejection, but you can't let this impact the energy level you bring to the pitch meeting. During the meeting, it's very important to be open-minded to any questions or criticisms from your potential partner. If you disagree with something they say, do so politely and offer reasons for it (the reasons need to be better than "just because" or "that's not how I want to do it"). I have witnessed pitch meetings take a sharp downward turn because the team leads vehemently disagreed with something said in a pitch meeting, and the meeting ended right then and there.

Partners will ask you tough questions about the game. Don't answer with what you think they want; be transparent and honest with the actual information. If the publisher is interested in the game, they will understand that there are areas of weakness that will be addressed during the development.

If the partner chooses not to move forward with your game, thank them for the time and feedback they've given. It's not out of the question for a publisher to call you about a future opportunity, so don't burn any bridges. The main goal of this initial pitch process is to get to the next step and closer to a deal.

In some instances, the partner will be interested in the game but not ready to move forward with the next steps. They may ask you to answer further questions or to revise the pitch based on the feedback they gave. Be open-minded about this because sometimes their feedback and requests will make a stronger game concept. If you are asked to come back and pitch again, be sure to highlight what changes were made to the concept based on previous feedback.

If the partner is interested in moving forward with a deal or you have successfully crowdfunded your game, congratulations!

9.6 Next Steps

If you've crowdfunded your game, the next steps will be to engage with the people who contributed to it and thank them for their support. You will also want to provide frequent updates on how things are going on with development so your supporters aren't left wondering whether the game will actually get finished. If you have the resources and time, it's a great idea to get your supporters engaged more fully in the development process. They already have a vested interest in the game's success, and they will tell their friends about it when it is released, which equals more players for you.

To get your supporters more involved, provide frequent updates via discussion boards, developer videos, or social media. You can have the community participate by offering opinions and feedback as the game progresses. As discussed earlier in this book, there are many examples of successful games (Minecraft) that actively sought feedback from the community while the game was still in development.

If partnering with an investor or a publisher, the next step before you receive funding involves contract negotiation and a vetting process.

9.6.1 Contract Negotiation

Chapter 3 provides more detailed information about the development contract and what to expect, so please refer back to that with any questions about what's included in a development contract. The partner will likely want to begin with a deal memo. This is not a legally binding contract, but it does outline all the key information that will be included in the contract, such as the milestone payment schedule, what the developer is expected to deliver, what additional support the partner is offering (such as testing or localization support), and anything that should be agreed upon before the actual contract is written. Once the deal memo is finalized, and both parties agree to it, the contract can be drafted. It is a good idea to have a lawyer involved in the deal memo process as he or she can catch any red flags before they are included in the contract.

Once the contract is drafted, a lawyer should definitely review it. Compare the deal memo to the contract to make sure all the terms from the deal memo are accurate.

The partner will probably want to use their contract template, which means that the terms listed in the contract will be more favorable to the partner and less favorable to you. So, when you have your lawyer review it, there will be places where they will request edits in order to limit your exposure. While the contract negotiation is happening, the partner will also want to more thoroughly vet the development team.

9.6.2 Vetting Process

Any potential partner will want to vet who they are going into business with to ensure that the team can do what it says it will do and that it has the proper tools, resources, and skills to do so. The vetting process is usually done by someone appointed by the partner. This person usually has a game development background and will be knowledgeable about development processes, including project management, development pipelines, and scoping features. In some instances, the partner will also want to do a deep dive on technical expertise, so they may also send someone to thoroughly vet the technology pipeline and the game's technical architecture. In general, these are the areas that the partner is interested in vetting:

- **References:** They will want to speak with people who previously work with the team to get answers to questions. For example, who has the team worked with before? What was the experience like? Is the team easy to work with? Do they deliver milestones on time? Are they good about raising issues in time to be solved?
- **Process:** They will want to understand how your team's development processes work. This includes how things are scheduled and tracked, how code reviews work, and what the testing cycle is like. They want assurances that the proper processes are in place to deliver milestones successfully.
- **Technology:** As mentioned above, they may want a full understanding of the technology being used. This includes any tools and security protocols that are in place to reduce unauthorized access to the game.
- **Team:** What percentage of the development team is working on the project (this is useful in cases in which studios work on multiple projects)? Who are the key people working on the project? What are their skills and background? Do you have enough people on the team to actually do the work? Are you outsourcing any of it?

The vetting process may take a few days. It begins by setting up a time for the people doing the vetting to do an on-site visit to the studio. They arrive with a list of questions to discuss with you and the team. If the team is small, the people who are doing the vetting will probably talk to everyone on it, either individually or in groups. If the team is large, they will focus on interviewing the key people and other discipline leads on the project. The purpose of the team interviews is to get a feel for the team, what the culture is, what the morale is like, and how well people work with each other. Another purpose is to confirm that you have the team you say you have. There are some cases in which a developer isn't the team it claims to be—either it doesn't have all the positions filled, or the people don't have the background and skills they claim to. This doesn't happen often, but someone vetting the team will be looking to make sure. Finally, the people vetting will want to review design documents, schedules, budgets, financial reports, and any other important documentation that will be helpful with the assessment.

During the vetting process, you should also be conducting your due diligence on the partner. Ask if there are references from previous game development teams you can talk to. You can also find out a lot about your partner with a good online search. Look at Reddit, game forums, or other places where people post comments about games the publisher or investor was involved in. Search game industry news websites to see what stories have been written. Contact developers who previously worked with the partner to find out if milestones were paid on time, how the feedback process worked, and if they were a good partner.

Once the deal is done, welcome them to the team! Your partner will be invaluable as your team navigates the process of making the game. Chapter 2 discusses in more detail how you can manage your relationship with your publishing partner.

9.7 Conclusion

Pitching your game is an important part of the development process, especially if you are looking for partners to fund the game. Preparing for a pitch takes time, and you don't want to cut corners. Your team is depending on the pitch to present the best view of the game and its potential. If the pitch is compelling and thorough, the game is more likely to move to the next step with your potential partner.

PART 4
Assembling the Game Team

Part 4 focuses on the most important team resource—the people! Spending time and attention on finding and retaining the best people for your team is critical. You want a team comprising happy, productive people who feel a sense of ownership for what they are making. This section touches on how to hire people, how to organize your team, and how to manage your team. The chapters are:

Hiring Talent;

Team Organization;

Managing Your Team;

Outsourcing.

CHAPTER 10

Hiring Talent

10.1 Introduction

People are the most important resources when developing games. Regardless of how much funding, publisher support, or fan support you have, the game can't get made without a team. Game teams come in all shapes and sizes, but one thing that all teams must have is the right mix of skill, personalities, and passion. When it is time to build or grow the team, focus on hiring people who complement the existing talent and are willing to collaborate. Making games requires a huge group effort, so people who aren't interested in collaborating will only make the game development process more painful. You also don't want to spend time managing personalities because it pulls focus from the game and lowers quality. As a producer, you may or may not have hire/fire authority. Regardless of whether you do, you will be involved in many interviews across different disciplines, so learn how to interview and hire the people who will make the team strong.

Finding the right person can be difficult, so remote workers are also something to consider. With today's technology, working with remote team members is easier than ever. Chapter 11 discusses this in more detail. There are a lot of ways to find talent, but be open-minded about what's needed. An entry-level person can show a lot of promise, so hiring him or her and investing in training might be worthwhile, especially if the position is hard to fill. People with relevant experience in a non-game-related field can transfer their skills to something in game development. There are some great project managers working in other industries who would do well as a project manager or producer on a game team.

If you work with a large company, you may have an HR and recruiting department to lean on.

If you are a small company, the burden may fall on the producer to advertise the job, screen candidates, and schedule on-site interviews. In either case, the HR department is usually the initial point of contact for all potential candidates and handles the logistics of creating and posting job descriptions, collecting resumes, coordinating phone interviews, making travel arrangements for in-person interviews, negotiating salaries, and extending final offers. The producer is responsible for informing the HR department of the hiring needs, providing details for the job description, and interviewing prospective candidates. They may also determine who else on the team needs to interview the candidates.

10.2 Job Descriptions

Writing a job description is the first step in the hiring process. It outlines the expectations and responsibilities for the role. This includes what the day-to day work entails, how this role interacts with other people and departments, and what the key goals are for the position. The qualifications must also be included. Having someone who perfectly fulfills all the qualifications is rare, so think carefully about what experience is really necessary to succeed in the role and focus on those aspects. Be aware of the language used when writing the job description. Include information about the company and why it's a great place to work. If writing a job description is difficult, it means there isn't a clear understanding of what the role is, which makes it difficult to hire the right person.

Finally, use inclusive language, and actively encourage a diverse pool of applicants. A team comprised of people with different life experiences and different ways of thinking makes for a stronger team. Diverse teams provide more points of reference and feedback when creating the game. They also have more options for thinking through a problem and finding a solution. Diverse teams are more successful, so being inclusive when hiring is important.

10.3 Finding Applicants

Finding applicants is the next step in the process. There are a variety of sources, so plan to utilize multiple to get a good sampling of applicants. Remember to be open-minded about the necessary experience and qualifications. When people switch jobs, they may be looking to challenge themselves in their next role, so they'll apply for positions where they don't meet all the qualifications but feel confident that they are qualified and motivated enough to do the job. Be open to these candidates as you will find some diamonds in the rough that can be mentored and trained on the job.

10.3.1 Working with Recruiters

The main focus of a recruiter is to find the right person for the job. Recruiters can be internal or external. In a large company, there may be an internal recruiter who works closely with the development team to staff open positions on the team. They will write up the job description, screen applicants, and come up with a shortlist of people to start interviewing.

In some cases, when more senior talent and experience is needed, an external recruiter may be used. An external recruit is independent from the game studio and can approach top-tier talent at other companies to see if they are interested in making a job change. An employer will pay a fee to the external recruiter for this service. An external recruiter needs the job description, information on the company culture, and an understanding of the type of person that is needed.

Internal and external recruiters are the main point of contact for potential job candidates. The recruiter works directly with the candidate and represents the company's interests in the first step of the hiring process. When working with recruiters, make sure that everyone is aligned on what the job position and benefits, including salary, key responsibilities, visas, and relocation expectations. This makes it much easier for the recruiter to answer the candidate's questions and to better screen candidates for the position.

10.3.2 Online Job Postings

Online job postings are the most common way to find applications. Companies can advertise open positions on their website and post on other job search sites, like Monster.com and Gamasutra.com. LinkedIn is also a useful place for posting jobs. Finally, for more game-specific postings, you can advertise open positions with the International Game Developers Association (IGDA) or at schools that offer game-related degrees.

10.3.3 Referrals

Referrals from current employees are very valuable. If someone has a prior relationship with a potential candidate and recommends them, it can be assumed that they have a positive relationship and want to work together again. The employee can also talk to the candidate about what it's like to work at the company, so the candidate will be better prepared for what to expect in the position. They will have a reliable resource to come to with questions and get the real story about what it's like to work for the company.

Some companies offer incentives to employees if people they refer end up getting hired.

10.3.4 Job Fairs

If a large number of job positions must be filled, having a job fair makes sense. The company may host a local job fair at the studio. It is also common for game industry conferences to host job fairs. This is a good place to find applicants from different geographical locations. Job fairs also provide an initial chance to meet the candidates face-to-face and do some initial screenings before time is spent routing them through the full interview process.

10.3.5 Interns

Interns are a great source of talent, especially for entry-level engineering, art, or design positions. They only last a few months, which is enough time to assess the intern on the job, then you can decide if you'd like to offer them full-time employment after they are finished with school. Work with the HR department to set up an internship. Keep in mind that interns are not just free labor; they are also there to learn about the game industry and the different roles on the team.

10.4 Interview Process

The job was posted a few weeks ago, a stack of resumes has accumulated, and it's time for the interview process. Start by looking over the submitted resumes and selecting a list of prospective candidates for an initial phone interview. If that goes well, an on-site interview is next. After this, the producer and other people involved in the process will provide feedback on the candidate's strengths and weaknesses to determine whether or not to extend an employment offer. The offer will be extended, and if accepted, you have a new team member! The following sections discuss some things to consider for each step of the interview process.

10.4.1 Screening Resumes

When looking at resumes, note any gaps in work history and ask the candidate about this. The gaps may be times when the candidate went back to school, took some time off, or was laid off and spent time finding another job. If the candidate's work history includes several instances in which they were at companies for short time periods, make a note to ask them about this if you choose to do an initial interview.

Consider checking up on a candidate's shipped title credits, especially if they are called out on the resume. It is not unheard of for people to exaggerate (or even outright lie) about their contributions to a game. However, also keep in mind that people may not be in the published credits of the game, even if they made a contribution. The best way to do this is to check references and talk to people that worked with the candidate. They can usually give you a fair assessment of what work the candidate actually did on the game. Reference checks come later in the hiring process, so if you still have questions about what the candidate did on a particular project, even after you interview them, talk to their references for more information.

Pay attention to how the candidate describes previous job responsibilities. If the descriptions are repetitive or contain little information, the resume might be padded. Be especially wary of any outrageous claims that don't seem to fit with the job title, such as an assistant designer stating, "I completely redesigned the single-player aspects of the game during production." When a candidate describes very specific things they did on the project, it gives you more information on what their skill set is and how they utilize these skills on the project.

Finally, pay attention to how much industry experience the candidate has. You probably do not want to hire someone with absolutely no experience for an intermediate position on a team, although there are some exceptions. For instance, if you are looking to hire someone entry level, you might be open to looking at someone with no industry experience but who has transferable skills from another industry.

10.4.2 Phone Assessment

The phone assessment is likely your first direct contact with a candidate, and the purpose is to determine whether you want to bring the candidate in for an on-site interview with the rest of the team. Prepare for the phone interview ahead of time, have a list of questions to ask, and know where you want to get more information on the candidate's capabilities and skills. Don't forget that they are interviewing the company, and you are a reflection of that company. Put your best foot forward.

During the phone interview, it's useful to begin by finding out what the candidate is looking for in the position. Is there a match between what the job is and the candidate's expectations? For example, is there alignment on the roles and responsibilities, the salary range, the working hours, and so on? If it becomes clear from this part of the interview that the candidate's expectations for the role don't match what is needed, it's unlikely that they will be a good long-term fit for the position.

If there is alignment with the candidate and the position, proceed to delve more into their skills and capabilities. Asking the candidate about their background is a nice icebreaker, but don't squander the interview time by discussing information that can be easily gleaned from the resume. Instead, use this opportunity to find out more about how the candidate solves problems, deals with stressful situations, collaborates with others, provides feedback, and deals with other types of interactions.

Ask the candidate to give specific examples from their own experience when talking about these interactions. The candidate doesn't need to have done the exact job you are looking to fill; they just need to show that they are capable of doing this job. While you may want someone with a certain level of industry experience, you also want to better understand how they draw upon this experience to solve problems, make decisions, evaluate risks, gather information, communicate to the team, and determine priorities.

10.4.3 Discipline Tests

After the phone screen, some companies may ask the candidates to do some type of discipline test. Tests can be useful to see how people work, what their quality of work is, how well they follow directions, how well they take feedback, and what skill level they are at. It is becoming fairly common in the game industry to send tests to engineers, artists, and designers to check their skill levels. Tests provide consistency checks between the candidates and allow you to compare their skills more easily to what you need for your team. They also help mitigate unconscious bias in the hiring process, which can make you hire someone that you like (or that is like you) instead of someone who can bring balance or diversity to the team.

Be mindful that these tests take time, so don't take advantage of candidates with a test that would take several days to complete. For example, don't ask a potential design candidate to write a full design document as part of the discipline test. Understand what the goals of the test are, then select exercises that will fulfill these goals. For art, engineering, or design tests, make sure the candidate realizes that the contents of the test can be considered work-for-hire (see Chapter 3) and are considered company property.

10.4.4 Face-to-Face Assessment

After the phone screen and the discipline test, a candidate may be invited for a face-to-face interview. Usually at this point in the process, the company is fairly confident that this person is a good fit and is willing to spend money to fly the candidate in for an on-site interview. More people are involved in the face-to-face assessment, especially key people who will work with the candidate. Sit down with the interviewing group ahead of time to discuss the questions each person will ask, so you avoid repeating the same ones throughout the day. Each person can focus on a different aspect of the job when talking with the candidate. As in the phone interview, you want to ask questions that will help you assess their capability to do the job.

When the interviews are done, get everyone together in a room to discuss their impressions. There will not be 100% agreement on whether the candidate should be hired or not. When people say that a candidate is not their choice, dig into their reasons for this. Perhaps they picked up on something that others missed. Do the same for the people that said the candidate should be hired. Are their reasons sound? Are they good judges of skill?

During this wrap-up, make sure that the group stays focused on the purpose. People should be able to provide specifics to support their feedback on the candidate. When the meeting is over, hopefully, everyone in the room will be in alignment with the next steps for the candidate. If there are a lot of concerns or red flags, but people don't want to flat out reject the candidate, a follow-up interview is always an option. If this does happen, be transparent with the candidate about the concerns and provide them an opportunity to address these.

10.4.5 Making an Offer

If the candidate aces the interview and is someone you want to hire, the HR person will start putting together an offer. The offer will outline the salary, relocation package, benefits, and any other hiring perks. The offer will be presented to the candidate; there will be some back-and-forth negotiating; and then, the offer will be finalized. Once this is done, work with the candidate to determine the start date. Be flexible with your expectations. While you may want the person yesterday, it could take them a few weeks or months to wrap up their current job and relocate. It's worth the wait if you have hired the right person.

10.5 Onboarding New Employees

Be sure to have a plan for onboarding new employees. Starting a new job is very stressful, and a good onboarding process can help alleviate some of the stress and uncertainty. Each company will handle onboarding differently, but the overall goal is to get the new employee acclimated and ramped up as quickly as possible. The reality is that it may take 2–3 months for an employee to learn the ropes and the ins and outs of their job—especially more senior positions who have direct reports. It will take time for new employees to connect with their direct reports, learn who all the players are at the office, and understand how all the processes work. Be patient and helpful in order to ease this transition.

A good onboarding experience sets the tone for the employee/company relationship. Employees want to confirm that they made a good choice by coming to work for the company. Here are some things that can be included in the onboarding process:

- Pair them up with a buddy, who will be their resource and guide for the first few weeks.
- Schedule their first 2 weeks of lunches for them. Make sure they have new people to each lunch with every day.
- Walk around with them, and introduce them to each person face-to-face (this may take place over the course of several days, if necessary).
- Get them set up to play the game they will be working on. Make sure they have opportunities to play other games the company is working on as well.
- Help them define goals for the first 30/60/90 days. This is a good way to track how quick and effective the onboarding process is.

- For people who relocate, be flexible when they need to take time off during the first few months as they will need to take care of finding a place to live, finding doctors, getting children settled into school, unpacking, and so on.

10.6 Training

Even the most experienced employees benefit from training, so it is good practice to offer training to both new and old employees. Training is essential for people's success in their positions. After all, you can't expect someone to know everything. While people may have the ability to perform well in their core responsibilities, they might not have all the necessary tools to do so. For example, if someone is asked to step into a lead position in the middle of development, he or she might not be prepared to switch gears from content creation mode to management mode. Although he or she may have the ability to make the shift, he or she might need some coaching or training in basic people management skills, such as conflict negotiation or team motivation.

Additionally, he or she will have to think about the game as a sum of its parts instead of just worrying about one aspect. An art lead, for example, needs to lead the artists who are creating the art content for the game—textures, models, levels, cinematics, and so on. So, it is important to take time out for training because this will save you money in the long run.

Some people are highly motivated self-educators and have a clear picture of the training and information they need. They know what classes and books will be useful; they ask questions and gather information; they are always receptive to performance feedback and may even request it on a regular basis. However, more guidance is needed to help some people determine their needs, so it is important to figure out where they need training and support those needs.

Good employers take an active interest in developing their employees and offering training opportunities. Key areas in which an employee might need further training are leadership, communication, and technical skills. Anyone in a lead position will benefit from training in all three areas, especially if he or she is new to the position. Training programs for improving leadership and communication skills can be difficult to find, but the local university may offer continuing education classes. Technical training can be handled internally, if necessary, by technically proficient people on the team. Books and online classes also are good training resources. In addition, several organizations, conferences, and websites provide information, and even classes, on improving game development skills.

10.7 Retention

Retaining good talent is a challenge for many companies because people are always looking for better opportunities or work situations, especially if they are not happy in their current position. Surprisingly, money is not the primary motivator for most people; trust and respect are. If given the choice, most people will choose to make less money and work at a company where they are respected by their peers, listened to by management, and trusted to make choices about their contributions rather than make more money in an environment where they are treated disrespectfully, ignored, and given no choices about their contributions. Money certainly helps, and bonuses are always welcome, but more than that is needed to keep people happy and motivated. People want to be rewarded for commitment, loyalty, and high-quality work. Again, this does not necessarily translate into a monetary reward; instead, recognition can be given in the form of more responsibility, increased respect within the company (especially from management), and higher-profile assignments. If someone feels like his or her contributions are not properly recognized, he or she will become frustrated and eventually leave the company. Check in with your team on a regular basis to find out how people are doing, listen to their frustrations, and provide recognition for jobs well done. If you cultivate an environment of respect and transparency, people will be more receptive to feedback and suggestions for improvements.

In addition to these intangible benefits, there are also some tangible benefits that contribute to a more employee-friendly working environment: medical, dental, eye care, vacation, 401k, stock options, and maternity/paternity leave. A good benefits package goes a long way toward showing employees that the company values them. If you are a small company, start out with a core list of benefits, and add them as you grow. Other types of benefits you can consider are the following:

- **Health club memberships:** Encourage employees to be fit; fitness contributes to better health and less sick time away from work.
- **Flexible work hours:** Flexible work hours allow people to tailor their work time, so they can put in their best work—some people work better early in the morning; others prefer working late into the night. To foster collaboration among all team members, set core hours when people are required to be in the office, and be sure to match or exceed those hours yourself.
- **Ability to work from home:** Remote work is becoming more popular. With today's technology, the ability to work from home and collaborate, attend meetings, and work on documents is getting better and better.
- **Hardware and software:** People become frustrated if they are expected to perform their tasks on hardware or software that is not suited to those tasks, so make sure they have the necessary hardware and software.
- **Free drinks and other snacks:** Everyone enjoys small treats, and they are something inexpensive the company can provide. Don't forget to provide healthy options too!

10.8 Conclusion

Finding and retaining good talent is important. People are a valuable (and expensive) resource, so you want to spend time during the interview process to fit the right ones. People are not interchangeable like blocks, so it is important to find the right ones that will gel into a team. Once they are hired, you want to keep them happy and motivated with their work. This chapter gave a high-level overview of the hiring process and some things to consider when onboarding and trying to retain employees. Chapter 11 discusses some ways in which you can organize the team.

Team Organization

11.1 Introduction

As you start staffing the development team, think about how it will be organized. Smaller companies may opt to have a flat management structure where everyone has an equal say, while larger teams may want to organize into sub-teams within a larger team. Organizing the team, in other words making an org chart, helps clarify the roles and responsibilities of each person, which, in turn, clarifies the chain of command and who needs to be consulted for decisions. This chapter provides a general overview of why defining people's places on the team is important and how to pick leaders who can help facilitate communication and productivity. It will also present a few ways in which you can organize the team, including working with remote team members.

11.2 Defining Roles and Responsibilities

Defining roles and responsibilities is critical to building a strong team. Everyone on the team can do better work if they know exactly what their role is and what the expectations are. If roles aren't clearly defined, this leads to team conflict.

For example, if there are multiple producers on the team, and it's not clear who is responsible for what, this can create situations where developers are approached by multiple producers regarding the same tasks. This is annoying for the developers because they have to keep repeating themselves (and it pulls them away from work). It also creates a sense of chaos on the production team—the producers get frustrated with each other because they don't understand who is responsible for what, and while some things are getting a lot of attention, others may be falling through the cracks and causing issues with other aspects of the game. When people start becoming frustrated with a situation like this, it leads to conflicts and less-efficient, lower-quality work.

These situations can be remedied by clarifying people's roles. James P. Lewis, the author of *Team-Based Project Management* (1997), has developed a simple role clarification exercise that can be done at the beginning of the project and should be done during the project whenever new people are added, or there seems to be role ambiguity. This is also a good exercise for the producer and leads to do throughout the development cycle so that everyone is clear on who is responsible for which aspects of the project.

The exercise begins with each person answering the following four questions:

- How does the company see your role on the team?
- How do you see your role on this team?
- What resources do you need in order to effectively carry out your role?
- What do you need to know about other people's roles in order to do your job better?

Each person writes answers to these questions and comes prepared to discuss them in a meeting. He or she begins by presenting his or her answers, and then everyone discusses and comes to an agreement on how that person's role is best defined. Ten to twenty minutes should be allocated to each person. If you do this for a large team, schedule a few separate meetings instead of a single meeting that lasts for hours. Once the team has done this exercise, publish the role definitions someplace so that the team can easily review them.

This is a very simple solution, but it is one of the most effective ways I've found to reduce conflict and confusion between people on a project. People want to work in harmony and can work together better if they understand their own role on the project and how other people's roles fit in. When everyone has a shared understanding of what is expected for each person on the team, it makes the team stronger. This is also a good way to ensure that people understand that everyone has a contribution to make to the game, which is important.

11.3 Picking Leads

When working with the team on their roles and responsibilities, you also want to think about who will act as a discipline lead on the project. Generally, leads don't have time to be content creators on the project. Instead, they manage the content creators and provide leadership and guidance. The most effective leads have expertise in their fields and strong people skills, which means they can advise people, such as the producer or junior team members, on what techniques and processes will be needed to get the desired result. For example, an art lead who is knowledgeable of the technical limitations of console hardware can converse intelligently with both art and engineering team members about what tools will be needed to create realistic terrain. In addition, the art lead helps the art team to successfully complete their project tasks by managing the schedule, providing useful feedback, answering questions, arranging for tutorials in new techniques, or defining the art production pipeline. A lead engineer and a lead designer provide the same types of services to the engineering and design teams, respectively.

As they develop in their career, it seems natural that they would want to take on more responsibility for the project. A lead usually has some number of direct reports and is responsible for reviewing and providing feedback on their subordinates' work; in many cases, he or she is also responsible for mentoring and growing people in their roles.

Strong leads are invaluable assets for any producer. If the producer can depend on the leads to manage the day-to-day art, engineering, and design tasks, he or she can concentrate on the other aspects of the project, such as localizations, managing external vendors, dealing with the marketing and legal departments, updating senior management on the project status, and providing the leads and team with the necessary resources to do their jobs.

If a lead's skills are lacking in one area, the producer must provide training in order to avoid problems down the line. For example, a talented lead designer who is not easily approachable cannot manage the design team effectively. The other designers might be reluctant to come to him or her with concerns for fear of being yelled at or rudely dismissed. If a lead designer continues acting this way, even with proper coaching and training, the producer may consider replacing him or her with someone who may not be as skilled in design but has better people skills.

When choosing leads, there is a tendency to appoint someone who is highly skilled and has successfully shipped a few games. The benefit of this is that an expert is readily available to offer technical or artistic guidance to team members. However, this person may not be prepared for the management and administrative responsibilities of the position. He or she goes from a well-respected content creator to someone who has to manage people, schedules, and office politics, and he or she may have little interest in accepting a lead position because of these types of tasks. This team member might prefer to remain a content creator, leading the team in a less official capacity.

In fact, a lead should not be the most artistically technically skilled person on the team. You want to keep these people doing what they do best— creating high-quality assets for the game. If you move high-quality content creators to lead positions, they won't have time to create content, and the quality of the game will diminish. You may also find that the production schedule suffers if you remove your most prolific asset creators to positions where they do not create.

When picking leads, focus on choosing the best managers for the job, not the most technically skilled person. Developers with strong management abilities have a tendency to be organized, work well with others, possess strong communication skills, are knowledgeable in their field, and have earned the respect of their peers. It is easier to help someone improve their knowledge of artistic and technical techniques than it is to train someone to be a better people person, so keep this in mind when selecting project leads.

Ineffective leads who do not improve their management skills can put a project at risk. How many times have you heard the development team complain about how ineffective or useless their lead is? If this complaint is common and isn't addressed immediately, the people under this lead will stop asking questions, pointing out risks, and making progress on the game. They will quickly lose interest in their contribution to the game and communication breakdowns between the team members cause the project to slowly erode.

In some cases, a producer might not have the authority to replace an ineffective lead who did not respond to coaching. In such instances, a liability will be created, and the producer will have to work around it. They might decide to take on part of the lead's role and provide the management or technical skills the lead is lacking, or they may unofficially grant lead status to a junior member of the team who shows promise as a future lead. If you are stuck with a lead who becomes a liability, try to deal with the situation without further alienating any of the team members who are under this lead.

ASHLEY JENNINGS, SR. TECHNICAL ARTIST, HI-REZ STUDIOS, FINDING GOOD LEADS

The best leads have compassion. They are clear communicators, cognizant of the needs of the people on their team, and passionate about training new team members. The best leads I've seen build up their team like a start-up—choosing new hires that they see as having great potential and checking in on the members of their team on the daily. Great leads make time to teach their new hires and provide challenges to the more experienced members of their team to help build their self-esteem. Nothing builds trust and camaraderie more than a leader who makes their team members feel like their role has a purpose, and they have someone watching out for them.

When choosing an existing employee for a lead, it's important to look at the qualities that this person has showcased during their time at the company so far. Do they frequently look for new solutions to problems they or other departments experience in the pipeline? Are they easily approachable, and do they have a natural inclination to communicate with other developers? Good leads aren't always the most talented member of a team—rather, they are the member that can bring people together and encourage others to work towards solutions.

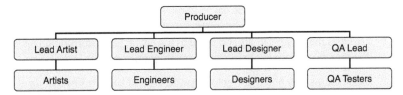

FIGURE 11.1 Org chart with producer-lead structure.

11.4 Organizing the Team

The team can be organized in several ways, depending on the team size and what roles are needed. Small companies might have a single person fulfilling multiple roles on a project, such as producer-designer, engineer-designer, or producer-engineer. Large teams will likely have a team comprising people who specialize in a specific, clearly defined role, such as user interface (UI) artist or Artificial Intelligence (AI) engineer. Be aware that when one person is fulfilling multiple roles on the project, it may cause some conflict. For example, you might be a producer-designer and find your producer side disagreeing with your designer side, especially if the design decision means adding more time or money to the project.

Whatever the team size, create a team organization chart so that people know who they need to talk to for information.

Figure 11.1 depicts a general organization chart for a team with a producer-lead structure. The producer manages the art, engineering, design, and QA leads, and the leads manage the rest of the development team. This is a very straightforward way of organizing the team, and the chain of command is very clear. This reporting structure works well for developing employees since the discipline lead is focused on helping subordinates improve and grow within their disciplines. The drawback to this structure is that it silos the disciplines and doesn't encourage cross-discipline collaboration. If you have a large team, you may find that organizing them into strike teams will provide a better result.

11.5 Strike Teams

Task forces or strike teams are cross-discipline groups that are responsible for designing and implementing features into the game. They work best when they have flexibility and autonomy to make decisions within a general set of project parameters. Being cross-discipline is a key component to their success; the group should have all the necessary people to design, implement, test, and iterate a set of game features. For example, a project might have a UI strike team who is focused on creating all the UI in the game. Because they are cross-discipline, the engineers, designers, and artists will be more knowledgeable about the technical, design, and artistic limitations of UI functionality, and will be able to more efficiently work together to create the full UI experience. Another strike team might focus on the player's character and how it interacts with the game world. This team will also have artists, designers, and engineers working together to design the player character, the activities the player can do, and perhaps the character customization system. Another strike team might focus on implementing enemies in the game.

Some teams may find it better to organize around strike teams than to organize around disciplines. When you organize around disciplines, it limits the exposure team members will have to people outside of their discipline. Doing it this way also fragments the tasks needed to implement a feature across multiple discipline teams. Instead, organizing strike teams around a set of game features provides a more holistic view of the feature and information on what effort will be needed to implement it in the game. With the rise of agile development (discussed in Chapter 4), game teams have become more open to utilizing strike teams to get things done.

If you utilize strike teams as a way of organizing your team, follow these guidelines:

- **Teams must be cross-discipline:** This includes art, design, engineering, and production. It is also nice to include testing. Having testers work directly with the developers is enormously helpful when creating and iterating on features.
- **Teams must have all the resources within the team to complete the features:** For example, if the team is tasked with creating mission intro cinematics, they should have animators, audio designers, and a scripter on their strike team. The team shouldn't be put in a position where they need to "borrow" someone from another strike team to do the work. If all the resources are contained within the team, they have the most autonomy to do what needs to get done.
- **Utilize an agile production methodology:** Agile and strike teams go well together. Strike teams can be created for certain feature sets, then they can be reconfigured as needed for others. At the end of a sprint or milestone, reassess the team configurations to see what changes need to be made.
- **Appoint a strike team lead or leads:** Within each strike team, it is helpful to have leads who are responsible for the implementation and quality of the feature. These people work closely with the strike team to research what needs to be done, collect information, task out the work, implement features, and check quality, and are responsible for the final version of the feature.

If organizing around strike teams, you will want to have a lead who is responsible for helping the team organize their work, unblocking any issues, and providing status updates to the appropriate parties. This is a role that can be filled by a producer or a discipline lead. If you utilize this format for the production pipeline, you can still utilize a structure where employees have a discipline lead who is responsible for performance feedback, mentoring, and career growth.

11.6 Working with Remote Team Members

Working remotely is on the rise, even within game development. As you put your ideal team together, you may find someone who is a perfect fit who, for one reason or another, is unable to physically be in the office with the team. You may also find yourself working with off-site freelancers, and while they are not full-time employees of the team, they should still be treated as members. There are pros and cons to working with remote team members.

One advantage of this is that the pool of available talent is larger. You have more people to choose from, and since they don't have to relocate, they have more choices as well. You may find someone in a different country who has the right set of skills for what is needed. People who work remotely are often more productive since they don't have to deal with the small interruptions that happen when working in an office. Remote workers have more autonomy over their schedule and work-life balance. All of these things make working remotely attractive.

Disadvantages revolve around relationships and communication with the team at large. As a remote worker, it can be hard to build relationships and trust with on-site team members, which, in turn, can impact the quality and speed of work. Communication can be fragmented since the remote workers won't have the benefit of face-to-face communication or people dropping by their desk to see what they are working on. There can also be some confusion in terms of tasks and responsibilities, especially if these things are not defined clearly from the outset. If people are located in different time zones, scheduling meetings can be difficult (especially if their working hours are opposite). Language could also be a barrier if working with people from different countries.

If you have remote team members, here are a few ways in which you can improve the working relationship and integrate them as fully as possible into the team:

- **Introduce them to team (in person is best):** When remote people start on the team, try to fly them to the office and have a kickoff meeting with them and the team. Ideally, they can stay the week, hang out with their teammates, learn how the pipeline is set up, ask questions about their work, and so on. The team will get to know this person, and it will be easier for them to establish a working relationship.
- **Establish multiple lines of communication:** Be sure the remote people are included in the appropriate mailing lists and meeting invites. They should also have access to any group chat areas (like Slack or Google Hangouts) and have the ability to do video conferencing. If they are integrated into the day-to-day communication outlets for the team, it is less likely that they will miss key information.
- **Have a "water cooler" area:** One of the biggest drawbacks of working remotely is that it is hard to establish camaraderie with the team. It's nice to create some type of virtual "water cooler" where people can ask questions, be social, and feel like they are part of a team. It takes a bit

more effort from both the remote and off-site workers to maintain this, but the results are worth the effort.

- **Schedule regular meetings:** Consistency is also important in creating a sense of camaraderie with off-site and on-site team members. If you have regular stand-ups, have them at the same time every day and be sure to dial in so remote team members can join. Make sure remote team members are also included in team-wide or company-wide meetings, if applicable.
- **Clearly define their work:** When people work off-site, make sure what they are working on is clearly defined. They will be working for several hours or days at a time on something without the benefit of immediate feedback from other team members. If they have clearly defined work and know who they should talk to with any questions, it helps improve the quality and flow of the work.
- **Integrate their workflow with your teams:** Make sure remote workers have their source control, email systems, calendars, and anything else integrated with those of your team. They should be checking their work into the same source control as the rest of the team, and they should also be part of the same approval workflows.
- **Check in frequently:** The person who is directly managing the off-site worker should check in with them frequently, at least once a day. Checking in during a stand-up is fine as well. The goal is to have daily contact to ensure that the off-site person hasn't run into things that are blocking their work, and they don't have anything else to discuss.
- **Have some working hours overlap:** It's nice if the working hours of the remote and on-sight employees can overlap. If the time zones are too far apart, this may be difficult. At a minimum, try to schedule the daily stand-up at a time when everyone can be present either in person or on the phone.
- **Give them a tech support contact:** When people are working remotely, they may run into issues that require tech support. For example, they might be blocked from checking things in, or they may not be receiving emails. A lot of time can be spent trying to troubleshoot, and I've found that it is much easier to make sure they have a reliable person in the company's IT department that can help alleviate any technical issues.

BRIAN SOWERS, ONE METHOD MONKEY LLC, WORKING EFFECTIVELY WITH VIRTUAL TEAMS

It's going to sound super obvious, but regular, structured communication with the team is the biggest force multiplier. I worked with a team of senior engineers that didn't set up any kind of meetings or daily stand-ups, and it was a train wreck—people would go off into their own corners and work on something, and when we started integrating, everything would fall apart. I remember there was a feature I wrote when I started that job that someone would break literally every 3 days.

Peer review becomes more important for distributed teams; it's easier for an isolated developer to stray when they're not involved in the regular day-to-day conversations that happen in an office. This has the caveat that peer review done poorly can significantly hamper productivity.

My best peer-review experience was when a single tech lead had ownership of the reviews and gave feedback in a one-on-one conversation after changes had been made. We were never blocked on reviews and could properly prioritize review feedback.

Conversely, my worst peer-review experience was when anyone could review work, the conversations about the review happened out-of-band in a forum, and the review was required before changes could go in. The undefined review ownership coupled with the elongated discussions meant that features could sit in the queue for days (or frequently weeks) before getting into the game. This pushed back integration and testing, and increased the likelihood of developers stepping on each other.

11.7 Conclusion

Time spent defining roles and responsibilities and picking the right leads for your team is worth the investment. A team organization chart is also useful for further clarifying people's roles and who is responsible for what. Now that you have an idea of how to organize the team, think about ways to manage it. Chapter 12 discusses things to keep in mind when trying to build an effective team that works well together.

Managing Your Team

12.1 Introduction

An effective producer must develop leadership skills to keep the team motivated, maintain morale, and take care of their needs. Motivation is challenging because it requires managing many different personalities; helping people discover their strengths; and neutralizing any risks to team morale, such as shortened schedules or difficult personalities. The producer must take this responsibility seriously; otherwise, people will stop collaborating with each other, and the quality of the game will suffer.

If the producer is committed to building and maintaining a strong team, many of the other risks on a project will be minimized, mainly because the lines of communication are open, and people are aware of these risks much sooner in the process. Because of this awareness, the risks have less chance of snowballing into more serious problems. This chapter discusses some ways in which to build strong teams and maintain project momentum, even when a project becomes stressful.

12.2 Team Leadership

Leaders are people who possess and exude confidence, a strong vision, values, and an appreciation for the people with whom they are working. They can pull together and help a group to achieve a shared vision, and hold them accountable for their work. They project passion, enthusiasm, and a positive attitude about work. Most importantly, leaders have the courage and initiative to take risks, make unpopular decisions, and do what is necessary to achieve project goals. Leaders are defined more by what they do than by their assigned position on the team, which means they can come from anywhere on the team.

The good news is that you can develop your leadership skills through training and practice. Check with your HR department about getting some leadership training or coaching, especially if you are a new manager. There are several good books on how to become a better leader, and these often include very tangible strategies.

There are a few basic leadership archetypes—someone charismatic who inspires people to aim high, the strong and silent type who leads by example, and the motivator who personally works with each member of the team to bring out their best qualities. Become familiar with them, and figure out which style or styles best suit you. Remember that different leadership styles work better for different situations. For example, if you are working with one of your entry-level employees, your approach to leadership is going to be more instructional (i.e., you will tell them the tasks to be done very specifically), while your approach with a senior person on the team will be more strategic (i.e., you will tell them what goal needs to be fulfilled, and it's up to them how they get done). If you are not consciously improving your leadership skills and utilizing a style that works most effectively with the team, you might find yourself in charge of a team that is demoralized, unhappy, and unproductive.

Keep in mind that even though you (or a group of you) are leading the team, it's the team that actually gets the work done. So, one of the most critical things you can do as a leader is establish and maintain a healthy work environment where people are not bullied or belittled. Do not let someone on the team bully or disrespect people, even if they are one of its most skilled members.

One of your main goals as a leader is to create an environment where people can do their best work and have a voice that's heard. This means that you should be transparent with your team about what's going on with the project. Teams tend to get nervous when they think something is going on that they don't know about, so try to stay ahead of any rumors by being up-front about things impacting the project. The team members also prefer to have autonomy in how they work. They come to the office every day because (hopefully) they are passionate and excited by what they do. Giving them leeway to make choices on how they do something contributes directly to their satisfaction. If the team thinks they are being micromanaged or dictated to, it impacts their morale negatively. Leaders need to listen to their teams, and be open, honest, and approachable. A great way to get an idea of how your team is feeling is to walk around and talk to people. Find out what is working for them and what's not, and figure out ways to improve their workflow. For a more in-depth discussion on the topic of team leadership, take a look at Seth Spaulding's book *Team Leadership in the Game Industry* (2009).

THE GAME OUTCOMES PROJECT

In 2014, a team of developers, headed up by Paul Tozour, did an in-depth study of the cultural differences between teams. They wanted to know what factors separated the best teams from the rest of the teams. The result was a five-part series entitled *The Games Outcome Project* (Paul Tozour, 2014). The articles are available online at Gamasutra.com (http://gamasutra.com/blogs/PaulTozour/20141216/232023/The_Game_Outcomes_Project_Part_1_The_Best_and_the_Rest.php).

This series is highly recommended reading if you are interested in learning more about the dynamics of game development teams. The articles in the series discuss the top 40 things that great game teams do. The series contains lots of great information and interesting things to learn. You may be surprised at what some of the top motivators are.

12.3 Team Building

Team building is a critical part of the game development process and often one of the most neglected. There is a common misconception that assigning a group of people to work together creates a team, but this is definitely not the case. A group is comprised of individuals whose work is directed by the head of the group. A team consists of a group of people who are working together towards a common goal and holding each other mutually accountable for the outcome, which is a big difference. Strong teams must be built and supported throughout the project.

Building a team is challenging; you must be able to deal effectively with different types of personalities and get them working together in harmony. There is some risk in getting people to participate in "team-building" activities, especially because such activities could be considered corny or cheesy. But it is worth trying something that helps a group of people develop trust and camaraderie, and eventually turn into a team. You want more than just a group of people doing work as directed. You want a team that is actively sharing ideas, collaborating, taking ownership or pride in a project, and exhibiting passion about their work. These actions and attitudes lead to quality games that are appealing to players. Some of the ways in which you can make a group into a team include establishing trust, providing motivation, establishing norms, and engaging in cross-training.

12.3.1 Establishing Trust

One way to establish trust is to be up-front about any news that impacts the game. This includes good and bad news. There may come a point during game development when bad news must be delivered to the team, such as a project cancelation or the departure of key personnel. Although it isn't enjoyable to be the messenger of bad news, do it with timeliness and sensitivity in order to minimize the negative impact. First and foremost, be honest about why something is happening. You do not have to get into the nitty-gritty details, but do provide the context of the decision, and answer any and all questions as honestly as possible.

Second, be sensitive about how the news is delivered. Even though something bad might be happening—such as layoffs—do not overemphasize the negative aspects. People will feel bad enough already for their friends who may be let go. Instead, discuss the reasoning behind the layoffs, what steps were taken to minimize the impact, and what is being done to take care of the employees who have to find new jobs.

Finally, deliver news in a timely fashion, before any rumors get out of hand. Rumors are often incorrect, and if they aren't quickly neutralized, they will impact the morale of the team. If there are rumors going around, schedule a team meeting to have an open discussion. Allow people to ask questions, and provide honest answers with context so they better understand how decisions are made.

12.3.2 Motivation and Buy-In

Team buy-in and motivation are important elements of a strong team. When people know their feedback, opinions, and concerns are considered when decisions are made, they feel more ownership of the project and are more highly motivated. Being thoughtful and supportive of the team's input also helps people to more clearly define the vision of the project.

For example, if a designer has a cool idea for a new feature in the game, work with them to understand the feature and determine if it is something that should be added. If so, talk with the rest of the people whose work will be impacted, and figure out how to prioritize other work to get the new feature added. If the new feature, while cool, is not something that fits with the vision and goals of the game, take time to talk about why it is not a fit with the designer so he or she better understands. If people can visualize and share the game's vision, and understand the goals, they will be more willing to work on a project for 6 months or 2 years to make this success a reality.

If people on the team are not motivated or do not have buy-in, you can have a serious problem. If one or two unhappy people are on the team, this number will increase quickly if these people are visibly unmotivated or vocal about their dissatisfaction with the project. When this happens, the producer must deal with the situation as soon as possible in order to prevent damage to the overall morale of the team. Try to identify problems as early as possible since it may be too late to solve them by the time they are clearly visible to you.

In order to minimize motivation issues, strive to create a work environment in which the team feels valued and appreciated. There are many ways to do this; for example, do a monthly birthday celebration, celebrate the completion of project milestones, or purchase movie tickets for a team outing. Above all, remember to tell your team "thank you" for a job well done.

DANIEL TAYLOR, SR. PRODUCER, PSYONIX. MANAGING PEOPLE

By far, the hardest part of being a producer is managing people (the work is easy by comparison). When I was greener, I cared more about being liked, but you get to a point where you don't worry so much about trying to make everyone happy. You compassionately tell people the truth and what can be done to help.

12.3.3 Getting to Know Each Other

How well do you really know your teammates? Even though you might have worked on one or two projects with them, do you know exactly what they contribute to the project? Do you know their first and last names? Small development teams of ten people or less may know this information, mainly because everyone on the team fulfills multiple roles and is dependent on the work of several others.

However, as development teams get larger, it is not uncommon for someone not to know everyone's full names or even who is on the team. This basic information is important for people to know. It might seem elementary, but there are instances every day of someone asking a friend in a loud whisper, "Hey, who's that guy? Is he on my project? What does he do?" Providing answers to these simple questions can go a long way in building a strong team.

One of the first things to do when a new team is assembled is have everyone introduce themselves and briefly describe what they will be doing on the project. They only need to spend a minute or less on this; most people will not remember everyone's names after this initial meeting anyway, but the exercise starts the getting-to-know-you process.

If anyone new is added to the team, send an introductory email a few days before the person starts working there; then, on his or her first day, make personal introductions to everyone on the team. There is nothing more awkward than someone coming into the office on Monday morning and seeing a stranger sitting at a nearby desk.

If there is money in the budget, consider having a project kickoff event at a local bowling alley or restaurant to give people the time to socialize with each other outside of work. Team members might feel more comfortable interacting with each other in this casual setting, and it allows them to get a better feel for the other people's personalities.

In addition, create nameplates with people's names and departments: for example, "John Doe, Character Artist." These can be displayed on people's desks and provide an unobtrusive way to reinforce their names and what they do on the team. As people put faces to names and see who is responsible for which cool features in the game, they might start talking with people they have never interacted with on a personal level. Nameplates also make it easier for a new person to become familiar with teammates and their job roles.

Set aside a few minutes at each weekly team meeting for one or two people to give a five-minute presentation on their game development background, favorite development techniques, hobbies, or anything else they want to tell the team about. People might learn that other developers have similar tastes in hobbies or music, which can create a rapport. In addition, these presentations are something fun and interesting that the team can look forward to.

12.3.4 Establish Norms

Establishing communication norms for your team can help foster good communication. Norms are guidelines for the typical and approved behavior that the group expects people to exhibit. These are formed in several ways: they can emerge naturally over time, they can be defined up-front, or they can be triggered by a problem that needs a solution. An example of a norm that emerges naturally is making it a habit to stop by your boss's office first thing each morning to give him or her a brief update on what you plan to accomplish for the day. If you miss a morning of chatting with your boss, you might both feel that something is off but not quite be able to put your finger on it. An example of a norm that is defined up-front is when your boss requires you to stop by each morning and provide an update on what you plan to do throughout the day. If you do not do this, your boss will want to know why you missed your standing appointment. And, finally, if there is an issue on your project that puts the ship date at risk, your boss might institute a policy in which you have to submit a task list each morning that you will review together—this norm is often established as a solution to a specific problem.

Involving the team in defining a set of norms can be an effective team-building activity—everyone has a say in what the norms are, and everyone agrees on the final list. After a set of norms is established, other norms will naturally evolve that will improve overall communication between team members, leads, the producer, and studio management.

For example, set up a time for the team to discuss communication norms. Get the whole team in the room, ask people to discuss some of the communication issues they are having on the project, and determine which areas need improvement. When team members define the issues, they can more easily formulate a set of norms. After the problems are defined, explain to the team what norms are, and ask them to brainstorm on what guidelines will work for them. When they have thrown out all their ideas, have everyone participate in narrowing down the ideas and defining the norms. Here are examples of some team communication norms:

- Know who the point of contact is for your questions.
- Be considerate of other people's time.
- Do not mumble or be a low speaker.
- Do not yell or raise your voice.

- Be constructive with criticism; do not complain.
- Act professionally towards your peers.

If establishing communication norms works to help build your team, think of other things that might be useful to establish norms around.

12.3.5 Cross-Training

Cross-training is a method in which people on the team are trained in disciplines they have not worked in before. For example, have an artist follow an engineer for a day and learn how to code features for the art tool, or have an artist spend the day testing the game with the QA department and learning the ins and outs of testing, logging, and regressing bugs. After people spend some time in someone else's role, they will be more appreciative of that person's role on the project.

This practice might even lead to improvements in the process. For example, if an artist walks an engineer through the process of importing a level into the game and then has the engineer do it, the engineer might realize there is a way to improve the current set of tools to make this easier for the artist. A designer with some basic training in creating 3D levels will gain a greater understanding of how to document his level designs on paper so they are more easily translated into 3D spaces by an artist.

Cross-training is a good way to integrate new people into the team as well. On their first week, they can spend part of each day shadowing an artist, engineer, or designer. Shadowing can help them to more quickly become part of the team and learn what people's roles and responsibilities are on the project.

ASHLEY JENNINGS, SR. TECHNICAL ARTIST, HI-REZ STUDIOS, TEAM COMMUNICATION

There are many challenges in game production, but people who have a true appreciation for the work that other departments do will be the most beneficial to the studio in the long run. While a poor developer will insist that they have the "best ideas," and only their methods will work, a great developer will understand the role the members of each department play and allow them to "do what they do best." Just as in any other industry, no one wants to be micromanaged. Game designers should be not telling animators the exact way they want a character to be animated or putting down concept artists when a design does not look exactly the way they'd envisioned it in their head. Producers need to provide clear communication from the start, so artists and developers can provide deliverables that don't need constant iteration. Iteration, although essential to the creation of extraordinary work, is a time-consuming process that should be handled early in the development process to reduce lost time and effort on the part of the developers. No one on the team wants to pour days into their work only to have it omitted from the game because the original vision was not clearly communicated by the producers.

12.4 Team Communication

There are many ways in which people communicate with each other on the development team. Effective communication ensures that members are in sync on the project goals and vision of the game. Since there are so many points of communication, information can get diluted or less accurate as it is passed from person to person. Establishing strong communication practices is critical to keeping the right information flowing to all people on the team. Think about all the different types of communication used on a team—emails, status reports, meetings, instant messages, feedback, and so on—and focus on what makes each type most effective.

12.4.1 Written

Most people would agree that there are too many emails and too many instant messages being sent on any given day. Producers and leads may get up to 100 emails a day from all over the company. The expectation that someone can read and act on this amount of email each day, and still get their actual work done, is unreasonable. Email is still a primary form of communication on a development team, although chat programs like Slack are starting to replace some of these (but they can also be overwhelming). When writing information for emails or chat messages, keep the following in mind:

- Lead with the most important information or a call to action.
- Keep the wording concise.
- Include specifics, especially for deadlines and other important information.
- Set up mailing lists or chat channels.
- Use the high-priority label sparingly, or people will ignore its importance.
- Use correct grammar, and write in coherent sentences.
- Use bulleted lists to quickly convey major points.
- Use a font that is large and easy to read.

When writing other types of documentation, such as meeting notes or status reports, many of the preceding guidelines apply. In addition, create a standardized format so that people can better understand the information being presented. In some instances of written communication, especially if the information is critical, you will need to follow up with people in person to confirm they got the email, notes, or report and are interpreting the information correctly. This follow-up only takes a few minutes, and if the information is vital, the time spent is worth the investment.

12.4.2 Meetings

A great deal of time when making a game is spent in meetings. Ideally, the team's focus should be on limiting the amount of meetings needed so that people can focus on actually doing the work. Producers and leads are most likely to be scheduled for back-to-back meetings, and it is important to keep these meetings as productive and effective as possible. Here are some simple ways in which to make meetings more useful:

- Before scheduling, define the goals and desired outcome of the meeting. For example, the goal could be to provide feedback on the game scripting for one of the missions. If you cannot define these goals, cancel the meeting.
- Invite the right people to the meeting. If a decision must be made, make sure the decision maker is invited. If something needs to be explained, make sure the person who can best convey the information is presenting. Keep to the smallest number of attendees that is effective. It's expensive to have too many people in a meeting, especially if they are key to the conversation or decision-making. You can always send around notes afterwards to anyone who should be informed about what the outcome of the meeting was.
- Include the agenda in the meeting invite so the people involved are prepared. Stick to the agenda during the meeting, and table any topics that aren't listed.
- Schedule the meeting for 30 minutes or less. This keeps people focused and is less of a time commitment. There's a lot that can be done in 30 minutes.
- Assign time limits to each topic to keep the meeting moving forward. Some topics take more time to discuss than others, but setting a general time limit on the agenda provides a better idea of how much material can be covered.
- At the beginning, state the meeting goals to the attendees. At the end, summarize any decisions made during the meeting (and include these in the notes).
- Start and end meetings on time.
- Do not combine information gathering and decision-making in one meeting. Meetings can quickly get off track if you try to combine information gathering and decision-making into a single meeting. People can get bogged down in the information part and never get to a decision, or they may want to make a decision quickly and not consider all the pertinent information.
- Appoint a moderator. The moderator is a neutral party whose job is to keep the meeting running on track; they shouldn't be involved in the discussion. The moderator controls the agenda and keeps people on topic so the meeting can start and end on time.
- Take meeting minutes. Minutes are a useful record of what was discussed and what decisions were made. This avoids the issue of people forgetting why the meeting was held in the first place and prompts them to follow up on tasks that were assigned during it. The minutes should list who attended the meeting, the meeting goals, the agenda, key points of discussion, key decisions, and action items. Action items should be assigned to a specific person and have a stated deadline for completion. As with the moderator, assign someone who is neutral to take notes so they do not have to be actively involved in the conversation.

- Follow up on action items. Action items are important by-products of meetings and are needed in order to come to a resolution on some of the topics discussed. Track these in the minutes, and make sure they are completed by the deadline.

Team meetings are an important way in which to communicate information to the team at large. The other benefit is that questions from the team can be addressed quickly before they turn into rumors. This meeting doesn't need to follow all the rules outlined above, but you do want to have some structure to avoid wasting anyone's time. If there isn't a burning need to have a team meeting, you should cancel it. How frequently you need to have a team meeting depends on the size and complexity of the project, and what other communication pipelines are in place. For example, it's somewhat cost prohibitive to have a team meeting every week if the team includes hundreds of people. Think about how much money is spent on having hundreds of people stop work for an hour to attend a weekly meeting.

The team meeting agenda is straightforward as it is just another venue for communicating with the team. Plan to include the following types of information in a team meeting:

- **Project update:** Discuss what progress has been made in the overall game plan, what marketing and PR events are being planned, how things are progressing with getting approvals on licenses, the current status of any hardware requests, and anything else that happened during the past week. Also include any schedule changes.
- **Introduce new team members:** Make sure people know who joined the team.
- **Questions and Answers:** Take questions; address any rumors. It's important for the team to have clarity about anything they have a question or concern about. If there is no truth to the rumors, make this clear in the team meeting.
- **Establish a regular meeting time:** The meeting becomes a fixture on team's calendar. Jot down notes of what items to discuss in the next team meeting. People will come to rely on the team meeting as a resource for useful information.

12.4.3 Seating Arrangements

Think about ways to arrange team seating so that you have the right group of people sitting near each other. Some companies sit people together based on discipline. The thinking is that you will learn more about your craft if you are near people you can learn from and talk shop with. In some cases, depending on what work they are doing, this may make sense. The drawback to this arrangement is that people have a tendency to focus on their discipline, instead of taking into consideration what the other disciplines are contributing. This can make it difficult for communication to flow effectively between engineers, designers, artists, producers, UX, and QA. Separating people by discipline also fosters an us-versus-them mentality that is not healthy or good for team morale.

A more valuable seating arrangement groups people based on what feature or functionality they are working on. This allows them to develop the feature as a whole, with input coming from every discipline about how to make the feature. Engineers can have better access to designers, and impromptu conversations about the design and technical feasibility of a feature will happen naturally and more frequently. For example, grouping designers, AI engineers, object artists, and mission scripters together creates a cross-functional team that focuses on creating a playable level in the game. You can set up a cross-functional team for other levels in the game and work on multiple levels in parallel. Once a level or feature is done, people may be assigned to work with a different group of people on a feature, and if this is the case, the seating arrangements should change as well.

The team might object to switching around the sitting arrangements, especially if they are not used to doing so. In addition, they may be concerned about the increased noise level in an environment where people are encouraged to talk with each other. To keep the working environment productive, inform people that any meetings lasting more than a few minutes or consisting of three or more people must be conducted in areas outside the team room so as not to disturb others. You can also invest in noise-canceling headphones for everyone on the team. This way, people can feel more comfortable in the more open environment. Designating certain hours of the day as "quiet hours" in which no talking is allowed in the room is also something to consider.

In addition, think about the personality types that are sitting near each other. If possible, make sure that positive and enthusiastic people are seated throughout the team rooms. These people bring a natural positive energy to the team and really get people excited about what they are working on. They also help mitigate the negative energy from people who have a tendency to complain.

12.4.4 Status Reports

Status reports are a common way in which to provide an update to a group of people about what's going on with the project. Consider who your audience is for the status report as each audience is probably looking for different information. For example, senior management is likely interested in overall progress, such as how closely the project is tracking to the milestone schedule, what things are at risk, and what key things happened since the last report. The development team is likely interested in a bit more detail: for example, what character models are finished, which levels are ready for scripting, and what is the next deadline the team needs to be aware of. The frequency of the reports is also determined by the audience. Senior management might want a weekly or monthly report, while the development team might prefer a daily rundown of what has been happening. Work with your stakeholders to determine what makes sense. As in meetings, you don't want to waste time writing status reports if they aren't providing value.

Here are some things to consider adding to a status report. The specific items you include should be determined by the needs of the audience:

- **Feature updates:** What features are in progress, and which features are ready for testing? Include anything that gets the team excited about the work they are doing.
- **Marketing and PR updates:** What trade shows will the game be at, what are the latest articles and reviews, and what other promotional events are happening?
- **New employees:** As teams get larger, new employees are bound to start mid-production. Introduce these developers, and give some brief background information so people can get to know them.
- **Upcoming deadlines:** It is always a good idea to note upcoming deadlines and what main items need to be accomplished in order to meet them.
- **Risks:** What are the top project risks, and what mitigation strategies are in place?
- **Resources:** What are the additional resources needed (including personnel, equipment, and outsourcing)? The report is a good way to keep visibility on these needs.

12.4.5 Key Project Information

There is a lot of information to track and organize during game development. Start thinking sooner rather than later about how you can organize this information. The way it is organized should be straightforward and easily understood by the team. The other thing to consider is the process for keeping all the information up to date. This can be a full-time job, especially if information is fragmented across different reports, schedules, task-tracking tools, etc.

A well-maintained team website or wiki can function as the central source of information about the project and is a great team-building resource. For example, let's say the art assets are tracked in Shotgun, the coding standards documents are in Visual SourceSafe, and the design documents are stored some place on a team Google Drive. You can create a website that includes hyperlinks to each of these different assets. So, while the assets and information are spread among different tools, the website can gather them all in one place for easy access. The website should be well-organized so that people can easily find the information they need. Here are some of the things to include in the website:

- Design documents and coding standards;
- Meeting schedules and minutes;
- Status reports;
- Calendar that shows vacations and key deadlines;

- QA test plans;
- Contact information for the team members.

The team can provide feedback on what other things to include. The goal is to have a central resource that is always up to date and that the team can easily navigate to get the information they need. Storing this information in a publicly accessible place allows team members to be as informed as they choose to be about the project. Some people will rarely visit the team website; others will make it their home page and check it on a daily basis. The team website is also a great tool for educating new people about the project or for directing management to the most current set of design documents.

To make the team website an effective tool, always keep it up to date. Then, the team can rely on it for the most current project information. This practice also ensures that everyone on the team has equal access to all the information—not just the people who constantly check in with the leads on the status of the project. The minute the team realizes the website does not contain the latest information, they will stop using it as a development tool and instead rely heavily on the producer and leads to directly supply them with the necessary information.

12.4.6 Performance Feedback

Most companies conduct annual performance reviews to let employees know which areas they excelled in and which areas could use some improvements. However, providing feedback to employees *throughout* the year is more effective. More frequent feedback allows an employee to continually improve throughout the year, instead of being weighed down with a list of improvements once a year. Here are some general guidelines for giving effective feedback:

- Ask questions to gain understanding. Sometimes, instead of going down a list of feedback for the employee, it's more effective to have a conversation with them about an issue so you can better understand their motivations. You may find that something which appeared to be performance related actually isn't—the employee may just have taken a different approach.
- Give feedback in a timely fashion. If you see that someone isn't meeting expectations, give them feedback immediately, and don't wait for the annual performance review. Do the same with positive feedback.
- Be constructive with feedback and provide examples. Work with the employee on ways they can improve and get back on track. Focus feedback on the behaviors the person is doing, and don't make it personal.

Empathy. My god, we need more empathy everywhere, but especially in game development. And when I say empathy, I mean it in many ways. Making a great, playable game means encouraging and fostering empathy for your players. Making a great game on a reasonable schedule means having empathy for the developers and their time and their needs. It means finding ways to take tasks they shouldn't be dealing with and taking them upon yourself. It means protecting them from occasional not-helpful feedback from publisher sources, yes, but it also means having empathy for the publisher who doesn't quite understand what you're making. You need the developers' help, so you need to figure out how to get them what they need, no matter what. Now, I'm going to be honest here—that was the hardest lesson I ever learned, and I don't think I ever really nailed it before I left my job.

12.4.7 Resolving Conflict

Conflict happens on any project, and some basic causes are personality differences, miscommunication, and disagreements over how things are done. As with feedback, you need to deal with conflicts in an assertive and timely manner. However, you don't want to try to resolve conflict when emotions are running high, so you may need to wait an hour or a day in some cases. Before attempting to resolve the conflict, make sure you understand exactly what's going on (and don't assume intent on anyone's part). These guidelines are a starting point for conflict resolution:

- Don't exaggerate the situation by saying words like "always," "never," and "constantly." Stick to the facts, and do not interpret or embellish.
- Don't assume you know what the person's motivations are for doing something or assume that the person has negative intent. There are many reasons why people act the way they do, and you will not know why until you ask them.
- Do not resolve conflicts publicly. If someone acts improperly during a meeting, do not reprimand the person there; instead, deal with the situation privately.

After you lay out the facts, describe the tangible impact this situation has on the project, so the person has a better understanding of the cause and effect. Give them a chance to respond, and then discuss what needs to be done to remedy the situation. Show the person how an improved situation benefits him or her and the project. For example, let's say a lead designer didn't agree on a feature that was cut from the game and was asking designers to continue working on it.

The conversation might go something like this:

- **Producer to designer:** "The team agreed to cut the feature from the game because there was not enough time to implement it. This decision was communicated to the team in the team meeting and via email. On Wednesday, I found out from another designer that you had instructed the designers to continue working on it. This direction has caused them to fall behind on their design documentation for the UI, and now UI engineering is held up until the documentation is complete."

After stating the cause and effect, allow the person a chance to respond. He or she will likely state why he or she wants to keep the feature in or have an emotional reaction. No matter what the person does, be prepared to assertively state your solution to the problem. However, you will want to tailor your response appropriately to the situation. Then, continue: "The designers need to get the UI design documentation finished, so please have them work on that until it is completed. If you feel strongly about this feature, we will schedule a meeting to discuss it again with the leads—maybe we can put in a scaled-down version or replace another feature."

When resolving conflict, you may try to achieve consensus, which can be a useful tool if a quick resolution is needed in order to keep making progress. But keep in mind that consensus means only that someone will accept a proposed solution, not that they agree with it. For example, you may have a designer who wants to have a specific feature functioning in the alpha version of the game, even though this feature is not as important as some of the other things that need to be completed for this milestone. The designer may agree to hold off on having the feature so that progress is not blocked in other areas, but he or she may still believe strongly that the feature should be implemented.

MATT IMMERMAN, PRODUCER, TEAM BUILDING

The goal, to me, should be to have a team, and ultimately a company, where people are as open and honest in what they are thinking during meetings as they are in the hallways, at their desks, or outside of work. Keep the following in mind when building your team culture with openness:

- People don't want to just focus on the negative. Find time to celebrate the team's successes. I've found people are generally more honest and open if they feel there is a balance between negative and positive. As a producer, I should try and facilitate that balance, and build a feedback system that fosters empathy among the team. If one person is struggling, then the team is struggling.
- Open and honest communication doesn't come right away. It takes time for any group of people to develop the level of trust needed to express criticism, concerns, and reservations. The goal is to establish an environment where everyone is free to make suggestions without fear of judgment.
- I talk about my own mistakes and failures as they happen, and people have tended to follow that lead. If I can't admit that I messed up or failed, then I can't expect my team to.

- Recognize that Impostor Syndrome is a real thing that a lot of people experience. People generally don't want to look "dumb" in front of their teams. Usually, before people say anything in a team environment, they will ask themselves, "Is this really a good idea, or will everyone think it's stupid?" and instead of throwing out ideas and suggestions, they are more concerned with appearing as if they have a handle on things. This is amplified depending on how many people there are on the team and what their positions are within the team/company. I have found that acknowledging this thought process at the start of our team's first few meetings and talking through it helps to ease people into the kind of open and honest collaborations I aim to facilitate among my team(s).

12.5 Conclusion

This chapter touched upon a few things to consider when managing a team. There are many valuable leadership and management resources available that delve into these topics in more detail. The game industry is not unique in the management and leadership challenges that are encountered on a daily basis. As a producer or a leader of the team, it is important to understand areas where you need to develop leadership skills so that you can be an effective team builder and team leader. You want to be a strong communicator and be on top of ways to grow your team's trust in each other.

CHAPTER 13

Outsourcing

13.1 Introduction

If you don't have enough people internally to handle all the development or if there is a requirement for highly specialized work (such as voiceover recording or localization), outsourcing is a solution. It shouldn't be considered something that saves time and money; in fact, outsourcing may end up being more expensive and take more time since you are hiring an expert to do what they do best. The vendor needs time to get familiar with the game, and their schedule will also be constrained by how quickly they receive feedback on their asset deliveries. In some cases, the vendor will actually be ahead of their estimated schedule but then fall behind because the development team took a long time to give feedback or dramatically changed the scope after the initial delivery. This chapter gives a high-level overview of things to consider when working with outsourcers, including using middleware and how to effectively manage outsourcing.

13.2 Outsourcing Overview

There are many types of game development services you can outsource without impacting the game's critical path. Most of these involve design, art, audio, and localization because these areas tend to have discreet sets of tasks that can be organized and worked on outside of the game's critical path. For example, the animation and audio for pre-rendered cinematics can be easily outsourced, especially if there is a clear script and storyboard for the vendor to work from. Narrative design and game dialogue is also something that can be successfully outsourced if the vendor is able to gain a good understanding of the game from design documents, playing the game, or talking with designers. Outsourcing audio and localization are quite common, and are discussed in more detail in Chapters 16 and 17, respectively, because of this.

Outsourcing engineering is not recommended because engineering tasks are more dependent on each other, and code merges can be time-consuming, making it difficult to test outsourced code on a regular basis. Additionally, an engineering vendor will need access to source code, which is highly confidential, and will need to set up a development environment that exactly matches what the internal engineering team is using. However, outsourcing engineering can be successful; it just requires more time and diligence from the internal engineers and production staff to ensure that any code merge conflicts are quickly resolved, that coding standards are being adhered to, and that any questions the vendors have can be quickly answered. In some cases, you may be able to bring an outsourcing vendor on site to work directly with the team; if this is the case, many of the hardware and software conflicts can be resolved more quickly.

The quality of the outsourced work is dependent on how well the development team defines what is needed, communicates deadlines and constraints clearly, and provides useful feedback in a timely fashion. If an external vendor is left to their own devices for an extended period of time and is working in vacuum without regular feedback, the quality of their work will suffer and may not meet the necessary quality bar. If this happens, more time and effort may be required to either work with the vendor to get them back on track, find another vendor, or bring the work in-house to be salvaged. If you plan to work with outsourcers, be prepared to spend a fair amount of time onboarding them, checking on progress, and keeping their work on track.

13.3 Pros and Cons of Outsourcing

As in any project, there are pros and cons to working with external vendors. The biggest benefit is that the team will be able to concentrate solely on their tasks for the game and have more time to iterate and fix bugs, and they won't have to take on work they are unfamiliar with doing. If there is a large amount of work to be done, a good outsourcing vendor can also augment the capacity of what the team can deliver. Selecting recommended vendors that are highly specialized in one area allows them to contribute to the overall quality of the game, leaving the team to concentrate on the areas they do best.

There are a few drawbacks to working with a vendor, one being the extra costs involved. However, if the project is large and complex, the cost of an external vendor might be worth the time and resources saved by the internal development efforts. Another drawback is that the developer will lose the flexibility to shift project deliverables and internal deadlines around. When working with a vendor, the developer must be organized and confident in the team's ability to meet key milestone dates. He or she needs to provide the vendor with the necessary assets when they are needed. For example, a cinematics vendor might need to have the final character models to complete the final version of the movies. Providing this information requires the developer to think months ahead in the production cycle in order to give accurate estimates to the vendor.

Another potential risk is that the vendor might not meet deadlines. This can severely impact the project if deadlines are extremely tight. In order to mitigate this risk, be sure to schedule ample time for finding a vendor, and check in with them frequently on progress. If it makes sense, you might have the vendor attend any daily check-ins with the internal team. This way, everyone can stay up to date on where things are with the project, and the vendor will have at least one chance per day to connect with the team face-to-face (even if it is just over video chat). Additionally, after you get the vendor's schedule, add some padding to it so there is some slack if needed. Don't schedule a vendor's deadline at the same time as a major milestone; it is better to have the vendor deliver the work at least a week beforehand so it can be integrated and tested as part of the milestone deliverable.

If the vendor is running behind schedule, and all necessary assets and documentation have been provided to him by the development team, this is a problem. In order to avoid this, schedule regular deliverables for the vendor. The vendor should get into the habit of making deliveries every week or every few days, depending on the work to be done. If any of these deadlines are missed, it is a red flag and should be mitigated as quickly as possible.

In some cases, the vendor might be good at convincing you everything is fine, then miss the final deadline by a long shot. If the situation is this bad, you might need to cut your losses and look for another vendor to complete the work or bring the work in-house and assign someone on the development team to finishing it. This is not an ideal situation because it will impact the amount of work, or the quality of the work, that the internal development team is responsible for.

13.4 Working Effectively with Outsourcers

After an external vendor is hired, work with them to set up an effective working relationship. You will get their best work if you are actively involved in checking in on status, being available to answer questions, and reviewing and providing feedback on their work in a timely fashion.

Start the working relationship with a project kickoff. The kickoff is an easy way to onboard the outsourcing vendor with the internal people they are working with. During the kickoff, do the following:

- **Clarify expectations:** Review the scope of work and what the vendor is expected to deliver. Answer any questions the vendor has. Include the necessary internal team members in the meeting so they also have a clear understanding of what work the vendor is actually doing. If there is any confusion, the internal team may duplicate work that the outsource vendor is already doing.
- **Discuss deadlines:** Review all the deadlines, and discuss contingency plans if the vendor runs into any delays. Establish a protocol for them to follow if they are blocked by waiting for something from the internal team. Discuss what will happen if the dates change (which they will).
- **Designate points of contact:** Most external vendors will have a project manager who is responsible for managing the vendor's part of the development process from beginning to end and acting as the primary contact for the developer. A single person from the development team should be the primary point of contact for the vendor's project manager. These two must communicate on a daily basis, even if it is just to provide a brief status update on what went on that day with the project. If more people are involved in the communication chain, it is likely that confusion will occur.
- **Establish communication channels:** If they are interfacing directly with members of the internal development team, make sure a clear communication pipeline is set up and adhered to. If the developer and the vendor do not establish the communication pipeline up-front, information will fall through the cracks, and key details will be missed. Poor communication might also impact the vendor's ability to meet proposed deadlines, especially if necessary information from the developer is not received on schedule. Consider adding them to any internal chat channels or email lists if it makes sense and is not a security concern.

The internal development contact is responsible for delivering all the necessary assets and resources to the vendor. They must also inform the vendor of any changes to the schedule, especially ones that affect the vendor's deadlines. If the vendor is not informed of a schedule delay that affects work deliverables, you might find yourself paying them extra money because they put in extra effort (beyond what was agreed to) to meet the new deadline. If the vendor is flexible, unforeseen schedule changes can be accommodated.

Provide resource to the vendor so they can get familiar with the game. It is helpful to show them concept art, playable prototypes, the style guide, and anything else that can help them get a good idea of the game's vision, and understand how the work they are doing fits into the development pipeline.

Think of the outsourcing vendor as an extension of the team, and treat them as such. Include them as much as possible in necessary meetings, make sure they receive important announcements, and try to establish a virtual "water cooler" where they can hang out and build rapport with the team. If possible, have the vendors come on site for a few days (ideally for an in-person kickoff meeting) to meet the team, play the game, and ask questions.

CHRIS SCHWEITZER, PRODUCER OF INTERACTIVE ENTERTAINMENT

I would say that in order to be effective with working with outsourcing, you should start small. The goal is to get both teams familiar with working with the other, start identifying and working through issues in the pipeline, and be able to define or change expectations before going into a long-term contract. Specifically with art outsourcing, the starting small period usually occurs while you have the outsourcing studio work on some "test" assets (these are game assets that are not high priority or that have an upcoming deadline).

I worked on a project that had a very unique art style. When we started looking into animation outsourcing, we had to find a studio that would meet the strong stylistic expectations while hitting our high-quality bar. When we found a potential company, we had the company animate a small set of character emotes, six in total, that ranged in animation difficulty. Since this was the first time we had this company working on emotes, the varying difficulty allowed us to judge the effectiveness and skill of the animators, with emphasis on receiving and interpreting feedback from the animation leads. This process allowed us to identify two major issues: there was a bottleneck in giving feedback on the submitted animation videos, and there was a broken dependency between animation and audio. Because we only had a set of six emotes, we were able to correct the pipeline and feedback process quickly, and have it ready for when we started the long-term contract.

The other thing I would say to keep in mind while working with outsourcing is that both sides (contractor/contractee) are a business, and dead time is wasted money. If you want to keep a good working relationship with the outsourcer, you need to make sure that the outsourcer is consistently fed tasks. What I found worked relatively well was making sure the next set of tasks/next contract was being discussed around the midpoint of the current task/contract. You do not need to have a new contract signed by the midpoint, but you should have the next task/contract done by the three-quarters point. Finalizing it at this time reinforces the deadline of the previous task/contract (because the new one will be dependent on it) and gives enough time to the outsourcing company to make a commitment to your studio.

13.5 Middleware

A quick note on middleware as this is another way to get more done with less resources. Middleware has become an all-encompassing term for any out-of-the-box software that can be modified for use in a game. Middleware is used for game systems, such as AI, animation, physics, rendering, and networking.

For example, developers can license an engine and modify it for use in their game instead of programming something from scratch. Cross-platform game engines, such as Epic's Unreal Engine 4, are considered middleware. Other third-party tools used for modeling, texturing, bug tracking, and project management could also be considered middleware.

One of the biggest benefits of middleware is that the developer can theoretically spend more time on creating and polishing unique features of the game than on creating a generic but necessary feature, such as lobby support for an online game. If the developer is familiar with the middleware technology (e.g., the developer used it on previous games), it is usually an easy decision to use it again on another game. However, if the developer is not familiar with the middleware, he or she needs to plan for a learning curve that may initially slow down development time as the team gets up to speed on how to work with the technology.

The biggest drawback to working with middleware is likely to be cost—you will need to pay a licensing fee (and sometimes royalties) to the middleware provider, and depending on the product, this fee can be costly. However, you may find the cost is justified after crunching the numbers for the budget. Many middleware providers price their products competitively and provide excellent technical support to make it easier for the developers to decide to use it.

After the license is in place (and in some cases before), the middleware vendor will provide a SDK that includes the Application Programming Interfaces (APIs), tools, and documentation. Most middleware providers offer technical support and will help the team to work through any technical issues they encounter while they are integrating the technology into the game's production pipeline.

After the middleware is integrated into the game, the vendor may request a build of the game in order to check how the software was implemented. The vendor may have a formal set of technical requirements that the game needs to fulfill before it will approve the middleware implementation in the game. This ensures that the technology is working as intended and that no surprises will occur when the game is launched. The approval process can be a benefit for the developer because testers who are familiar with any common problems that may occur when implementing the middleware will check the game and flag any issues that need to be addressed. Be sure to include time in the production schedule for this approval process.

13.6 Conclusion

Outsourcing and middleware are proven ways to add value and capacity to the development team. Both have advantages and drawbacks that should be considered when making a decision on whether to use them. Don't assume that using either one of these will save time or money; instead, view them as ways to get more general work done so the team can focus on what's unique about the game they are making.

PART 5
Making the Game

Once the plan is complete, and the team is assembled, the game development process gets into high gear. During this phase of the process, everyone is busy executing the tasks and iterating on the game. Each chapter in this section discusses some aspect of executing a set of tasks for the game. The chapters are:

Executing the Plan;

UX;

Audio;

Localization;

Testing.

CHAPTER 14

Executing the Plan

14.1 Introduction

The concept is approved, the pitch goes well, requirements are established, and now the team is ready to execute the plan. The hope is that all the contingencies have been planned for up until this point, and the plan will go smoothly. The reality is that there will still be a fair amount of change and iteration during this phase. If an agile method is used to develop and manage the game, there is already a process built in to accommodate iteration and changes while in the execution phase. However, using an agile method doesn't mean that the development of the game is chaotic and unplanned. Instead, agile provides a framework in which the team can commit to executing a defined set of work for short periods of time.

During this phase of game development, the team has defined the work that needs to be done and is working hard to complete it. By now, they should be working well together, especially since they spent time together planning and iterating on the prototype. At this point, they have a clear idea of what they need to do for a specific milestone and should have all the pieces necessary to work together towards this goal. As they begin to execute the work in earnest, they will encounter various issues and roadblocks that need to be resolved; much of the producer's time during this phase is spent resolving these issues and making sure the game is staying on track. This chapter provides an overview of what types of things occur during the execution phase, including project reviews and postmortems, managing feature creep, setting up a process for compiling game builds, and submitting the game to the rating boards. Let's begin by discussing two more major pieces that need to be in place before the team can fully start executing all the planned work: namely, the development pipeline and documentation.

14.2 Development Pipeline

The development pipeline is the series of steps that are followed to actually get assets and code working together in a playable version of the game. Most features rely on work from art, engineering, and design; each of these disciplines works with a different set of tools and file formats. For the pieces from each discipline to fit together in the game, a development pipeline must be defined and established. The pipeline must smoothly incorporate all the tools, assets, and production needs. For example, if a character is added to the game, the pipeline might look like this:

1. 2D concept art is created (Artist);
2. 3D model is created (Artist);
3. 3D model is textured (Artist);
4. 3D model is rigged for animation (Artist);
5. 3D model is animated (Artist);
6. Textured and animated model is imported into the game (Artist);
7. Character skills and attributes are added (Designer);
8. Character is added to a mission scenario and objectives (Designer);
9. Audio and voiceover are added to the character (Sound);
10. Character performance is optimized (Engineer).

For each of these steps, there are different people working with different file types, and they need to set up a consistent process and pipeline to ensure that all the file types work well together so that the final game asset can be generated and used in the game. Pipelines can get complicated, so it's something the team will want to map out ahead of time to ensure that there are minimal bottlenecks. More content going through this process means that the pipeline can get quite large, so the process and pipeline need to be able to scale up and scale down as needed. When thinking about the pipeline, consider the following:

- **Tools and Software:** The tools and software needed for the pipeline will be determined by what the technical needs are for the game. The software is used to convert file formats and import/export assets into the game. This includes thinking about which compilers and coding language will be used.

- **Two-way functionality:** The pipeline should support functionality for assets to be converted for game use and the ability to convert game assets back into their original source assets. This is useful when a change needs to be made to an in-game asset. If it can easily be converted back to a source file that a developer can work with, it will save them the trouble of having to remake the entire asset from scratch and put it through the pipeline again.
- **Critical Path:** The critical path is the key series of steps that every asset must complete in the pipeline. The game can't be finished until all the necessary assets have gone through the critical path. Make sure that one person doesn't have a disproportionate amount of work to do in the pipeline as this will create a bottleneck in the process. If the person can't keep up with all the work needed to keep the pipeline running, the process will back up, and delays will occur.
- **Number of steps:** Limit the number of steps in the pipeline; assets should be viewable and playable in a build as quickly as possible. Fewer steps mean fewer people involved, which means a more efficient pipeline.
- **Fully Functional:** The pipeline should always be functional. Earlier in the game development process, all parts of the pipeline may not be needed, so it will be tempting to try to work as long as possible with the pipeline in a partially functional state. Avoid this if you can as it will create scheduling and development problems later on in the process.
- **Asset Management:** Decide which source control software to use so that team members can check out assets before working on them. Everything should be kept under version control to prevent multiple versions of a file from causing confusion in the pipeline.
- **Automation:** Automate as much of the pipeline as possible in order to reduce time and human error.

For a more detailed discussion of production pipelines and how to create them, refer to Renee Dunlop's book *Production Pipeline Fundamentals for Film and Games* (2014). This book walks through the foundational layers of the production pipeline, including IT needs, best development practices, and asset management.

CHRIS SCHWEITZER, PRODUCER OF INTERACTIVE ENTERTAINMENT, SETTING UP A PIPELINE

What worked for me was first understanding the beginning and end of the pipeline. The end of the pipeline is usually the easiest (as it's usually QA or some publishing work), and it helps to start there and work backward. If you keep asking yourself, "What do we need to make sure happens before this step?", you will get a great start on defining the pipeline. Eventually, you will probably hit a point where a couple of branching paths can be identified, and it will become considerably harder to work backward. When that happens, you move onto the beginning of the pipeline and then go towards where you left off from there.

I found that it's best to identify a single owner at the beginning of the pipeline. This doesn't necessarily mean that the person does the work; instead, it means that they will be responsible for defining what the expectations are when going through the pipeline.

Once you have a general idea of what needs to happen and how the tasks flow down the pipeline, you should make it visual. It's much easier for the team to visualize the pipeline if it's in simple shapes and colors representing the identified tasks and owners, and this helps with rolling it out and with the team adopting it. There are a few things that need to be easily recognizable on this visual pipeline: who is the owner of each step, what discipline is responsible for that step (character art, systems design, audio, etc.), and a clear dependency chain. The idea is that if the developers know who the owner of each step is, then this can help to promote cross-team communication. It's no longer a group that owns that step but an identified owner that a developer could get an answer from or send an email to about a suggestion (it's a lot less intimidating if you are communicating with a person than it is with a group).

In order for the team to engage with the pipeline process you will need to track it and make that information visible to the team. This will all depend on how the project is set up and if you are using a tracking software, bulletin board, etc. But to help with team adoption, give everyone access at the beginning, keep all information up to date (producer's responsibility), and share the knowledge on how to access that information.

Let me use the Weapon Creation pipeline, from one of the games I worked, on as an example. We realized that in order to finalize a weapon, we need QA to do a pass. So, QA testing is the end of the pipeline. Before QA starts, audio will need to be finished. Before audio can start, visual effects (VFX) needs to be finished. Before VFX, we need animation to be complete, and so on... We identified the pipeline steps needed and represented the dependencies; the next step was to identify the owner. This came down to our Lead Systems Designer. This person would be the one to identify what weapons were needed: for example, a shotgun that is mid-tier and needs to pump. Once this person identifies the need, the pipeline kicks in. To help visualize the pipeline, we used Visio to create a simple flow graph. I passed this around to the team, and the feedback I got was that it was super helpful as it opened up communication lines that had been hidden from the rest of the team. Originally, the tracking was done on a shared Excel file kept in our perforce repository. This wasn't the best option as only one person could edit the document at a time, and the look of it was intimidating to the developers. We looked into possibly creating a JIRA entity that had the workflow mimic the pipeline, but eventually, the team rolled the pipeline into Shotgun instead. One thing that did not work out with the Shotgun integration was that not all the developers on the pipeline had access to Shotgun (accounts had not been created). Over time, we eventually got more and more developers into Shotgun, but until that happened, it fell on the producers to make sure the communication was bridged (by utilizing weekly emails and weekly reviews with stakeholders, and calling meetings when necessary).

14.3 Documentation

Each development team has a different philosophy on documentation. Some teams prefer to keep things light and use a prototype to communicate the major aspects of the game. Some teams pass along information verbally, while others document everything thoroughly. The benefits of documentation are clear—this is a good way to communicate on the game's design, schedule, budget, technical constraints, and so on. It is the one source of truth for questions about the game. But, in order for the documentation to be consistent and reliable, it must be updated on a regular basis. Once documents are out of date, they quickly lose their usefulness and can create more confusion since the team may not know if the information is current or not. Documentation can be time-consuming to create, so talk with the team to see what makes sense. You also want to make sure that the right people are reading it and using it as intended; otherwise, writing it is a waste of time.

The QA department usually uses design documentation when writing the test plan. For example, if an artist creates a working prototype of the game's UI shell and does not document the functionality, it will be difficult for QA to write an accurate test plan to check that all the buttons, boxes, and screens in the game are working correctly. You cannot expect QA to load up the UI prototype on a computer, then play through the game and compare the actual game UI screens to the screens in the prototype. This creates additional work for them, which they do not really have time for; they might also miss a large chunk of functionality if they forget to click a button.

Each discipline creates different types of documents. Each of these documents has a specific purpose and intended audience. Examples of art documentation are as follows:

- **Style guide:** Details the look and feel of the art style for the game. It contains concept art, style guidelines, font choices and usage, color palettes, and any other necessary information about the game's visuals.
- **Asset list:** A list of every art asset that needs to be created for the game. This includes character models, levels, cinematics, textures, and any other visual elements in the game. This list should be organized into some type of asset tracking program, such as Shotgun, to ensure that nothing is overlooked when making the assets.
- **Tool instructions:** Technical documents that discuss how to use the various tools in the art pipeline. This is especially useful if the pipeline uses proprietary tools.

Examples of design documents include:

- **Character Bible:** This includes descriptions, backgrounds, and art for all the characters in the game. It will include the character's abilities, strengths, and weaknesses, and any other identifying traits.

- **UI Wireframes:** This is a set of functional diagrams of the UI screens. It includes information on how the player transitions from screen to screen and details the functionality of each UI screen. It also includes information on the game controller set-up and what each button does on the controller.
- **Story Bible:** This includes the high-level story for the game, including the game lore, history, locations, politics, and anything else that helps set the background and context for the game world. It will include a breakdown of key story elements in the game and how the player will progress through these elements as they play the game.
- **Game Script:** Similar to a movie script, this contains all the dialogue spoken in the game.

The documents need to provide enough detail for an engineer, artist, QA tester, or designer to read them and understand how to implement the feature as designed. After the feature is implemented according to the specs in the documentation, it can be playtested and adjusted as necessary. The documentation must be updated with any changes because it is the central written resource for the game design.

Technical documentation includes:

- **Coding standards:** This details coding conventions, hardware and software specs, naming conventions, which technology is used, and any other technical information.
- **Technical design:** This outlines the technical architecture of the game. It discusses at a high level all the components of the game and how they will function from a technical standpoint. It includes diagrams of various systems and how they interact with each other.

Production and QA documentation include:

- **Budget and Schedule:** This is the estimated budget and schedule for the game. It should be updated throughout the development process.
- **Staffing Plan:** This shows how people will roll on and off the project.
- **Test Plan:** This details how all aspects of the game will be tested. It includes a checklist to show which parts of the game have been tested and what the results were.

Each development team will have a different format for design, art, and technical documentation. The key is to have a format that is easy to read and provides clear information about how the game works. There are several books on game design that discuss how to format design documents in detail. These same lessons can be carried over to art and technical documents. Tracey Fullerton's *Game Design Workshop a Playcentric Approach* (2018) is a good resource to consult about writing effective documentation.

14.4 Measuring Progress

As the team executes the plan, finding ways to measure their progress is important. Project reviews are one way in which to do this. During the review, the established development plan is compared with the game's actual development progress to determine if it is running behind or ahead of schedule. The review is also a good opportunity to discuss risks and gather feedback. As noted earlier in this book, it is important to continually assess risk and gather feedback throughout the development process. The project review is a logical place in which to do this, especially if reviews are conducted every 4–6 weeks. Set up a regular time for the reviews, and add them to a recurring schedule to ensure that the team actually does them. Focus on the quality of information presented in the review so that all the people involved will find them useful and worth doing.

In order to conduct a successful project review, begin by defining the goals and objectives. This ensures that the review will be beneficial to the people involved and that it will be geared toward the correct audience. For example, the review will likely include the publisher, project leads, studio management, and other stakeholders on the game.

Next, establish a consistent format for review. This keeps the information focused and makes it easier to compare data from past and present reviews. Some examples of information to include are:

- **Current progress in comparison with the baseline progress:** This includes things like what features were scheduled to be completed by this point in the development process as compared with which features are actually completed. A review of the budget is also useful to show whether spending is on track or not. A status update from each strike team is also useful.
- **Accomplishments since last review:** This is where tangible examples of what was completed and checked into the game can be discussed. If there haven't been any accomplishments since the last review, the project is probably in trouble.
- **Status of project risks:** Chapter 5 discusses how to assess project risks. Provide an update on all past risks, and present any new risks and potential mitigation plans.
- **Any roadblocks that need to be removed for the team:** Roadblocks are problems that can be identified and quickly removed so that progress does not come to a standstill.
- **Any additional resources the game needs:** This includes things like personnel and large hardware and software purchases. Talking about resource needs at the review keeps them visible and provides a good opportunity to remind management why they are needed.
- **Any changes to scope, milestones, or feature sets:** If the team is iterating on the game, there will likely be changes to the game design or

scope that need to be discussed by the stakeholders. In some cases, these changes will also need to be approved by the stakeholders before they can be implemented in the game.

Project reviews are beneficial because they keep everyone focused on the high-level goals of the game and provide a formal way to gather feedback from stakeholders. It is much easier to track feedback given in a project review than to have the stakeholders directly approaching members of the development team and asking for changes. By providing the feedback during a formal project review, the project leads can synthesize and prioritize it before presenting it to the team.

DANIEL TAYLOR, SR. PRODUCER PSYONIX.
CREATING QUALITY OUTCOMES

Simple stuff really. Be genuine, honest, and of service. Manage the scope of work and create a focus on what's important. Iterate as much as possible.

These are the questions constantly running through my head as a producer:

- What is our vision (desired UX)?
- Where are we at in achieving our vision (status)?
- Who is working on it (talent)?
- When is it due by (schedule)?
- How much can we afford (budget/scope)?
- How do we get more (process improvement)?
- Do we have the tools we need to do our best work (productivity)?
- Does the team believe we can achieve our vision (moral)?

I believe that if we make sure these eight questions are consistently met with pragmatic action for the duration of a project, then we will have a quality outcome.

14.5 Managing Feature Creep

During the project review, the stakeholders usually have a lot of feedback about things they'd like to see in the game, ways to improve existing features, or things they want removed or completely redone. When this type of feedback is given, carefully assess and determine which feedback needs to be prioritized highest and implemented sooner rather than later. If you take all the feedback at face value and just start implementing it, the game vision will become diluted and could result in a lower-quality game that feels very disconnected from the original vision. The other thing that feedback can do is cause feature creep.

Feature creep occurs when additional features are added without adjusting the other project variables (time, resources, and quality) to accommodate the additional work. It is something that developers are always fighting against because feature requests are made on a regular basis by the team, studio management, publisher, marketing, fans, and so on. Some feature creep can be good because it improves the player's experience with the game.

For example, if the control scheme is implemented as designed, new feature requests to improve usability might come in after UX testing. On the other hand, some feature requests can be damaging to the project—they are completely unreasonable given the other project parameters, they impact a lot of work already done, or they are so small that it is not worth putting the project at risk to include them.

When a stakeholder makes a feature request that will cause feature creep, it can be awkward to explain why a pet feature can't be included in the game. This could be because the feature doesn't fit the design vision or art style of the game, the feature is going to negatively impact the players' experience, or the feature can't be done within the current schedule and budget. If you are the person responsible for controlling feature creep, make sure you have a good understanding of the game's cost, schedule, and resources so that you can properly assess the impact a feature request will have on the development pipeline.

For example, if marketing requests that an online ranking system be added, research how long the feature takes to design, implement, and test as well as who is available to do these tasks. Most likely, a feature of this nature will take several weeks and several people to implement, requiring a shift in the schedule and resources, which directly impacts the work already being done. Essentially, if someone asks for a new feature to be added after the game is in production, a feature (or features) must be removed in order to finish without changing the schedule, resources, or quality.

Striking a balance between the schedule, budget, and resources is a challenge for any project, and when feature creep occurs, this balance is impossible to maintain. Hopefully, you will realize when feature creep is having an impact on the game and be able deal with it quickly to get the project back on track. If regular project reviews are done, this is more likely to happen. When it does, there are four fundamental areas to review to see which solution is the best path forward:

- **Increase scheduled time:** More time is something that teams always request on a project, but sometime, the deadlines can't be moved. For example, the game must ship before Thanksgiving or ship in conjunction with a movie release.
- **Increase resources:** Adding more people to the project seems like an easy solution. However, adding more people to a project doesn't necessarily help, especially if the new people need to be trained and ramped up on the project (which could extend the schedule).
- **Cut features:** Review the features to determine which are key to the game's vision and goals, and which are secondary. Don't cut the key features, but find some secondary ones that can be deprioritized and shipped in a future release. It's also a good idea to try to cut secondary features that have the most pressing resource and schedule constraints.
- **Reduce quality:** If cutting a feature isn't an option, explore ways to reduce its quality. You may be able to ship a bare-bones version of the feature and improve it later with a content update.

MATT IMMERMAN, PRODUCER, PRIORITIZING WORK

While a JIRA board is what most of the projects I have been on have utilized, there have been instances in which this wasn't the best approach. One project I was on had been tasked with putting together a playable demo based on pitch material in time for the Game Developer's Conference (GDC) to show to potential publishing partners, and we had about 12 weeks to throw something together. The team was relatively small (around 15 people), and we would only have dedicated engineering for about half of our allocated time. Given the circumstances, we wanted to eliminate as much overhead in tasking and prioritization as possible, so instead of focusing on maintaining a JIRA board and setting up sprints, we developed a Burndown List. This list was broken down by discipline and had everything we knew we wanted to be prioritized from top to bottom. As people finished their tasks, they looked at the list and took on the next task related to their discipline. This not only helped to keep the team moving at a rapid pace but removed any questions from the team as to what the next task they should tackle should be (with traditional JIRA usage, developers may be tasked with multiple priority 1 tasks and not know which one is truly the most important). It also had the added side effect of boosting team morale in what could have been an extremely stressful situation. During stand-ups, we would pull up this list, and the team would be able to see all the items getting crossed out as we worked our way closer to the bottom of each discipline list. While this approach to organization and prioritization worked well for a small prototype-style team, it does have its issues: primarily that it doesn't scale well, and there is no great way to account for dependencies. It's important to remember that there is no "one-size-fits-all" solution when it comes to task organization and prioritization, but that doesn't mean you shouldn't have a toolbox or template for prioritization and organization that you can utilize and adjust based on developer's preferred workflows.

14.6 Postmortems

Usually, postmortems are conducted at the end of the game development cycle because they provide closure to the process. They are an opportunity for the team to discuss the ups and downs of the development process and use what they've learned to improve future game development. I've found that conducting a postmortem after a major milestone delivery is more useful since there is an opportunity to learn and improve within a shorter time frame. If you think about the postmortem in terms of performance feedback, it is far easier to correct process and development issues continually than to wait to make these changes on an annual basis.

A postmortem focuses on answering the following questions:

- **Did we achieve the goals of the game?** The purpose of this question is not to highlight where the team fell short of the goal but to evaluate why the goal was not achieved, such as changing scope, shifting priorities, or limited time.

- **Were the project's expectations realistic?** This isn't an opportunity for the team to launch personal attacks. Instead, focus on discussing where the project expectations were unrealistic. For example, three levels had to be cut from the original plan because the first five levels took a lot more time than anticipated.
- **What went right? What went wrong?** By discussing both the positive and the negative, the team can do more of what worked and less of what didn't. If things went wrong, the team can discuss solutions to prevent these problems going forward.
- **What lessons were learned?** These lessons should focus more on big-picture items and less on small details. The details can be used as methods for implementing the lesson learned on the next project. For example, "communicate deadlines clearly to the team" might be one lesson learned, whereas the methods for communicating these deadlines (email, status reports, and weekly meetings) provide the details on how to accomplish this.

During the development process, encourage people to take notes of things to discuss in the postmortem. This will ensure that the details are not forgotten and can be used to formulate solutions for the Lessons Learned document.

14.6.1 Lessons Learned

The Lessons Learned document is a tangible outcome of the postmortem process. As discussed earlier in this chapter, the lessons learned focus on big-picture items that can be applied to future projects. Ultimately, the Lessons Learned document will be published to the team, the studio, and perhaps even the publisher so that everyone can benefit from the learnings.

Limit the number of lessons learned in the document to five. Anything more than that is daunting to implement, thereby reducing the effectiveness of publishing the lessons in the first place. Focus on lessons that have the highest probability of being implemented. For example, one lesson might be "schedule time for risk assessment after each phase of the project." This is something that can be implemented fairly easily and does not require any up-front monetary investment. Conversely, a lesson that states, "Send everyone on the team for training in team software process," might not actually have a chance of being implemented due to schedule and budget constraints. However, lessons like these can be implemented if the company is committed to them, so gear each Lessons Learned document towards what the company can willingly commit to.

14.7 Build Process and Pipeline

Have a process in place for compiling daily builds so that features and assets can be checked in-game. While developers usually have local versions of the game running on their computers, it is important to compile the build on a daily basis to check for any issues that may not occur when viewed on an uncompiled build. For example, there is a noticeable visual difference between the way a console game's art assets display on a PC and how they display on a television. There are numerous settings on televisions—some with lighter displays and some with darker displays—which can affect how something looks in-game. The developer will not see these differences unless he or she creates a build and looks at the assets directly in the game.

If there is difficulty creating a build, it can also indicate that there are bugs in the game that are preventing the code from compiling. The developers may not be aware of these bugs until they see the reports with the compile errors.

At the point when daily builds are being made, the QA department will work with the team to decide how often builds will be submitted for testing. It is counterproductive to give QA a new build to test every day. They need to spend several days with each build to make sure that they have tested all aspects of the game thoroughly. The frequency of builds submitted to the QA department will increase as the game gets closer to launch.

An automated build process is usually simple to set up and saves a lot of development time. If the process is automated, the person responsible for making the build does not have to take time to manually complete all the steps necessary to compile it. All of the build tasks can be automated by setting up a separate "build" machine which has a programming script that will instruct the machine to pull out all the updated code and assets from the version control system, and compile them. When these are compiled, it will generate the latest build and copy it to an appropriate place on the network. This programming script can be set to run on a regular basis. For example, it can be set to run at midnight each night, so there is a new build waiting for the team in the morning.

The automation process can be taken a step further in reducing time in other areas of development. For example, on certain days, the build script could be instructed to copy the latest build to all the QA machines so that when the QA testers report to work in the morning, the latest build will be ready for testing. The process can also include scripts that check the build for errors, such as misnamed files, missing assets, or incorrect file formatting. The error log can be automatically emailed to the team so that developers can begin fixing the errors before the next build is created. The lead engineer can work with the team to set up the best way to automate the build process.

14.8 Software Ratings

Software rating boards are important to understand as they regulate ratings for game content. Familiarity with the rating process for each country is important so that your team has a clear understanding of what content is allowed for each type of rating.

Publishers need a rating for each country in which the game is released. The normal procedure is for the publisher to submit a beta or near-final version of the game, along with documentation, to the appropriate rating board, which then reviews the materials and assigns a rating. A game that is to be released in the United States, Europe, Asia, and Australia needs to secure ratings from at least six different rating boards, and each one has a separate process and set of guidelines for securing a rating. For example, the Entertainment Software Rating Board (ESRB) rates games that are released in the United States, Pan European Game Information (PEGI) rates games distributed in most of Europe, and the Australia Classification Board (ACB) rates games released in Australia.

The guidelines are fairly subjective, so it can be difficult for publishers to determine the rating a specific game will receive. For instance, the ESRB does not have specific rules on what constitutes a Teen (T) or Mature (M) rating. While they are happy to offer some feedback on what rating the game might get, nothing is guaranteed until the game is officially submitted and reviewed by the rating board. Other countries have different guidelines, and so something that is rated as appropriate for teens by the ESRB may be rated as inappropriate for teens by the ACB. When in preproduction, think about the game's target audience, and determine what ratings best suit this audience, then develop the game within acceptable guidelines.

The boards' main goals are to prevent children and teenagers from being exposed to content that is deemed inappropriate for their age groups. As mentioned previously, this is a subjective process, but the boards make a concerted effort to provide ratings within reason. The main areas of concern are:

- Violence (cartoon-like included);
- Bad language;
- Drug use (including tobacco and alcohol use);
- Adult themes;
- Sex and nudity;
- Criminal acts.

The rating boards are not opposed to games containing these elements; they just prefer that the depiction of these themes is age appropriate to the rating. In addition to the overall rating, which indicates the general age range the game is appropriate for, there are content descriptors that provide more information about which areas of the game had an impact on the rating.

If the game does not have a final rating, and the publisher wants to release a demo or game trailer, the publisher will need to submit this type of content for review in order to be classified as "rating pending" or some other equivalent. The boards will not use a demo or trailer to determine the final rating for a game; only a full version of the game can be used to determine the rating.

If the game is released on multiple platforms, the board may require that each platform be submitted separately for a rating. If the content is exactly the same across all platforms, the rating will be the same as well. However, if one platform has some additional content that may be considered mature, then that version of the game may receive a higher rating than the other versions.

Build time into the production schedule for submitting the game to the rating boards. After a game is submitted, it can take anywhere from 10 to 45 days (depending on the board) to receive a final rating. If you wish to contest the rating and resubmit, it will take another 10–45 days to get another rating. Most boards want to review a game that is at beta, meaning that all the content is in, and the game can be played all the way through. Some boards will also require the game to be fully localized before they review it. Finally, third parties require the rating certificates as part of the final submission process and will not allow any game to begin the process without having the appropriate age ratings confirmed. See the sidebar for a list of some of the software rating boards and their websites.

SOFTWARE RATING BOARDS

- **International Age Rating Coalition (IARC):** www.globalratings.com— check website for territories covered
- **Entertainment Software Rating Board (ESRB):** www.esrb.org—the United States
- **Pan European Game Information (PEGI):** www.pegi.info—EUROPE
- **Unterhaltungssoftware SelbstKontrolle (USK):** www.usk. de—GERMANY
- **Office of Film and Literature Classification (OFLC):** www. classification.gov.au—AUSTRALIA
- **Computer Entertainment Rating Organization (CERO):** www.cero. gr.jp—JAPAN
- **Korea Media Rating Board (KMRB):** www.kmrb.or.kr—KOREA

Currently, any games released in China are reviewed by the Chinese government and they decide if the game can be released in China and what the rating will be. This process can take a long time, and you will need assistance from your publisher in getting the proper materials to the Chinese government.

14.9 Conclusion

There are a lot of plates spinning when the team is fully executing the plan. Producers will spend a lot of time juggling these plates to keep things moving on the project. Remember that while you can plan for your desired outcome, the actual outcome is going to be different, so making sure you are doing project reviews and postmortems can help you maintain some semblance of control during the production process. This chapter contained overviews of a lot of different activities that occur during this phase of the project; the intent wasn't to discuss all these things in detail but to provide a starting point for discussing these activities with your development team.

CHAPTER 15

User Experience (UX), UX

Written in Collaboration with Celia Hodent

15.1 Introduction

UX, or user experience, is a mindset placing the end user of a product, system, or service at the center of the development process. UX practitioners, now well established in industrial design and many tech companies, are eager to work in the video game industry; however, many teams view UX as an afterthought. While the UX team may provide valuable insights early in the game development process, there are many other critical issues for the development team to deal with at this time. They can be less enthusiastic about UX because it can be viewed as one more input that needs to be considered when making the game. However, UX is a mindset more than a discipline, and much can be gained if the UX team and development team take time to understand each other and learn to work together. This chapter, co-authored with Celia Hodent, discusses why UX is important. It begins with a discussion of what misconceptions UX and development teams have about each other, and ends with suggestions on how to build UX effectively into the game development process.

15.2 What Is UX?

UX encompasses what it's like for the targeted user to perceive and interact with the software, including how engaging the experience is (cf. Isbister and Schaffer, 2008) relative to the design intentions (Hodent, 2017). It is mainly about making sure that the design and the business intentions are experienced the way they were intended by the target audience of a product, system, or service. UX practices employ knowledge of cognitive science and psychology, and apply user research methodologies (e.g., playtests and analytics) to ensure that the game has good usability and is engaging. It's about adopting a human-centered approach: looking at how a user understands and interacts with a system without the guidance of the humans who designed it. Therefore, UX should be the concern of everyone on the development team and everyone in the studio. UX practitioners are just providing tools and methodologies to help everyone accomplish their goals with the game. In some studios, a separate UX team can be put together to accompany and guide the development team in achieving the experience they want to offer to their audience (users).

15.3 Developer Misconceptions about UX

Until very recently, game developers were somewhat resistant to the idea of adopting a UX mindset and methodology into their development pipeline. UX practitioners entering the video game industry are often confronted with misconceptions regarding what UX is, and this can make it hard for them to work with the development team (as well as other teams in the studio). The top five misconceptions encountered are:

1. **UX will hamper the team's creativity and make the game too easy for the players:** In reality, the main purpose of UX practices is to offer the experience that the designers and artists intended to their target audience. Therefore, if your audience is made up of hard-core gamers, and the experience you want for them is a very challenging game, UX guidelines will absolutely help you to accomplish your design goal.
2. **UX design is merely common sense, so there's no need for UX testing—the player will quickly understand what they're supposed to do:** The truth is that the human brain is filled with perception, cognitive, and social biases that affect both the developers and the players. It's for this reason that researchers from all fields use standardized protocols to test their hypotheses—it's very easy to miss or misinterpret what's going on. Perception is a construction of the brain; therefore, it is subjective. What developers perceive and understand about their game can be vastly different from what new players perceive. A UX mindset and methodology will help developers figure out what the real problems are faster and more precisely.

3. **The UX team merely provides another opinion to the game development team, and that the opinion is neither more nor less meaningful than those of someone from the marketing team:** Admittedly, the core team has to deal with many opinions: from within the game team, from the marketing team, from the publishing team, from the executive team, etc. However, UX processes are meant to test hypotheses through rigorous research and to anticipate problems through analysis. Therefore, in reality, UX experts do not give opinions; instead, they provide an analysis based on their knowledge of the brain, past experience, and data when it's available.

4. **There's not enough time to focus on UX, because the development team needs to make the actual game:** They point out that the money would be better spent elsewhere, like on art or programming. However, no one makes this argument about QA testing because it's quite clearly necessary to spend money to make sure the game ships without bugs. However, if a game ships with critical UX issues, this will affect sales. The development team will be unhappy because the game won't achieve what they'd hoped for, the executives will be disappointed because the game won't make money, and the players will be frustrated with the game experience. The UX process is an investment. The question isn't "Can we afford to think about UX?" The question is "Can we afford not to?"

5. **The UX process can be started later in the development cycle; early in the process, the development team already knows where the game is broken and looks ugly:** The end result of this thinking is that the UX team gets involved too late. The game is only tested and evaluated when there's not enough time for a major overhaul; the architecture is in place, and important decisions about the game have already been made. There's enough time for a few quick fixes and patches, but that's all. Moreover, testing low-fidelity prototypes and iterating on them are much faster and less costly than waiting until the feature is implemented or, worse, has final art and is complete for all intents and purposes.

15.4 UX Misconceptions about the Development Team

Similarly, there are misconceptions that the UX team has about game development. Let's examine the most common ones:

1. **The development team doesn't really understand all the subtleties of UX:** In truth, while the team members may not have doctorate degrees in UX, they generally understand that providing an easy way for the player to interact is part of good game design. The development team can be reluctant to take game design feedback from the UX team since they might perceive UX practices as separate and different from game design. The reality is that UX practitioners are here to help the whole development team accomplish their goals.

2. **The development team doesn't want to work with UX teams:** However, most development teams are happy to utilize resources that will ultimately make the game better for the players. If a process is in place that works well for both, the development team will be happy to work with UX as a partner. The real issue is that UX practitioners may offer feedback that is too detailed and not applicable to where things are in the development process. For example, the team may create a placeholder UI screen for switching inventory items, that they already know be completely changed in design and functionality. Therefore, receiving UX feedback on the placeholder UI is not useful to the development team. UX teams need to be aligned on what feedback will be useful at a given time. Also, if the development team is not used to UX practices, time will be needed to establish a working relationship.

3. **The development schedule won't be impacted by UX testing, especially if the UX team handles all the tests and reports:** While a good UX process can streamline things for the development team in the long run, the reality is that adding a UX-centered pipeline to the process requires additional time. The team has to schedule time for testing, reviewing, and tracking feedback; educating the team on UX practices; and so on. This all needs to be integrated into the schedule; otherwise, it will be ignored. It's important to note that UX practices can't just be shoehorned in to the development process. It's necessary to prep the team, get buy-in, and come up with a way to gradually introduce it. Simply having tests and generating reports is not actually integrating UX practices into the development process.

4. **Implementing UX feedback isn't hard—just a matter of prioritization:** The reality is that while UX research findings and suggestions may seem simple to implement, they're actually another form of feedback in the development process and must be weighed against all the other priorities. Rewriting text or changing colors may seem easy, but these items still need to be tasked out, completed, and tested. Larger changes require more people, more testing, more iteration, etc. Fixing UX issues can be a big deal, especially if planning has already been completed.

15.5 Working Together

Ultimately, the UX team is another source of input that production has to account for. The key is to determine which inputs are going to have the most value for the game team at whatever point they are currently at in the process. The development team also needs to understand how to prioritize UX feedback against things that the executives and marketing team want. Since UX feedback is based on data, it is easier to determine when a piece of feedback is useful to implement. Once it is implemented, it can be retested to see if it had the desired impact. To create a strong working relationship, both sides need to be willing to work together and put effort into the process. As UX practitioners start working with development teams, they need to find ways to work with the development team within the development team's established processes. This approach will make it easier to get people on board with incorporating UX practices into the process.

15.5.1 Establish Trust

First, it's necessary to overcome misconceptions on both sides. UX practitioners (when they are not embedded in the development team) must listen to the development team and understand their needs. Since the latter is probably less interested in strengthening this relationship, UX practitioners should make themselves readily available as a resource. There should be ample oppurtunity for a developer to talk to someone on the UX team and get feedback. Ideally, production will evangelize having a UX mindset and make the related work more visible to the team (for instance, reminding people in meetings to consult with the UX team, inviting people to view UX tests, and inviting UX practitioners to team meetings). It's important to show the developers that having a UX mindset is fully part of the development process without becoming another "gate" the game has to pass through.

15.5.2 Find Advocates

It's important to find UX advocates on the development team who can act as intermediaries who negotiate on behalf of external UX practitioners. Advocates can communicate to all parties—they ask questions of designers to understand their intentions and of executives to understand the business plan. An advocate can ensure that developers have clear information on what to expect from the UX team and that the UX team has someone who can keep them in the loop about what's going on with the development team. Typically, the production team can make excellent advocates for UX. A bonus is that the production team can also work UX tasks into the schedule and development pipeline.

It's also important that the team knows that the UX group is a resource, and the development team are free to use them at any time. Encourage your designers to check in with the UX group on a regular basis and give them updates on some of the design problems they are trying to solve. Invite the UX group to team meetings so they can get firsthand information on what's going on with the game and can mingle with the other team members.

15.5.3 Start Small

The UX team should partner up with designers, artists, and engineers who are interested in UX. The groups can start addressing concerns on a smaller scale instead of doing a comprehensive review of the game's entire UX. For example, initial discussions can revolve around specific design questions about elements like icons, in-game User Interface (UI), or the core game loop. This provides the core development team and the UX team with a way to begin a working relationship. As smaller concerns are successfully addressed, the teams' relationship will grow stronger so that bigger concerns can be discussed in the future.

At this stage, UX and core teams can schedule meetings to identify areas where the process needs to evolve, which makes it easier to track and implement UX feedback. For example, the process may change so that UX information can be tracked in software like JIRA. This makes UX issues more accessible to the core team and gives UX more visibility within the priority stack. The development team can then easily see what needs to be implemented, triaged, and retested.

15.5.4 Align Goals

There are other methods that can be used to increase the touchpoints between the two teams, resulting in more closely aligned goals and priorities. For example, the team might look at major milestones for the next 6 months and prioritize which features to UX test. By closely aligning the UX-related priorities with the other priorities, the UX team can establish the value of what's being tested. It's also important to formalize the points at which testing will occur in development as well as what type of testing this will be (for instance, a 3-day UX test vs a 1-day UX test). If these UX tests are part of the development schedule and publicized to the team, then all teams will be aware that they need to plan for UX tests at these points. It's good to make efforts to invite the team to the UX tests (after all, it's really valuable to watch other people play your game) and to make sure they use the UX team as a resource early and often.

15.6 UX Process

Once the UX and development teams are working together more closely, start defining a process. This process is important because it provides consistency to how the UX team works with the development team to iterate the game. The UX process includes the following phases: hypotheses, planning, testing, reporting, iterating, and retesting.

15.6.1 Hypotheses

The hypothesis phase begins when the team specifies the key questions they want to answer. For example, will players understand how to open doors, pick up items, or interact with NPCs? How often will players switch weapons, and how quickly can they do so? What features are players interacting with the most? The least? Questions can come from anyone— the developers, analytics team, marketing team, or executives. The UX team works with the others to determine what set of questions can be answered in the UX test. Once the questions are defined, the UX team prepares an experimental protocol and defines which data collection resources will be needed to produce answers.

The goal at this stage is to get everyone in sync with what is needed for the test.

15.6.2 Planning

Once the focus of the test and its protocol have been established, the UX team can plan when to run the test, how to perform it, and who should be present. Then, they choose which version of the game will be tested. If testing a game that is still in development (i.e., a prototype, alpha, or beta version), allot time to make sure the game doesn't have any major bugs, missing features, or technical issues that will impact the UX test. Ideally, the version of the game being used will be ready a few days beforehand. This will give the UX team time to set up on the test machines and confirm that all the necessary functionality is working.

Work with the UX team to identify the dates of the next few UX tests and what the goals of the test are. It's useful to establish a consistent schedule for UX tests so that the team can plan their feature work around it. This ensures that high-priority features are tested as soon as possible (and thus, there is more time to retest any iterations on the feature).

15.6.3 Testing

Once the tests are planned and scheduled, the UX team will establish the test protocol and recruit participants. Any potential participants must fill out a questionnaire about their game habits, which will be used to screen for a set of participants that will provide the most relevant data on what is being tested. For example, the questions may ask what types of genres they play, how many hours they spend playing a specific game, what platforms they play on, and so on.

On the day of the test, participants will sit down and play the game. Depending on how the test protocols are set up, they may play through the game without any additional help or prompting, just like a real-life player. If there are specific areas of the game being tested, a UX researcher might walk them through an explanation of a feature and how it works. All of these testing activities will be predetermined as part of the testing protocol.

It is extremely beneficial for the development team to observe the UX tests' being conducted. Testing may occur over the course of a few hours or a few days. During this time, the development team should observe the participants in real time (ideally behind a one-way mirror so they are literally watching over participants' shoulders without biasing the test).

Try not to schedule meetings or other obligations on test days so that the development team is free to watch the tests along with the UX group. Developers can learn a lot about their game by watching someone actually play it.

15.6.4 Reporting

Once the test is over, the UX team analyzes the data and generates a detailed UX report. The report should focus on the specific hypotheses that were being tested or at least present this information first. There's a risk of overdelivering since there is always going to be a lot of data. However, if there are pages and pages of reports, the development team may feel like there isn't enough time to thoroughly digest the feedback and determine which should be applied to the game (and at what point it should be applied). Less is more, so targeted tests are certainly more actionable and less overwhelming.

After the report is sent, a quick meeting should be scheduled; during this meeting, the UX and development teams can review the report together and decide what actions to take based on the findings. For example, an issue could be classified as:

- **By Design:** It means the feature remains as is, and no iteration is needed.
- **Needs Addressed:** It means the UX test revealed areas of the feature that need to be changed to improve UX. This is added to the task list, and the work is prioritized and planned.
- **In Progress:** It means the development team was already aware of the UX issue and is already working on a solution (although they might want to take the UX feedback into account as they work on their solution to ensure that it will be relevant).

Once all the issues have been reviewed and classified, the development team can start iterating on the game. There will be disagreements. In some cases, something that the UX team marked as high priority may be viewed as a lower priority by the team. Some of the feedback may require large revisions that can't be addressed immediately and will thus have to be part of future planning. Perhaps some feedback will be in opposition to design's intentions and will require a longer conversation with UX about what experience is intended and if this aligns with the business goals.

15.6.5 Iterating

The development team can then iterate the features that revealed UX issues. As part of tracking open UX issues, and to make it easier for the developers to understand what the issue is, everything should be added to the task list and scheduled for work. If you are using an agile development process, integrating work into the schedule to address UX feedback should be easy since it can be included as part of a sprint. When the UX team enters the information into the tracking database, they should include a detailed description of what was observed, along with screenshots and videos from the UX test, if applicable.

As the UX issues are addressed in the game, the developers should mark the corresponding tasks as complete. This way, when the next UX test is scheduled, it will be very clear which UX feedback was implemented and thus which sections of the game should be retested.

15.6.6 Retesting

Once the UX feedback has been addressed in the game, it should be retested. If you have regular tests set up in advance, you can just send a list of what to check in the next test to the UX team. They will include the retests in the testing protocols and recruit the right group of people to test these changes.

Early on in the development process, an area of the game might be tested many times in order to achieve the right UX for the player. Later in the process, it will be more difficult to do multiple iterations and tests on a feature. If the feature is critical, and its UX is still not good, the team should have discussions about how to mitigate this—as they may need to delay the launch or completely redesign the feature.

15.7 Conclusion

This chapter gave a high-level overview of UX practices and how to incorporate them into your development pipeline. For more specific information, you can read Celia's book *The Gamer's Brain*: *How Neuroscience and UX Can Impact Video Game Design* (2017). Key things to take away are that development and UX teams should be proactive about talking through their misconceptions and setting up a process that allows them to effectively work together.

CHAPTER 16

Audio

16.1 Introduction

Players have come to expect high-quality audio design, which encompasses voiceover (VO), music, and sound effects. As a producer, there are a lot of pieces to juggle when producing game audio. This chapter provides a high-level overview of things to be aware of when producing voice and music for a game. Most game studios will outsource VO and music composition. This is one case in which it is more cost-effective to hire an expert who can do a better job for less time and money. If the audio needs for the game are large and complex, however, it may be necessary to assign a full-time producer to manage the process.

16.2 Voiceover

Start planning ahead for the game's VO needs. VO is difficult to design, record, and implement at the last minute, especially if the work is being outsourced. Developing a rough timeline in advance gives the writing and design team a better understanding of when dialogue needs to be finalized.

It is a lot easier to record VO if the dialogue is final and won't be changing after it is recorded and implemented. Sometimes, this can't be avoided, but if a plan and VO pipeline have been established, making changes and updates is much easier. There are lots of components to the VO production process, including design, asset management, finding a studio, recording, and implementing. Each of these phases will likely have different sets of people doing the work, so from a production standpoint, there are many tasks to be scheduled and managed.

16.2.1 Design

VO is an important component of bringing characters to life and immersing players in the game world. Executed correctly, it communicates a great deal about a character's emotional state, personality, location, and even origin (e.g., are they human, alien, dragon, or robot?). To get the most out of the VO work, start thinking about the design early in the concept and pitch phases.

The VO design determines the overall cost of recording and implementing the VO files; the design specifies how many characters are in the game, how many lines of dialogue are spoken, and which lines will require additional processing for effects (such as radio static, distortion, or echo). Typically, the sound designer and the game designer collaborate on VO design.

Often, the game's genre has a major impact on the scope of work. Role-playing games, for example, tend to feature a large cast of characters and a large number of spoken lines. Games that are not story driven feature fewer characters and speaking parts, and can usually get by with a smaller-scale VO design. A game like World of Warcraft will feature thousands of lines of dialogue with each major update to the game, while a puzzle game like Bejeweled may not feature VO at all.

You also want to consider how the game will be localized. If the VO can just be subtitled into the appropriate language, it is going to be a lot cheaper than recording localized VO. This type of decision is usually made within the publishing department—they will do financial projections to determine if the cost of doing fully localized VO is worth it or not.

If you are working within a budget and want to have a variety of VO lines for each character, you can consider using concatenation. Concatenation is a method of playing VO that offers a few advantages; however, it creates significant problems during the localization process. During concatenation, different lines of dialogue are spliced together in the game engine and played one after the other: for example, "No, I'm not interested in a new mission" can be created in-game by playing the recorded line "No, I'm not interested" and then another recorded line, "in a new mission." Alternately, the game engine might play a different second line, resulting in "No, I'm not interested in buying anything today." Or the character might say, "Yes, I want to try a new mission."

Concatenation cuts down on the amount of memory needed to find the correct audio asset and reduces the number of game assets to track. However, it introduces complications for localizations because different languages have different grammatical rules.

Furthermore, it's hard to record concatenated dialogue effectively because voice actors sometimes have a hard time matching pitch and inflections for each line of dialogue. This is especially true if there are thousands of lines that must be recorded, and the actor must maintain a consistent tone across the board. When a concatenated line is played in-game, there's a good chance that the player will notice that two lines have been joined together.

VO cost also increases with the number of different voices that are needed for the game. If it features a large number of speaking characters, the cost of hiring actors and managing different sets of character voice assets will increase. When talking with designers about what they envision for the VO, talk through all the cost, schedule, and management issues so they have a better understanding of the boundaries they must design within.

16.2.2 Asset Management

Another thing to plan ahead for is how all the VO files will be managed. If thousands of VO files are being generated, the team needs to have a system for tracking and managing them. At minimum, they'll want to establish where the VO script, audio assets, and character descriptions will be stored in the source control database.

If a project features numerous speaking parts, it's worth exploring a database to track all VO assets. A database allows developers to sort by different variables, such as character name or whether the dialogue has been recorded or not. It allows a team to track any and all changes to scripts, assets, and character notes. It also prevents costly rerecording sessions because it keeps developers from accidentally using the incorrect version of a script or audio file. If the assets are managed properly, then team members can also track whether a recording studio has furnished all that is required.

A file naming convention should be established prior to recording any VO; otherwise, different team members, such as the game designer, sound designer, and recording studio team, may establish different naming conventions on their own, resulting in confusion.

If placeholder VO files use the same file names as the final versions, then the files can simply be replaced when the final versions are recorded. The optimal file name is one that permits someone to look at it and immediately determine who says the dialogue and where the file is located in the game. Your audio and design leads can work together to establish what naming convention makes the most sense for your game.

Consider having an engineer create an automated process for comparing the file names listed in the script against the actual audio files that are delivered. This can save a lot of time when trying to vet the delivery of audio files. If the process is automated, it will be quicker and more accurate than someone who is manually reviewing the files and checking them against the file name list.

16.2.3 Script Preparation

The VO script is the main resource for tracking all of the VO information needed for the game. The script must be well organized and contain the information needed by both the actors and the development team. The ideal format for this is a spreadsheet because it allows you to display all required information clearly. In addition, developers and actors can sort the spreadsheet by using filters and hide columns in order to see the necessary information. For instance, a sound engineer can sort by "effects" to see which sound files need echo effects, radio static, or what have you. Voice actors can sort by character name. Creating a version of the script in traditional cinematic format can be useful—particularly when recording cinematics. However, any dialogue presented in cinematic script format should be converted to the spreadsheet to ensure that it remains the primary source of dialogue.

A VO script contains all the dialogue for the game, with each row in the spreadsheet representing one audio file. For example, if there are 20 rows on the spreadsheet, then there are 20 audio files. This becomes critical when dealing with a large number of files. In addition to the actual dialogue that is recorded, the VO spreadsheet must include file names, audio effects, narrative context, and voice inflection. Ideally, all this information should be included in a single document to minimize the number of assets that have to be tracked and to lower the risk that one document will not be updated along with all the others (resulting in mistakes). Be sure that the necessary information is labeled consistently in order for the filters to work. Figure 16.1 is an example of a VO spreadsheet. In this example, the dialogue is arranged in chronological order.

The line number is in the first column; this allows actors to quickly reference lines during recording and makes it easier to rerecord a line (also known as a "pickup"). The second column shows the names of the characters. The third column features the actual dialogue to be recorded. The fourth column lists the location where the dialogue is found in the game (e.g., Map 1 or Level 1). The fifth column describes the type of the dialogue (e.g., whether it's an argument between characters or instructions given to the player character by someone). The sixth column describes any special effects that should be added, such as an echo or distortion. The seventh column provides context for the dialogue. The eighth column gives information about how the voice actor should be directed for this line. The context and voice direction columns help actors prepare for recording sessions, and they aid the translators and actors who will record the localized VO. The ninth column lists the file name. Be thorough when putting the VO spreadsheet together. Missing information increases the risk that something crucial will be forgotten, resulting in additional unplanned recording sessions, which can be expensive and difficult to schedule.

Line #	Character	English	Level	Type	SfX	Context	Voice Direction	Filename
1	Jane Doe	Geoffrey, help me get this person to safety!	1	Mission		There has is a tornado and Jane is asking Geoffrey to come help her get someone freed from a crashed car.	Yelling, panicked.	M01_Jane_01
2	Geoffrey	I can't, I'm stuck underneath this tree.	1	Mission		Geoffrey is caught under a tree that was knocked down by the tornado.	Yelling, panicked.	M01_Geoff_01
3	Civillian #2	Help me!	1	NPC		The trapped person is scared, they are in a car that has been flipped upside down.	Scared, weak, injured.	M01_Civ2_01
4	Jane Doe	Ok, I'm on my way to get you out.	1	Mission		Jane starts running over to Geoffrey to help free him from the fallen tree.	yelling, decisive.	M01_Jane_02
5	Geoffrey	I'll call 911.	1	Objective		Geoffrey can get to his phone and is going to call 911.	Decisive, panicked.	M01_Geoff_02

FIGURE 16.1 Example of VO spreadsheet.

16.2.4 Voiceover Timeline

Recording and implementing VO takes time and isn't something to leave until the last minute. Start thinking early on in the concept process about what the VO needs will be, and plan accordingly. If VO recording and processing is being outsourced, plan for additional time to find the vendor and set up the pipeline. If the vendor is popular, you may need to book with them well in advance to ensure your recordings can be completed in time to coincide with your development schedule.

One person, usually a sound designer or an associate producer, should be responsible for producing the VO. Depending on the number of lines and VO sessions, this could be a full-time assignment lasting for weeks or months. This person needs to remain in constant communication with the game's writer, audio personnel, and recording studio to make sure that all deliverables are handled on time.

During development, designers can record placeholder dialogue and integrate it into the game to gain an understanding of how it will fit. The designers can evaluate the pacing, get a feel for how information is delivered to the player, and make any adjustments to the VO script before a lot of money is spent on professional recordings. Using placeholder audio also provides a way for the team to set up and test the audio asset pipeline. Placeholder VO files and the final VO files should have the same file name so that files can be easily switched out.

From a scheduling standpoint, the recording session should be scheduled as late in the production as possible because additional VO needs will arise during production and testing. If the VO is recorded too soon, costly retakes will become necessary; this gets complicated if the original actor isn't available. It may be necessary to schedule multiple recording sessions, depending on timetable and number of lines. In general, 50 lines can be recorded in an hour (a line is typically eight to ten words).

Usually, dialogue for the game's cinematics is recorded earlier in the project in order to synchronize character animations and lip-syncing. For this reason, it's best to schedule one recording session for the cinematics earlier in the production cycle.

Numerous variables can impact a game's schedule, including:

- **Number of lines of dialogue:** More dialogue equals more time.
- **Production schedule:** Does VO recording need to be done in weeks or months?
- **Amount of Cinematic VO:** Cinematic VO needs to be recorded sooner so there's enough time for animation and lip-syncing.
- **Actor availability:** Actors might not be free when the team wants them; they might be booked by other studios, working elsewhere, or on vacation.
- **Recording studio availability:** A studio might be booked by other projects, so it's a good idea to tentatively block out some time with it prior to settling on a definitive recording date.

Establish some time frames for the entire VO recording process when creating your initial schedule. Include time for writing the script, casting actors, doing the actual VO recording, editing the final takes, and integrating it into the game. Your audio lead will be helpful in determining what these timelines should be.

16.2.5 Choosing a Studio

As mentioned previously, VO recording can easily be outsourced to a recording studio. The VO needs for the game will help determine which recording studio is a good fit. If the game features a small cast and a few hundred lines of VO, then a smaller studio and nonunion actors may suffice. On the other hand, if the game requires a large group of actors and thousands of lines of VO, look into contracting with a larger, more experienced recording studio. The ideal studio will assist with the process of auditioning and casting actors, help coordinate the recording sessions, and deliver high-quality audio files in a timely manner. They might even help with VO direction, audio processing, and asset tracking.

When evaluating the studio, start by asking the following:

- Does the studio have experience with recording dialogue for video games? If so, that will help them to understand and anticipate the team's needs.
- Is the recording studio a union signatory? If so, then they're authorized to pay union actors. If not, then the development team will need to set

themselves up as a signatory or else hire a union payroll service to act as a signatory for them.

- What kind of equipment and software does the studio use? Will these be adequate for the work?
- How large is the studio space? Can its recording booth handle multiple actors at once? Is the studio large enough to accommodate multiple members of the development team?
- Can the studio work with remote participants? Can members of the development team attend via video chat?
- How quickly can the studio turn audio assets around after the recording session?
- How will assets be delivered? What compression schemes and file formats are available? Can the studio convert files to a proprietary format if they are given access to the conversion tools?
- What are the studio's hourly or daily rates? What will they charge for processing the audio files? What are the rates per actor? What fees are charged if you cancel the session?
- What are the additional costs? For instance, what is the cost of casting and/or directing voice actors?
- How far in advance should the team book studio time? What's the studio's typical availability for last-minute pickup sessions?

Once you've researched a few studios and have a shortlist of ones you want to explore further, put together a bid package. The bid package outlines the specific VO needs and is sent to prospective studios so they can evaluate and provide a time and cost estimate. The bid process also gives valuable insight into each studio's responsiveness to questions, level of professionalism, and ability to communicate.

Studios may have a preferred format for the bid package to ensure that they have all the necessary information, so check with them before you send over information. Typically, a studio needs to know how many lines of VO there are, how many characters have speaking parts, and how many voice actors are required. An accurate line count is a key factor in estimating time and cost for the recording session. Recording studios usually consider a line to be a single sentence (roughly eight to ten words). Don't just count the number of rows in the spreadsheet as a row may contain multiple sentences, and this will result in an inaccurate line count.

Other items to include in the bid request are:

- **File processing:** Will it be necessary for the sound studio to process all audio assets and remove pops and clicks? Will the studio need to process any special effects, such as radio static?
- **Number of actors:** Generally, a single actor can voice up to three different characters. It will cost less if a single actor records multiple characters, as opposed to using a different actor for each game character.
- **Uniquely skilled actor:** Is there a need for an actor who speaks a particular language or uses a specific accent?

- **Union/nonunion:** Will the project require union actors? Union actors are going to be more expensive but are likely more skilled and able to work more efficiently. For more information about union actors, visit the Screen Actors Guild and the American Federation of Television and Radio Artists (SAG-AFTRA) website at www.sagaftra.org.
- **File formats:** What file format is needed for the final audio files? Will uncompressed versions also be delivered?
- **Tentative schedule:** When will the final line count and VO script be given to the vendor? When should the final audio files be delivered by the vendor?
- **Character descriptions:** What are the key characters like? What are their personalities? What do their voices sound like? What are their ages, genders, ethnicities, tones, and speech patterns?

16.2.6 Casting

Once you've picked a recording studio, they will help you cast the parts. The right actor really brings a character to life, so the casting process is critical. The first step in the casting process is to determine whether union or nonunion actors will be used.

The decision to use union or nonunion actors will impact the game's budget, scope, and schedule. Nonunion actors don't require additional union fees, so they are cheaper. However, it is harder to find high-quality nonunion actors, so additional costs may be incurred because it takes longer to find the right voice actor or because multiple takes are required to get a line right. For a smaller project, nonunion talent is a lower risk.

Union actors in the United States are members of SAG-AFTRA. Because they can be reached through databases maintained by SAG-AFTRA, union actors are easier to find. Their rates include an additional fee, which goes to the union for the actor's pension and health benefits.

Work guidelines for union actors are very strict, and they must be paid according to the union's fee schedule. Though they're more expensive (and, as mentioned earlier, must be paid for a minimum of 4 hours of work), the cost is justifiable because the actors are certified professionals.

Celebrity voice actors lend a bit of cachet to a game and can imbue it with a cinematic quality. However, they require additional contracts, and the final VO files might need their approval, which requires additional time in the schedule. Furthermore, the actors might have restricted availability, depending on other projects. It's best to start preproduction on VO sooner if working with celebrity actors. The celebrity may also need to approve any actors used for his or her character in localized versions of the game. For Apocalypse™, a PlayStation® game published by Activision, Bruce Willis performed the English version of the game, and then specific actors, approved by Bruce Willis, recorded the versions in other languages.

Once a decision has been made about union or nonunion actors, the recording studio can start finding actors to audition for the various character parts. This can be done in one of two ways: a casting decision can be made solely from listening to the actor's voiceover reel, or formal auditions can be held where actors are brought in to specifically record dialogue from the game.

In a typical audition, actors arrive at the studio at the scheduled time to record sample dialogue. If a VO director is present, they will prepare the actors for the audition and walk them through the script. The actor will then record the audition dialogue, which will be processed by the recording studio and sent to the development team. Based on these auditions, actors will be chosen. It's a good idea to provide sample dialogue from the game for these auditions. This will give the actor a better idea of what the character will say during the game, and you will be better able to compare and contrast actors when you hear them recite the same dialogue. The sample should reflect a broad range of in-game dialogue: whispered, shouted, angry, happy, and so forth. There should be some short phrases and some longer dialogue; this will provide a better idea of how well the actor fits the role.

Ideally, someone from the team should be present at auditions, either via video chat, phone call, or in person. A member of the team can give the VO director more details about the character and the desired voice performance. Also, this person will be able to get an idea of how well actors take direction, how wide their ranges are, and whether they can perform multiple voices. To ensure that there's enough time for a robust audition process, be sure to schedule auditions well in advance of the recording session.

As the development team listens to the audition tapes, they should consider the following:

- **Enunciation:** Are the words clearly articulated? Does the actor's performance include mouth noises, such as clicks, pops, lip-smacking, or audible swallows?
- **Breathing patterns:** Does the actor take loud gulps of air between sentences? It's possible that a good sound editor can minimize these if they're during breaks in the dialogue.
- **Pitch:** Is the voice a high squeak or a low rumble? Can the actor find a better pitch? An actor with a good range should be able to modulate their pitch.
- **Cadence:** What's the speech rhythm like? Is it natural or a singsong voice? An unusual cadence in the actor's delivery can be distracting.

Once final actors have been chosen, the recording studio will start the booking process. Hopefully, all of your preferred actors are free when they are needed for the recording sessions. First, the studio finds out if the actors are available during a specific time frame. If so, it is noted that the actor is "Available," which means they are penciled in for the session and can participate in the recording. Money is not owned to them if they are merely marked as "Available." Once the final schedule is determined, the sound studio will officially "book" them. This means that they're fully committed to your project; are unavailable for other projects; and will be paid for their time, even if the recording session is canceled or rescheduled.

16.2.7 Recording Session

After the recording session is scheduled, and the actors are booked, the developers must prepare for the session. First, choose a single point of contact for the actors. Multiple people from the development team, such as the producer, designer, and sound designer, can attend the recording sessions, but only one should work directly with the voice actors. When working with celebrity talent, it's possible that the publisher will send someone to the recording session. The game's writer should also attend because they will be best-prepared to answer questions about a line's context and delivery.

Once a VO script is final and ready for recording, it will be sent to the recording studio so that they can prepare it for the actors.

The original audition files should be brought to the recording session; these can be used to remind actors of the voices they created for the characters. They're also a good starting point for discussions of changes to a particular take. If there are multiple shoots over the course of several months, then audio files from earlier recording sessions should be made available to the actors so that they can match the previously recorded dialogue.

Bring a video with gameplay footage that the actors can watch so they can learn about the game. Bringing a playable demo isn't as useful because it takes time to set up and play, which takes away from recording time.

The development team should create a pronunciation guide for key words that need to be pronounced consistently. This is particularly useful for words created just for the game, like fictitious names and locations. Any real-life words of uncertain pronunciation should be included, such as foreign language phrases, international names, and locations.

Using a professional VO director is highly recommended. They will know how to get the best performances out of the actors and be able to utilize the recording time more effectively. If voice direction is handled by a member of the development team, it should be an excellent communicator who can put people at ease. The voice director will be providing instructions to voice actors and communicating feedback to them; this person must be able to do this respectfully and with sensitivity to the actors' feelings. Ideally, this is the kind of person who remains focused and positive, even if the session isn't going well.

Actors will perform multiple readings, or takes, of a line during a recording session. Each sound studio has a different method of tracking these. For instance, for a reading of line 28, the takes might be labeled 28a, 28b, and 28c. A pickup recorded for this line would be 28d. The final take will be selected from these choices, and the resulting script notes will be handed off to the sound editor. There may be situations in which more than one take sounds good. An alternative take can be chosen for a single line and should be marked that way in the script; it's best to find a distinctive way in which to identify alternate takes (e.g., "28d-Alt") in the script notes.

The VO session is recorded by a sound engineer, who then hands off the files to the sound editor for processing. The sound editor refers to the script notes, which list how many takes were recorded for each line and what was chosen for each final take. Since each sound studio has its own process, it's important to discuss the plan for recording and selecting takes prior to the VO session.

Here are some standard guidelines for VO recording:

- The actor should start by warming up with some dry runs of the dialogue. If it takes the actor a while to really warm up and relax, it may be necessary to redo the dialogue recorded at the start of the session.
- The actor should know about any dialogue involving raised voices (such as yelling or screaming) prior to the session. A raised voice will tire out an actor's vocal cords and will require some rest between VO recording sessions. All yelling should be done at the very end of the session.
- If there's feedback for an actor, it needs to be specific. For example, the actor may not be enunciating clearly, or may not understand that a line of dialogue is supposed to be sarcastic. If the feedback isn't specific, the actor won't know what to do during the retake of that line.
- It's best to let the actor record large chunks of dialogue at once. If the actor is stopped after each line reading (e.g., so that the director can review each take), it will break their concentration and increase the time and money spent on the recording process. Most actors can run through a page of dialogue without taking a break and can perform multiple takes of each line.

16.2.8 Asset Delivery

After the sound recording is complete, and the final takes for each piece of dialogue are selected, the sound editor will process the files. Basic processing means removing pops, clicks, and mouth noise. If any special audio effects are needed, they can be applied at this time. This is also a good time to review the VO spreadsheet against the final set of audio files to ensure that everything was recorded correctly. Use the spreadsheet to track which audio files you have and which are still needed. Some studios will furnish the developers with all of the raw data from the recording session, if requested. This can come in handy if the development team wants to edit the files or use a different take. Once you have the final and processed files, these can be implemented into the game.

16.3 Music

Music is an effective tool for setting the tone of a game, and it makes the game world feel more immersive. The Silent Hill series uses music and sound to great effect to enhance the creepiness of a world inhabited by demonic creatures. In some cases, music is one of the last things considered on a project, and the producer starts looking for a composer well after the game has started production. In others, music is an integral part of the entire game and planned for during preproduction. For example, the Guitar Hero games were built around licensing music tracks from different bands—something which is very time-consuming and needs to be planned for well in advance. When working with the design team on what type of music is needed, consider technical limitations, budget, and schedule, and how music will be used in the game.

16.3.1 Design

The sound designer and creative director usually work together on the music design. They will review the different areas of the game and figure out what is needed. For example, if the user is navigating the UI screens, music might play in the background. If the player is fighting enemies in a heated battle, the music in-game may change to reflect the increased energy and violence. For cinematics, music is integral to making an emotional connection with the viewer. These are all areas that will require different types of music that are consistent within the overall music design.

Think about how music is utilized in the game. Is it coming from an ambient source within the game world (such as a car radio), or is it constantly playing in the background? The UI shell might include one piece of music that continuously loops or consist of several songs that cycle while the player is in the UI. The cinematics might be scored directly to the image, or several generic music loops might be composed and placed in the soundtrack by the cinematic artist.

There are also technical limitations to consider when creating the music design. These constraints create some challenges but also provide opportunities to come up with creative solutions. The following are some technical things to consider for music design:

- **Memory limitations:** Consoles and cell phones have memory limitations to consider when designing the sound for games. If the game is going to be played on these platforms, discuss these limitations with your sound engineer.
- **Streaming audio:** Streaming audio consists of sound files that stream directly off the disc and play in real time. Streaming audio does not have to be stored in memory, which means that memory limitations can be mitigated if this is used to deliver audio in the game. The sound designer will want to specify which audio files to stream and which to load into memory so there are no performance issues.
- **Compression:** As with cinematics, music files will need to be compressed for the final version of the game. Compression allows more music and sound effects to be included in the game because it reduces the file sizes. The sound designer will want to determine which compression scheme gives the most beneficial result in terms of both sound quality and space needed on the disc.

- **Custom soundtracks:** If your game supports functionality for custom soundtracks, this means that the players can import their own soundtracks into the game.
- **Audio formats:** Which music formats will your game support? There are several to choose from, each with its own pros and cons. In general, the sound designer and audio programmer will want to support the format that gives the best-quality sound and stays within the memory limitations.

As with VO, it is helpful to implement placeholder music to get a better idea of the final music needs and how things sound in the game. Don't forget to remove any placeholder music before the game ships, especially if it consists of licensed music to which you don't have the rights. Also, be sure that no early marketing footage of the game features any licensed music that you do not have the rights to because this can turn into a legal issue if the musician or the musician's publisher finds out.

16.3.2 Licensed Music

There are two approaches to licensing music. The first is to license royalty-free music. Here, you will pay a one-time fee for the rights to use a music track as many times as you'd like without paying additional fees. The company from which you license the music will have some terms and conditions for how the music is used, so when you are looking at libraries of music, become familiar with these terms before making a final decision. Royalty-free music is generally inexpensive (compared to composing original music or licensing a track from a music publisher). You won't have exclusive rights to the music with this type of license, so there is a chance that another game will use the same track as you, but in my experience, this does not happen very frequently. Also, royalty-free music generally has fewer restrictions on altering the music with different mixes or arrangements, or using it as a sample track in a larger piece. PremiumBeat (www.premiumbeat.com/), owned by Shutterstock, is one of many royalty-free music libraries.

The second approach is to license music directly from bands or other music publishers. Negotiating the licensing deal is going to be time-consuming, so start contacting music publishers or bands early in the process so that the contracts can be finalized before the game's launch. When licensing music in this manner, it is likely that you won't be able to alter it in any way. The contract may also limit how many minutes can be used, how much additional mixing can be done on the track, or what other bands or musicians can appear in the game. The rights may cost a flat fee or may entail an advance against royalties on each copy of the game sold. If you have the budget, you might also be able to get the band to record a special version of the song or even record an original song for use in the game.

The contract should clearly define how the music can be used in the game, how the music can be used in marketing materials, and whether the music can be used on demos or game trailers. It should also detail whether the track can appear on a game soundtrack.

16.3.3 Original Music

Some game studios have in-house composers who create original music for all their games. The benefits of this are that the music will be unique to the game, it can be mixed or altered in any manner, and use is not restricted. An in-house composer can work directly with the team and has the ability to create music that is well-integrated into the gameplay experience.

The other option is to hire an external composer under a "work-for-hire" contract to create original music for the game. A work-for-hire arrangement is necessary to ensure that the game company owns the intellectual property (IP) rights to the music, not the composer. See Chapter 3 for more information on work-for-hire agreements.

Most composers charge by the minute when creating original music, and the rates can vary from $300 a minute to upward of $1,500 a minute. The rate depends on who the composer is and whether the music is recorded with live musicians or created digitally. Additionally, if live musicians are used, you might also need to compensate the musicians; your composer can work out the details with you and the musicians. If you choose to go this route, carefully consider your budget and schedule, and how many minutes of music are needed.

The amount of music varies for each game and might be dependent on the budget. For example, if you need 30 minutes of original music and can spend only $10,000 on music, you will need to find a composer who can do the job for around $300 a minute. On the other hand, you can reduce the amount of music needed for the game and spend money on a composer who charges more per minute. If you find a composer with whom you want to work, and the composer also wants to work with you, more than likely, you will be able to agree on fair terms.

16.3.4 Choosing a Composer

When choosing a composer, start by researching available composers and narrowing the list down to a few that you like. Next, create a bid package that outlines what your needs are, and send it to the potential composers. This allows you to get an idea of prices, how responsive they are, their music style, and how long it will take them to compose the music. Composers might have a preferred format for receiving bids, so check with them first for any necessary forms. In general, the bid packages must include as much information about the game's music needs as possible. Things to include are:

- Grand total number of minutes of music needed;
- How many different pieces of music are needed;
- How long each piece of music must be;
- Specifics on where each piece of music will be located in the game (UI, in-game, cinematics);

- Any sound, VO, and music mixes that are needed;
- Format for music deliverables;
- Deadline for receiving all final deliverables.

In addition, you will need to provide some documentation and samples on what you want the music to sound like. The music vision document should provide general information on the music genre, gameplay themes, and any other special considerations (such as regional flavor). It should also include samples of music from other games, soundtracks, bands, or composers, or any other audio that can closely convey the look and feel you want for the game.

Once you've made a decision, you can start giving the composer more in-depth information on the game. Send them a build of the game or a game trailer, concept art, character descriptions, and story line. The composer can review these elements, along with the music vision document, to determine the themes and inspiration for the music.

As the composer works, plan on several rounds of feedback between them and the game designers.

The feedback process needs to be well-defined beforehand so that time is used wisely, and the composer is not waiting weeks for feedback. It's best for feedback to be communicated in writing to all appropriate parties. If verbal feedback is provided via a conference call, write up the notes from the conversation, and email them to everyone who was on the call as a written record. Establish deadlines for when feedback will be provided and when it will be implemented. For example, when the composer delivers samples for review, he or she should expect to hear feedback within a few days. If no feedback is given, he or she can assume that everything is fine and proceed with the next phase.

Finally, when anyone is giving feedback, make sure that it is useful and constructive. It is not enough to say, "I really don't like this, but I can't put my finger on why" because that gives the composer nothing to work with. The composer will not know what to change in order to get it the way you want. Instead, be specific about what you do not like, even if you think it sounds silly. For example, "I really don't like the screeching at the end of the song; it is too shrill and may annoy the player. Maybe it can be toned down or replaced with something else." This type of feedback is much easier to work with. Provide specific time codes on the areas of the music you are critiquing.

16.3.5 Music Timeline

When putting together your music schedule, include deadlines for any music needed for marketing purposes. For example, marketing may need 1 to 2 minutes of music for a game trailer. If the game is at an alpha stage, the final music might not be ready, or the final tracks might not be legally licensed. In this instance, you want some placeholder music that marketing can use free and clear, and that evokes the same mood as the final game music. If the final game is using an orchestral soundtrack, placeholder orchestral music can be used for the trailer.

The composer should plan to deliver the final music mixes about 6 weeks before launch. If this is in the contract, the final music deliverable should also include the stems. Stems are the individual instrument tracks that exist within the final music mix. They can be used to compose variations for commercials, game trailers, or future games.

Plan to have all the music rights finalized and the contracts signed about one month before launch. This will ensure that everything is ready to go in time for the game's ship date. If you cannot get a music track secured by this time, consider replacing or removing that track from the game.

16.4 Conclusion

Define your audio needs early in the development process so you have time to find the right partner for creating the VO and music. Budget and schedule have a huge impact on audio design, so work closely with your design team to work within these limitations. When looking for partners, be clear about what your needs and deadlines are to ensure that you end up with the right audio partner.

CHAPTER 17

Localization

17.1 Introduction

Localization is the process of modifying a game for sale in other countries. Since this can account for more than 50% of total sales, international markets are not something to be ignored. Plan ahead to release your game in multiple languages during the initial launch; common languages for launch are English, French, Italian, German, and Spanish (sometimes referred to as EFIGS). Asian and Middle Eastern languages are also routinely released but sometimes take more time due to technical constraints with displaying Asian or Middle Eastern fonts and other features that must be added to comply with government requirements. Player's expectations for localized versions are high; they expect a localized version of a game to maintain the same quality as the original.

If a team plans ahead for localization and includes it as part of the core development pipeline, time and effort can be minimized; however, if localization is an afterthought, and if the game code isn't set up to be localization-friendly, then localization can be frustrating and time-consuming. It is a large and complex topic, and this chapter provides just an overview of the process. More information can be found in *The Game Localization Handbook, Second Edition* (2011), by Heather Maxwell Chandler and Stephanie Deming.

17.2 Cultural Awareness

Cultural awareness is a huge and complex topic, and definitely requires the team to really understand and acknowledge that creating localized versions of games needs to be handled with care and sensitivity. This chapter focuses on the nuts and bolts of how to localize a game; while it's beyond its scope to delve into a deeper discussion about cultural appropriation and diversity, and the impact this has on games, it is still an important topic for you and your team to educate yourselves on. It's helpful to talk with the ratings boards for various countries to gain a better understanding of what is acceptable or not acceptable to include in localized games. If you have access to native speakers, it's also useful to talk with them about the game to see what feedback they have on the game content.

In general, the development team and the publisher must consider how content will be received in other countries. Be aware of how characters, settings, and stories around other cultures are likely to be perceived within the context of the game. In addition, humor, figures of speech, and vernacular slang may not translate well and either won't make sense or, in some cases, may be offensive.

Content should be tailored to individual markets as much as possible to provide the player with a sense that the game was made for them and isn't just a translation of the original game. There are many ways in which to do this, with some requiring a bit more time and effort than others. For example, on a small scale, if a sports title includes teams from various countries, then the game should display the team from the player's country by default (a French player turns the game on and sees the French team; the same goes for the German team, the Italian team, and so on). A larger example is what Bethesda did with the Japanese version of Fallout 3. Fallout 3 has a quest where you can make a choice to either defuse a nuclear bomb or accept a bribe from an NPC named Mister Burke and detonate it instead. Because of Japan's history with two nuclear bomb attacks, Bethesda choose to remove the character of Mister Burke and the ability for the player to detonate the bomb.

When creating and implementing the game content, developers should seek input from cultural natives so they can be aware of whether content is culturally sensitive, offensive elements, or things that don't make sense or translate well. If you can learn about these things early in the development process, you can solve them before they become bigger issues that are more expensive to solve later. Experts can also advise on what kind of content best appeals to their culture. One great example is the game Never Alone, developed in partnership with the Cook Inlet Tribal Council and E-Line Media as way to celebrate and share the Iñupiat culture. An inclusive development process was used, in which a group of Iñupiats worked directly with the development team from concept to release to ensure that the game authentically portrayed the culture and values of the Iñupiat people. Never Alone is the recipient of numerous awards and praise for its inclusive approach to making games.

Finally, each country likely has a government entity that regulates the content of games and assigns a rating to a game before it is released. Chapter 14, "Executing the Plan," provides more detail on specific rating boards and where to find the most up-to-date information about what content is acceptable. For example, Germany does not allow depictions of Nazi imagery. The Wolfenstein series, published by Bethesda, includes Nazi imagery, so when the game is released in Germany, these images are replaced with something else.

17.3 Localization-Friendly Development

If developers plan ahead in the development process, they can create localization-friendly code, which will help them to avoid obstacles and delays later, when the game needs to be localized. Localization-friendly code takes into account technical, translation, integration, and testing needs. It's easier to localize because text and other language assets can be swapped into the game, and builds can be quickly compiled for testing.

It's always best to prepare code this way, even if a team isn't planning for localization at the start of a project (because things may change later). Retrofitting code to be localization-friendly isn't recommended because this typically results in numerous bugs, and it's both challenging and time-consuming. Here are some questions to think about when creating the game:

- How are language assets organized?
- What support is included for fonts and special characters?
- How are international keyboards supported?
- Does the game support subtitles?

The following provides a quick rundown of things to consider when building your game to be localization-friendly. Putting these things in ahead of time is good practice in general.

STEPHANIE O'MALLEY DEMING, FOUNDER
XLOC, INC. LOCALIZATION EXAMPLES.

I've been doing this for a while, but I was most impressed early in the simultaneous development trend with Civilization: Call to Power. This was in the late 90s, and the directive was to make this text-heavy game localization-friendly, which had been virtually unheard of before. We worked with engineering to define localized directories, to export string files (so the text wasn't hard-coded), and to use universal symbols and text in the user interface (UI) so that text spacing wasn't an issue. Yes, it was a while ago, but this team went to great lengths to understand the localized possibilities and build the proper infrastructure to make the game localization-friendly.

The quality of the translations is another aspect in "good localizations"—this means that translators are an integral part of the team and understand the concept and tone of the game. We were lucky in that regard as well. As gaming translation has become a more viable business, having that depth of experience is invaluable, and many companies will look to use the same translation team (or, at the very least, reference a glossary) for sequels and additional content.

17.3.1 Text

To make the translation and integration process more efficient, all language assets should be centralized and organized into separate language-specific directories. For instance, in each of the folders for French, English, and German, there should be subdirectories for audio, cinematics, and text.

The text itself shouldn't be hard-coded into the game. Instead, it should be accessible from string tables; this will make it easier to organize, integrate, and test translations.

17.3.2 Art

Text shouldn't be embedded into art assets unless there's no alternative; whenever possible, game code should be used to display text. If text must be part of an art file, then it should be included in a separate layer in the source file so that it can easily be replaced with translated text. For example, if there is a "Cancel" button in the UI screen, the word "Cancel" should not be part of the actual UI art. Instead, the UI text should be displayed programmatically and stored in a strings file.

17.3.3 Audio

A well-defined naming convention for voiceover (VO) files will allow the files to be easily identified. It will also permit someone to quickly understand which language is being used for any given VO file. The same goes for localized VO files.

Music, VO, and sound effects should be stored on separate tracks so that dialogue can easily be replaced with translated VO. Organize the VO assets the same way for all languages to make recording and integrating it easier. See Chapter 16, "Audio," for more information on how to organize VO and music assets.

17.3.4 Fonts

Fonts are another thing to consider in localization. The game engine should be able to display both uppercase and lowercase versions of special linguistic characters, such as ä, Õ, and Ç. At the time of this writing, Unicode is the standard for text characters. Regardless of platform, software, or programming language, Unicode provides a unique number for each character, which makes it possible to display more than 65,000 unique characters, including Asian and Cyrillic. It's worth noting that if the language uses an Asian or Cyrillic font, the engine must be double-byte-enabled, and it must be capable of displaying bidirectional text.

When choosing fonts, remember that they must be easy to read on both computer monitors and televisions (even when displaying international characters). Typically, televisions display at a lower resolution. You also want to choose a font that supports special characters as fonts don't always contain all the characters that are needed to display text in the game. If a font doesn't have a particular character, it will likely display as "□" in the game. If the font was purchased from a design company, contact the company about creating special characters for the languages that need to be supported. You might need to pay for this work, but if you have a specialized font that you want to use in all versions of the game, that's what you will need to do. Google has a free font library called "Noto Fonts" that are free and support all languages (www.google.com/get/noto/). You might be able to find a free font here that closely matches the font you are using in the game. This is a cheaper alternative than creating a custom font.

Some languages are easier to read in larger fonts; if this is the case, the UI text and layout may need to be adjusted in order to accommodate the larger fonts. Be sure to view the text on a variety of monitors and resolutions to check legibility.

17.3.5 User Interface (UI)

The game's UI presents numerous challenges for localization, the main one being the amount of space that is available on the screen. For example, German words are typically longer than English words, so if the game UI is built around the English language, you will run into UI issues when trying to translate it into German. In cases like this, the translator will need to find alternative terms or use abbreviations—both of which lower the quality of the localization.

When designing the UI layouts, be mindful of the following:

- Because localized text is about 25%–30% longer than English text, there should be extra space allotted in the UI to accommodate these longer words.

- Use scalable UI elements whenever possible; if buttons, menus, and text boxes can be scaled dynamically, then these can accommodate localized text more easily. This includes things like drop-down or scrollable lists and buttons that resize according to the length of the text.
- Using easily recognized icons allows your team to avoid text altogether, eliminating the need for localization. For example, a small gear is the universally recognized icon for "Settings," and a question mark is recognized as the icon for "Help." Using icons eliminates the need for text and presents a consistent look through all the versions of the game.
- Dates and currency should always be displayed in the appropriate regional formats. Some countries display dates as month/day/year, while others use a day/month/year format. Some currencies utilize decimals, while others use commas, and so on.

17.3.6 Controllers

On PC games, the keyboard is the main input control, and not all international keyboards have the same layout. There are two approaches to localized keyboard layouts: location mapped and character mapped. Location mapping means that the keys to control game actions are mapped to the same location on all keyboards. For example, the far right key on the top row reloads the player's weapon, regardless of which character is displayed on the key. Character mapping is when the game actions are mapped to the same character, regardless of location. For example, the tilda might be used to open up the chat box, and it will always open the chat box, regardless of where the character is located on the keyboard. Some characters don't appear on all keyboards; avoid mapping any actions to those characters. During testing, you will want to test the game with all types of keyboards to uncover any of these issues.

17.3.7 Subtitles

Subtitles are useful for both localization and accessibility, so it's always advisable to include them as an option in the game. Sometimes, in order to save money, only the subtitles will be localized. Thus, money isn't spent on recording VO and implementing it into the game. Also, with the need for localized VO eliminated, the size of the game will be smaller since it won't contain VO files for multiple languages.

17.3.8 Lip-Syncing

Lip-syncing is typically handled via dubbing for in-game speech and prerendered cinematics. In such cases, localized dialogue replaces the original source dialogue, and an animator attempts to synchronize the mouth and lip movements. In some cases, it can be very costly to spend time making sure all the characters' facial animations are perfectly synced with VO files. However, there are some software solutions that can be investigated to make this easier.

17.4 Localization Approaches

The scope of a game's localization usually depends on return on investment for a localized version. For example, it may cost $100,000 to make a fully localized game in Portuguese, but the cost of localization won't be recouped with the number of game sales. Publishers will do financial forecasts for different territories to determine how much they want to invest in localization costs. There are three common levels of game localization:

- **The packaging and manual:** Often referred to as "box and docs," this level focuses on the localization of the game's packaging and the user manual. The game's code is unchanged, and there's only one language option, but the aforementioned supporting documents are localized into the target language. This is something that was more common in the past, when a lot of boxed product was sold. Today, most games are available as digital downloads, which means there aren't any paper elements to be localized in the first place. For a game that is digitally distributed, the publisher may opt to just localize the text in the storefront that describes the game to the player, while the game itself remains unchanged and in the original language.
- **Partial localization:** Only the text is localized. Any VO in the game is subtitled, and the VO audio files remain in the original language. This is less expensive since money is not spent on localized VO recordings. If there is text embedded in the art assets (e.g., in signs), it may also remain unlocalized after evaluating the effort required to change it. As Chapter 16, "Audio," shows, a lot of work and money goes into recording VO. So, when publishers do financial forecasts, they will determine if the additional cost to record VO makes sense.
- **Full localization:** This is where everything in the game is fully localized—in-game text, VO, and art. It is the most costly and challenging level of localization. It also takes more time since VO recording sessions need to be done, and then, the VO files need to be processed and delivered so the team can implement them.

17.5 Localization for China and Korea

All territories worldwide have specific guidelines on what type of content is acceptable and usually have some type of software ratings board that regulates the game content that can be released in that territory. Chapter 14, "Making the Game," has more information on these rating boards. However, there are a couple features that (so far) are specific to games released in China and Korea.

One of these features is intented to notify players how much time they have spent playing the game. The idea is to remind players to take a break from games and spend time away from the screen. China requires the game to include in-game pop-up windows at regular intervals, telling people how much time they have spent in a single gaming session. If the player continues gaming without a break, the in-game rewards and progression start decreasing at regular intervals so that, after a few hours, the players will not receive any type of in-game rewards, loot, XP boosts, etc. while playing. When releasing a game in China, work closely with the publisher to ensure that you have the most up-to-date information about how this feature (and any other feature) should be implemented.

Korean games also have features to combat game addiction. In addition to reminders about how much time a player has spent online, Korean games have a feature that allows parents to set how much access children can have to the game (they can set it up so that the game is only available for limited periods of time). There is another required feature that prevents children under the age of 16 from playing online games between midnight and 6 a.m. (in accordance with South Korean law). As with games released in China, you must work closely with your publisher to ensure you are in compliance with all the laws and regulations in Korea.

Another feature to be aware of for Korean versions of games is specific to PC Bangs, which are very popular in Korea. PC Bangs are social cafes where people gather to play online multiplayer games for an hourly fee. The bangs are equipped with high-end computers and broadband internet access, which allows people to have a high-quality game experience, with their friends, for a low cost. There need to be support and features added to the game that make it possible for PC Bangs to charge the hourly fee and collect money. This can be a complicated feature to implement since you have to deal with different ways of handling monetary transactions, give players the ability to log into their personal game accounts from PC Bangs, and still ensure that rewards are credited to their accounts properly.

All of these features for China and Korea can be added after the original game launches, but as usual, they are much easier to implement if the need for them is anticipated and planned for ahead of time.

17.6 Asset Translation

Once a decision has been made to localize a game, the fun begins. Localizations are usually managed by an Associate Producer since there are a lot of different parts to coordinate to ensure success. First, you have to find a vendor who can translate the text for you. If the game is released in multiple languages, multiple vendors might be required. During the vendor search, work with the engineers to set-up a pipeline for easily importing and exporting the language-specific assets in the game. For example, the engineers can create a process for exporting all the text in the UI screen into a spreadsheet, which can then be delivered to the translators. When the translators have completed their work, the process will easily allow the translated text to be integrated into the game correctly. This process takes time, so this also needs to be accounted for in the schedule. The localization vendors rely heavily on the development team to answer questions about any of the game content and work through any technical issues that may arise when trying to translate the assets.

17.6.1 Organization

By planning ahead for localization, you can hopefully create a nicely organized localization kit that contains all the assets that need to be translated, including text, VO, and art files. If you separate the languages into different folders within the game, this should be pretty straightforward. In an ideal world, you can send the kit to be translated and then simply integrate the translations into the game. This series of events works well if the game has already been released, and the language assets are all finalized. For example, if you are adding Russian translations a few months after the game is released, you can just send the kit and take care of the localization fairly easily.

On the other hand, if you are planning to release localized versions simultaneously with the main game, you will run into a few scheduling issues. This is because it will be hard for the development team to finalize the game text in a timely fashion. Think about it this way: if the game has 100,000 words to translate, this will likely take a few weeks; while the translators are working, it is highly possible that there will be major changes to the source text. Now, you have two different sets of text that aren't in sync with each other, and you have to figure out a good way to provide the updated text to the translators. As you can imagine, localizing a game in active development can be challenging.

Therefore, you want to create a comprehensive process for tracking and updating assets so that localization proceeds as smoothly as possible. Involving the localization vendor in the creation of this process will give the vendor a sense of ownership and a personal stake in the game, which will have a positive effect on workflow. If the localization process is disorganized, time will be wasted as developers and translators attempt to figure out which assets (and/or versions) have been sent for translation and which have not. XLOC (www.XLOC.com) is a tool that specializes in a localization pipeline for games that is centered around organizing, tracking, and updating assets in an easy-to-use process. If you don't use a tool like XLOC, you will probably want to build some type of proprietary tools that help you to manage the pipeline.

Localization-friendly game code will make the organization of text and art assets much simpler. If the game's assets haven't been organized, and there isn't a defined pipeline, it will likely fall upon the producer to pull all art and text assets into a central location and create a spreadsheet to track which files have been sent for translation.

Now that you have a solution for how you will export the language assets and get them to the translators, you will want to make sure that the translators have everything they need to properly localize the game. The translators must understand the context of what they're translating in order to produce the highest-quality translation. This will take time as they need to play the game, review the design document, review the character descriptions and VO scripts, and so on. They will need the following in order to do their best work:

- A playable version of the game;
- Design documents;
- Cheats and walkthroughs;
- VO casting notes;
- A glossary;
- A technical overview, including information on file delivery formats and any tools the translator will need to work with.

For VO assets, the translator will also want the original versions of the source VO to aid in casting actors for the localized VO. These files provide localized voice actors with a reference so they can better understand the tone and context of a line reading. If the localized cinematics use lip-syncing, the audio vendors will also need the time codes for the original files to make it easier for them to match the timing of the cinematic.

In addition to all the text that appears in the game, other things need to be sent for translation, such as:

- Game website;
- Digital storefronts;
- Paper packaging;
- CS information;
- End user license agreement.

Plan for these in your schedule, and get these assets organized and sent off for translation as soon as possible so there isn't a last-minute scramble to get this done.

17.6.2 Integration

As mentioned, the asset translation and integration pipeline is critical to an efficient localization process. If the asset integration process isn't automated or organized as a part of the primary production pipeline, then it can involve numerous file modifications and become very time-consuming. The size of most games today means that manually integrating translations for multiple languages is too time-consuming and error prone.

The way in which assets are laid out in the game can affect the ease of integration. For example, if text is hard-coded into art assets, then a developer will need to manually cut and paste text within the source art file; there's no way to automate this process, and there's a high risk of introducing bugs into the code. If you have multiple art files that need to be manually translated, you risk impacting your art schedule if you need to pull an artist way from the main game to spend a few days making translated art assets.

If you layer the art files and have the game set up to pull text and display it on top of any art in the game, this is more efficient. It is possible to automate this process, so if there is the ability to do that, it is highly recommended.

Depending on how the pipeline is set up, the translators may also be able to integrate the translations into the game. If a tool like XLOC is used, the translator inputs the text directly into a database, pushes a button to generate a set of translated assets, then drops these assets into the game and immediately sees the results of their work. If there isn't an automated process, and spreadsheets are the main method of exchanging information between the translator and the development team, a developer may need to spend time manually integrating the assets, which is not the best use of their time. If you rely on the translators to manually integrate text into game-specific assets, you run the risk of introducing more bugs as the translator could easily delete a space or semicolon from the game code and cause entire sections of text to display incorrectly in the game.

If there is not an easy-to-use, automated integration process, the developer must handle asset integration themselves. This way, technical difficulties can be more easily addressed, asset integrity is maintained, and the developers have more control over schedule and resources. However, the developers will need to allocate production time for these tasks. From a schedule standpoint, this means that the translators won't be able to immediately see the result of their work in the game as they will have to wait for the developer to send them a version of the game that has all the translations integrated. This adds time to the schedule, and it is likely that the translators will spend more time fixing linguistic bugs since they have to wait until the entire game is localized and ready for testing (it also removes the luxury of checking translations at regular intervals).

When the first set of assets is integrated, it must be checked into the team's version control system so that it can be tracked through the development process. Then, after each update to the English language version, the new assets must be checked into source control. It's important to verify that the correct set of assets for each language has been checked in; it's easy to mix these assets up by mistake. In addition, it might be necessary to update other text elements for different territories, such as software registration and CS information.

Developers may elect to outsource the bulk of localization work by hiring a localization vendor. This allows the core team to focus on the game but requires them to appoint someone from the team to answer questions and troubleshoot issues. They'll also need to furnish the vendor with a full localization kit. The downside to this approach is that the developer will have limited control over the process and will have to trust that the vendor can deliver the work on time. Problems and delays will cause the cost of outsourcing to increase.

17.7 Testing Considerations

Localization testing includes linguistic and functionality testing, which must be done separately for each language. Be sure to allot enough testing time in the schedule for this. There will likely be rounds of testing and bug-fixing before the localized versions are deemed ready for release.

17.7.1 Linguistic

During linguistic testing, the team checks all language assets; they test for incorrect grammar, overlapping text, and truncated or misspelled text. Native speakers should conduct the linguistic testing because they're most likely to find errors.

The team may opt to have linguistic testers on-site, especially if the localization is complex. This can accelerate the bug-fixing process because these testers can furnish corrected translations immediately. To make the most of the testers' time, the travel plans and on-site schedules must be well organized. Linguistic testers should be familiar with the game's core features prior to testing; the functionality test plan can help with this.

A localization test plan will show the testers where to check the translations. For example, they can check the in-game text against the translation spreadsheet.

17.7.2 Functionality

During functionality testing, developers check for bugs that were created during localization, which are typically fixed via a code change. Ideally, an asset swap will not introduce functionality bugs. However, code changes might be required if special characters and increased text length weren't planned for properly.

The same QA team that tested the core game can conduct functionality testing since they're the most familiar with the game. They don't necessarily need to know the language they're testing; they can check for incorrect language assets, text overruns, and other functionality bugs.

In the central bug-tracking database, be sure to include which language is being tested so that the bugs can be sorted by language.

17.8 Localization Timeline

Prior to a game's localization, it must be decided whether such an effort will prove profitable based on sales. First, the team must calculate how many assets will need to be localized, at what cost, and over how much development time. This information is also useful when external vendors are bidding on localization tasks.

The schedule for localization encompasses these areas:

- **Asset organization:** This defines the amount of time it will take to convert text assets into a format that can be translated.
- **Translation:** This is how much time will be needed for translation. As a rule of thumb, one translator can typically translate 1,500–2000 words per day. This might take more time with games because the translators aren't doing a straight translation—they will have to make changes to the text to make it more culturally relevant. Machine translation is an option, especially in projects that have hundreds of thousands of words to translate, but then, time is taken by the translators to review all the machine translation and make sure they work with the game context.
- **Audio Recording:** After the translations are done, audio recording can begin. Depending on how much VO is needed, this could take several weeks. Time to cast and onboard actors also needs to be considered.
- **Integration:** This is how much time is needed to get the translations integrated into the game. If this is done manually, it could take days or weeks. If it is automated, it can go more quickly, if there are not issues with the pipeline.
- **Testing:** This includes both functionality and linguistic testing. The time needed for each depends on the size of the game. You can usually get a ballpark estimate from looking at how long it takes the QA team to run through their full test plan for the game.

While each project's schedule is different, it's not uncommon to spend 2 or 3 months in production on localized versions. This assumes that localization has been planned for in advance and that it proceeds according to schedule; if these conditions are not met, the process can take longer. Establish a schedule early in the process to make sure you are staying on track. This also gives the development team a better idea of how localization will impact their scheduled tasks. Start with the big picture schedule, and as you get more information, you can refine the dates.

After the team has created the initial schedule and an overview of all assets, a budget can be established. This should include costs for all required personnel, including external translators, part-time engineers, part-time artists, part-time associate producers, and testers. Typically, testers comprise the most significant development costs, particularly if the game is complex and content-heavy. These costs quickly add up when there are multiple languages, so be selective about which languages you choose.

Appoint one production person to manage all aspects of localization. This includes building the schedule and budget, finding translation vendors, and managing the integration and testing process. If one person has a deep understanding and is actively managing the process, the localizations will go more smoothly.

17.9 Conclusion

Localization is not a glamourous part of game development, but it is a necessary one. There are lots of pieces to the localization process, and it can be complex to manage. Make sure your team is aware of how localizations fit into their development processes so they can plan accordingly when making technical and artistic decisions on the project. In addition, be mindful of the game content to ensure that it is culturally appropriate for any territory in which the game is released. Remember that players expect a high-quality localization and will not forgive poor voice acting and typos. Plan ahead for localization to increase the chances of creating high-quality localizations that ship on time.

CHAPTER 18

QA Testing

18.1 Introduction

QA testing occurs throughout the development process, and it is more than just playing the game to see if it's fun. Testing is a stressful and difficult job as testers are the last round of defense before the game is released to the players. Avoid confusing this with UX testing, which has a different purpose. QA testing focuses on the functional aspects of the game—is it behaving as intended? UX testing focuses on the user's experience with the game—does it provide a satisfying and engaging experience for the player?

If a game launches with a critical issue, it is often the QA team that gets the blame for not finding the issue while testing. Testers spend a good deal of time testing the game day in and day out, looking for defects, confirming bug fixes, and playtesting. As you can imagine, this becomes pretty tedious after a few weeks, no matter how fun the game is. Oftentimes, because testers are looking for specific issues with the game, they do not even have a chance to just play and enjoy it. This chapter provides a general overview of testing, from a production point of view, and touches on the types of testing and test plans, and how to track and resolve bugs. For more information on QA testing and how to do it, take a look at a book called *Game Testing All-in-One, Third Edition* (2016), by Charles P. Schultz and Robert Denton Bryant.

18.2 Working with QA

The producer and QA lead work closely together to ensure that the development team and QA team are in sync on what areas of the game are ready to be tested, which bugs have been fixed, and any changes or updates to the schedule. If the game needs more development time, the time is often taken away from the testing schedule, which adds stress to the QA team. Since QA is the last thing done in the development cycle, the QA team may be expected to make up for this lost testing time by working overtime to ensure that the game is ready in time for its launch date. Thus, it is important to ensure that the development team delivers things in a timely fashion so that QA has an enough time to thoroughly check all areas of the game.

The QA lead is responsible for testing the game and regressing bugs, and is a key stakeholder in determining whether a game is ready to be code-released. The lead should be involved in the development process from the beginning to provide feedback and guidance from the QA point of view. Knowing how to test a potential feature and how long this might take can have an impact on how the feature is scoped out and designed. In some cases, the scope of the feature may be too large for testing to accommodate within a reasonable time frame. If this is discovered early in the development process, the scope of the feature can be reduced so it can be tested more reasonably. This still allows the feature to grow and iterate as needed for future updates but also accommodates the testing constraints and release dates. Open dialogue between the development and QA teams during the preproduction phase creates a tighter loop between the teams, which will hopefully translate into more manageable testing schedules.

Because testing time is often cut short to accommodate other schedule slips, work with the QA lead to create a high-level testing schedule during preproduction. The most basic way to do this is to count backward from the launch date to figure out the key testing points in the development process. For example, if you are releasing the game on a console, the internal testing needs to be done a few weeks before launch so there is time for the platform holders to do their testing. Define these types of requirements, and add them to the testing timeline. This ensures that everyone on the team will have a clear understanding of the testing schedule.

Think about how major game milestones will be tested and how long that will take. If you are utilizing Alpha and Beta milestones, thorough testing on just these milestone builds will take a few weeks (depending on the scope and complexity of the game). Ideally, the QA group can spend an extended amount of time with a single build. Although builds will be available on a daily basis, it is not useful for QA to test every build because they would never make it through the entire game before a new build was ready.

Instead, if the build is stable, the QA department can spend a few days or a week with a single build and test that as much as possible. This also allows QA to more accurately evaluate the game's progress against the list of expected milestone deliverables.

Other things to include in the testing schedule are:

- **Playtesting:** During production, schedule time for QA to playtest the game, and offer feedback to the developers. Ideally, find testers who haven't spent months testing the game and still have a pair of fresh eyes.
- **Marketing builds:** Marketing will need versions of the game to demo at conferences and to show journalists. These are additional versions that may need to be tested separately. They may just include a small portion of the game, with specific features accessible or inaccessible. Oftentimes, the development team will need to make a special build just for marketing purposes because the marketing team will want a demo that can provide a good understanding of the game experience in a limited amount of time.
- **Launch candidates:** When the game is ready to launch, make sure that the QA team has enough time to thoroughly check the version of the game that will actually launch. It may take a week or more for them to check all the areas of the game against the test plan.

During the concept or prototype phase, the testing team will be small—perhaps just one or two people. If the development team is doing a lot of prototypes, more QA people might be needed if there is a need for more formalized testing on these prototypes. During this phase, the QA lead can start working on the test plan and getting the test pipeline established. The QA pipeline and testing resources should be ready and in place before the development process begins in earnest. When the QA team is larger, the QA lead will play more of a managerial role and will no longer be working on actually testing the game. Instead, they will be defining the best strategies for testing features, managing the test team, and advising the project leads on any testing issues.

As development progresses, and there is more to test, the QA team will check different sections of the game on different builds. For example, when a level artist checks in a new level, the testers will examine the geometry and textures on the level, and submit any bugs to the database. This level will not be tested again until the artist has fixed all the bugs and resubmitted the level for testing, which could take several weeks. Meanwhile, the testers will concentrate on testing other levels and features in subsequent builds.

Once the build is in testing, the testing cycle is fairly straightforward. The testers will run through the test plan, find bugs, and enter them into the database. When the bugs are in the database, they are assigned to the appropriate person for fixing. This person fixes the bug and resubmits his or her work for verification in a future build. The tester will then check the fix in the build and close the bug.

18.3 Types of Testing

Different types of testing occur during the development cycle. The development team and the QA team should work together to determine when each type of testing is necessary.

- **Playtesting:** This type is focused on the fun factor of the game. The focus is not on finding bugs but on experiencing the game as a player would. Is the game fun? Is the UX good? Which features work well? Which features don't? Playtesting can be done by anyone on the team. You can also set up external playtests to get feedback from your target audience or other people outside of the game. Someone needs to be responsible for gathering all the playtest feedback and synthesizing it into actionable items for the team.
- **Functional Testing:** This is a more structured type of testing where a test plan is followed, and the game functionality is checked for bugs. QA spends the majority of their testing time doing functional testing. A bug-tracking database is used to collect all the issues, which are then vetted and assigned out to the developers to be fixed.
- **Compatibility Testing:** PC hardware can have many different configurations of graphics cards, memory, and processing speed, which impact how the game will run. Compatibility testing checks different combinations of operating systems, processors, and graphics cards to determine the minimum system requirement for playing a game. Android and iOS systems also have multiple hardware configurations, so work with the testing team to determine what configurations needs to be tested. Compatibility testing helps determine what the minimum hardware specifications are for a particular operating system.
- **Performance Testing:** Performance is how many frames per second (FPS) the game runs at. At minimum, games on any platform should be running at 30 FPS. On higher-end systems, 60 FPS is ideal in order to show the highest fidelity graphics. Game performance is directly impacted by hardware configurations and by how much information the game is trying to process and display at any time on the screen. Performance testing will happen throughout the development process as the team tries to optimize the game tries to optimize the game performance as much as possible on the target hardware platforms.
- **Compliance Testing:** Each platform holder has a predefined set of technical requirements that must be met. If the game is released on a console or mobile device, it must meet these requirements. Before the game can launch, the platform holder will test the game to make sure it complies. If it fails compliance testing, the issues it failed on will need to be addressed and retested before the platform holders will approve the game for launch. There are many examples of games that missed launch dates because they were unable to pass the platform requirements testing.
- **Localization Testing:** This is when you check the translations in the localized versions of the game. Localization testing will be done by native

speakers of the language being tested. Outsourcing localization testing is very common.

- **Ad Hoc Testing:** This is random and unplanned testing. The idea is to interact with the game the way a player might: have multiple programs open, leave the game sitting idle for long periods of time, interact with the game in ways that are counter to the design intent (i.e., trying to break the game), and so on. Ad hoc testing may uncover some issues that wouldn't be found by the normal test plan.

18.4 QA Outsourcing

QA outsourcing is something to consider if you have a small or nonexistent QA team and want to get a second pair of eyes on the game. If you have a large game and a large QA team, outsourcing is also useful. For example, a Battle Royale game hosts 100 live players, so an outsourced QA team may be needed to get 100 live testers into the game to confirm that everything works as intended. If there are a lot of areas of the game to test, an external QA vendor can focus on a specific area during development, which will help keep the testing schedule under control. External testing also occurs when the localized versions of the game need to be tested by native speakers of each language. Finally, money might be better spent on external testing if there is a specific area to test that requires specialized resources. For example, checking PC compatibility on a variety of computers, video cards, and sound cards might be best handled by an external vendor who has a compatibility laboratory already set up for testing. It may be worthwhile to hire a testing vendor that has extensive experience checking platform holders' technical requirements to increase the chances of the game getting approved more quickly.

If utilizing an outsourced QA team, do your research on the vendors and ask for recommendations from other clients. Things to ask potential vendors include:

- What's the process for getting them a version of the game to test, and how far in advance do they need it?
- Will they create their own version of the test plan, or will they need one provided? If they write the plan, how much will this cost, and how long will it take? What information or resources do they need from the development team in order to write the plan?
- Are the testing costs calculated on an hourly or a daily rate? When do overtime rates go into effect?
- What additional costs are added to the testing rate? Do they charge a project management fee or tack on an additional percentage of the total testing cost for overhead?
- What's the deadline for canceling or rescheduling the test? What are the penalties if the test is canceled or rescheduled after the deadline has passed?
- Can they provide an estimate of how long it will take to test the game? Will they do a free gameplay evaluation in order to determine how much testing time they need to fulfill your request?

- Who will be the main point of contact? Will they provide a project manager who you can contact on a daily basis? Will the project manager send daily progress reports?
- What bug-tracking software do they use? Do you have to use their software, or can they accommodate other types of bug-tracking software?

After a vendor is selected, work closely with them to make sure they get everything they need to test the game. If the vendor isn't getting what they need from the development team, the quality of the testing is going to be sub-par. The team should be doing the following when working with an outsourced QA team:

- Check builds before sending them to the vendor to ensure they install and load correctly. If the vendor has to spend a few hours troubleshooting a broken build, the costs can add up quickly. These delays can be avoided if the build is checked before leaving the building.
- Provide clear direction about what needs to be tested. Do you want them to check only the third-party technical requirements, or do they need to test other areas of the game as well? Are they only supposed to check multiplayer functionality, or are they also supposed to check the single-player campaign? Are they only focusing on regressing bug fixes from the previous build? If so, be sure the bug database clearly indicates which bugs are ready for regression.
- Establish a schedule for sending new builds. Are they supposed to test a build from start to finish and then wait until you are ready to do another round of testing? Are they supposed to continually test for the next 2 months—if so, how often do they need a new build (every day or every week)?
- Answer questions as quickly as possible. If the vendor has a question, get the necessary information as soon as possible because testing may be put on hold until the question is answered. The longer the wait, the more testing time is lost and the more money is wasted.

18.5 Creating Test Plans

The QA department follows a test plan in order to thoroughly check all areas of the game. The QA lead uses existing design documents (or sometimes prototypes) to create the initial test plan. They will then work with the development team to keep the test plan updated. It's ideal if the development team can be proactive about informing QA of any changes to the game. If a feature is added or changed, and this isn't communicated to QA in a timely fashion, they may assume that the game is broken and will waste time testing the wrong thing.

As mentioned earlier, the QA lead should join the team as soon as possible so they can start flagging potential testing issues and writing the test plan. Depending on the scope of the game, the test plan could be hundreds of pages. It is usually presented in some type of pass-fail format or as a checklist. For example, a checklist may include a list of playable characters, and the tester needs to start the game, go to the character selection screen, and confirm which playable characters are in the game. In phase two of this check, the tester might need to select each playable character and play through one level with them. In a pass-fail format, the tester may need to check each button on the UI screen and note if it passes (meaning it functions as expected) or fails (meaning it does not work at all or does not function as expected).

It is critical for the test plan to be updated to reflect the latest changes to the game and the design documentation. Valuable production time can be lost if the QA department is using an outdated version of the test plan to check a build. For example, the lead artist may have approved cutting some of the playable characters in the game but not informed the QA department or updated the character asset lists. A QA tester starts checking the list of characters against the test plan and finds that several characters are missing. This gets logged into the database as a bug and now needs to go through the established process for verifying, fixing, and closing a bug, when, in reality, all that is needed is an update to the test plan.

Because QA will not fully test every build they receive, they will focus on specific sections of the game for each build. For example, they may focus specifically on multiplayer modes for a few days; then, on the new build, they may focus on weapon upgrades. The engineering or design departments might also have specific things they want testers to check in a certain build. QA will cycle through sections of the test plan over the course of a few builds. If they started testing at the beginning of the test plan each time they received a new build, some parts of the game would get a lot of testing, while others would get only a small amount.

If the testing department receives a milestone build and needs to verify that it is content and code complete, QA is likely to test it against the full test plan. This will ensure that they touch all areas of the game in the milestone build and can accurately check what is working and what is not. Also, during the code release process, the testers will need to work through the entire test plan from start to finish to verify that everything is working correctly in the potential gold master build.

18.6 Reporting and Resolving Bugs

Before testing begins, the testers and the development team need to determine the pipeline for tracking and resolving bugs. If this is not established, there will be confusion about how the testers should be reporting bugs and which bugs are most critical for the development team to fix first. In addition, everyone needs to understand how to access and use the bug-tracking database.

The main goal of the testing pipeline is to set up a process so that any bugs entered into the database can be found, assigned, fixed, verified, and resolved. This process can get complicated on a large team since so many people are involved in entering and assigning bugs. Establish a clear process for how the bugs should be reported and tracked through the bug-fixing pipeline. The QA lead and producers are usually responsible for making sure that any new bugs found are prioritized and assigned to the appropriated person to be fixed. If there is a breakdown in the process, bugs will start slipping through the cracks, won't get resolved, and will go live when the game launches. In general, the process works like this:

- **Found:** Someone on the development team or the QA team finds a bug and enters it into the bug database.
- **Assigned:** The bug is assigned to a developer to be fixed. The person doing the bug assignments is likely a producer or a discipline lead.
- **Fixed:** The assignee fixes the bug and marks it fixed in the database. When the bug is marked as fixed, the developer will note which version the bug was fixed in. This helps QA to know which build they need to verify for the fix.
- **Verified:** On the appropriate build, the QA tester will verify the fix and note it as such in the database. They will include which version of the build the fix was verified on. This becomes important if the bug is reopened later. It could be that it was verified on the wrong build or that the bug was fixed but has now reoccurred due to other changes in the game.
- **Resolved:** The QA lead confirms that verified fixes are working as intended and closes the bug in the database. The bug is archived in the database and removed from the bug-tracking process. If the bug occurs in the future, the issue will be reopened, and the process will start again.

18.6.1 Bug Database

In order to efficiently track bugs, a centralized bug-tracking database is critical. Do not rely on emails as a reliable form of bug-tracking. Instead, set up an online database that is accessible to everyone, such as JIRA or Bugzilla. Both of these programs offer robust bug-tracking functionality for writing and closing bugs.

After the database is set up, the QA lead should train the development team and the QA team on how to use it. In addition, this should be when the overall bug process is defined, and people are assigned to manage specific steps in the process. The development team should be trained on how to enter and write bugs as they are likely to encounter them on a daily basis. If they don't write up the bug correctly, it is harder for it to be fixed. During this training meeting, the QA lead can also review how bugs are defined so that everyone has a common understanding of the differences between crash bugs, critical bugs, minor bugs, and feature requests.

18.6.2 Bug Definitions

When bugs are added to the database, make sure the correct bug definitions are used so that they can be fixed in the most efficient order. For instance, crash bugs should be addressed well before any minor bugs or feature requests. If a bug is not properly defined in the database, crash bugs might not be addressed for a while and will ultimately become more difficult to fix as production continues. Additionally, if feature requests are defined incorrectly as bugs, feature creep will sneak up on you before you know it.

Common bug definitions include:

- **Blocker:** This is a bug that completely blocks testing for which there is not a workaround. The only solution is to get the bug fixed and make a new build. An example would be a game that doesn't even load or crashes to the desktop within a few minutes of play.
- **Crash bug:** A crash bug is extremely serious because it prevents the player from progressing in the game. Crash bugs can freeze the game or, in the worst cases, kick the player out of it. When QA encounters a crash bug, they will look for a workaround so they can continue testing the game.
- **Critical bug:** A critical bug is a major functionality problem with the game, but it does not prevent the player from progressing. A critical bug is a level missing all of its textures or a major gameplay feature not functioning as designed.
- **Minor bug:** A minor bug is one that is noticeable to the player but does not detract greatly from the overall game experience. Stretched textures and typos can be considered minor bugs.
- **Feature request:** A feature request is not a bug, so be sure that everyone entering bugs in the database clearly understands the difference. A feature request is additional functionality that would be nice to add but is not part of the defined feature set. For example, someone might request an option to toggle the in-game heads-up display (HUD) off and on, but if this feature was not an original part of the design, it is considered a feature request. However, if the user is supposed to have the ability to toggle the HUD on and off, and this is not working in the game, then this is a bug.

18.6.3 Bug Priority and Severity

The terms "priority" and "severity" may sometimes be used interchangeably in the context of bugs, but they are two different things.

Severity indicates how seriously the bug impacts the gameplay and is usually defined as blocker, crash, critical, minor, or feature request. Some bug databases will assign a numerical value to severity that ranges from 0 (blocker) to 4 (feature request). Generally, blockers are addressed immediately so that the QA group can get back to testing as soon as possible. Crash bugs are normally classified as a 1 since they need to be addressed before the game is launched. If there is a workaround, or the likelihood of encountering the crash during normal gameplay is low, it is not going to block testing and therefore doesn't necessarily need to be fixed immediately. Generally, a critical bug is listed as a 2, a minor bug as a 3, and a feature request as a 4. Your development team may choose to define Severity differently. As long as everyone is in agreement on what the Severity numbers indicate, you can use whatever norms and guidelines work best within the development pipeline. Priority is used to indicate if the priority for fixing the bug is high or low. This becomes useful if developers have multiple bugs assigned to them, and they need a way to prioritize their work. The developers should focus on fixing the highest-priority bugs first and then go down the list (based on priority). You will have cases where a Severity 1 bug might be deemed a Priority 2 for fixing. For example, imagine a case in which there are three Severity 1 crash bugs: one crash is at the beginning of the game, while the other two happen at the end. The crash bug that happens at the beginning might be considered Priority 1, while the other two might be considered Priority 2. Usually, the producer and leads will work together to determine priorities in a situation like this.

18.6.4 Writing Bug Reports

Require members of the development teams to input any bugs they encounter or feature requests they have into the issue-tracking database. While feature requests are not bugs, it is good to include them in the database so they can be tracked. If a feature request is not approved for inclusion in the game, it can be moved to the backlog and considered for future releases.

Establish a standardized process for writing bugs, and enforce it. The bugs must contain the necessary information so that the team can figure out what the bug is, find it in the game, and fix it. Most bug-tracking databases have a standard set of information fields, including:

- **Version:** This indicates the version of the build where the bug was found. If the bug pops up again later, the version history will be useful for tracking down the cause of the bug.
- **Category:** This indicates if it is an art, design, or engineering bug. Usually, this is fairly easy to figure out, but, if in doubt, the tester should make a best guess as to the category. When the appropriate lead takes a look at the bug, they may recategorize it.
- **Component:** This subset of "category" offers more details on the behaviors the bug is exhibiting. For example, subcategories in "engineering" might be networking, AI, UI, physics, graphics, and so on.
- **Summary:** This is a quick one-sentence summary of the bug. The team may establish specific guidelines for how to write the summary so that the bugs can be easily sorted. For example, all art bugs found in the first level of the game need to begin with "L01—Art."
- **Description of bug:** The person writing the bug needs to describe what happened. In some cases, he or she may want to include information on what was expected versus what actually happened. This allows the

team to easily identify any bugs that are not working as designed or, in some cases, features that are working as designed but are incorrectly perceived as bugs.

- **Steps to reproduce:** This provides step-by-step information on how to reproduce the bug (if it is reproducible). If the bug is not reproducible, the testers should write down the list of actions taken before the bug was encountered. Team members should make it a practice to reproduce the bug before doing the fix to make sure they understand the issue.
- **Screenshots:** Including a screenshot of what was happening in the game at the time the bug occurred is very helpful in pinpointing the location and cause of the bug.
- **Crash log files:** The engineer can create a debug executable that will generate a log file each time the game crashes. The log file will note which line of code the crash occurred in so there is a good starting point for tracking down a bug.

Work with the team leads to determine what information needs to be included about the bug. Work with the QA lead on how the steps to reproduce should be written, and make sure that everyone understands when screenshots, crash logs, and other supporting information need to be attached to the description.

18.6.5 Resolving Bugs

Assigning bugs is a large part of the testing cycle because the bug has to get to the right person in order to be fixed and verified. The process for assigning bugs should be clearly defined and presented to the team. The goal of assigning bugs is to get bugs addressed as quickly as possible.

Here is a simple process for assigning bugs that involves the tester, the QA lead, and the discipline lead:

1. The tester finds a bug in the game, writes it up, and submits it to the database.
2. The bug is automatically assigned to the QA lead, who checks to ensure that it is indeed a bug and that the bug is written up correctly.
3. The QA lead assigns the bug to the appropriate lead. The art lead receives all the art bugs and so on.
4. The lead reviews the bug, verifies that it is assigned to the appropriate discipline, and assigns it to someone to be fixed.
5. The person doing the fix implements it and assigns it back to the QA tester for verification. If the bug can't be fixed, the person attempting to fix it should add a comment to the database with that information and recommendations for next steps.
6. The QA tester verifies the fix and marks it closed. If the verification fails, the bug is assigned back to the developer for further work.
7. The QA lead reviews all the closed bugs at the end of the day (or week) and marks them resolved.

Fixing every single bug in the game is not possible, especially as the launch date nears. Most developers have a list of "will not fix" bugs that will remain in the game when it ships. Some of these bugs may be addressed later with an update or a patch, but most will not. Bugs categorized as "will not fix" are minor bugs that will not demonstrably impact the player's game experience. The bugs may be cosmetic—there is stretched texture or a visible seam in a 3D model. Other bugs may be related to gameplay but are prioritized as low risk and not worth jeopardizing the ship date to fix. Each developer has different standards for designating a bug as "will not fix" and will likely need to get approval from senior management for anything on this list. The "will not fix" list provides the basis for a "known issues" list that will be part of the release notes for the game. Refer to Chapter 20 for more information on release notes.

18.7 Conclusion

QA testing is a critical component in the game development process. The best QA results are achieved when the QA team and the development team are working together to track and resolve bugs. Consider having some QA testers sit with the development team in order to facilitate communication between the two departments. Make sure that everyone on the team has a shared understanding of the testing pipeline and how to write useful bugs in the database. Utilize a process that ensures all the bugs are reviewed and resolved before the game ships.

PART 6
Launching the Game

The game is done, and it's ready for the players. The hard part is over, but there are still some challenges ahead with launching it and keeping it healthy for the player. This section provides information on activities that happen during the game launch and beyond. The chapters are:

Getting the Word Out;

Releasing to Players.

CHAPTER 19

Getting the Word Out

19.1 Introduction

As the game gets closer to release, you will want to think about how to market and sell it. If you are working with a publisher, they will handle this bulk of this work, with support from you and your team. This chapter focuses mainly on the relationship between an external marketing group and the development team. The discussion revolves around what marketing and sales needs from the development team and how to make the most of this relationship. Discussing how to actually market a game is beyond the scope of this book. If you want more specifics, check out Joel Dreskin's book *A Practical Guide to Indie Game Marketing* (2015).

19.2 Working with Marketing and PR

The marketing team creates and manages the marketing campaign around the game. Marketing is one of the tools to generate sales for the game; they handle the paid advertising and determine the branding and how to communicate it to the players. The PR group, working in conjunction with the marketing team, focuses on ways to generate free publicity for the game from websites, news organizations, and other outlets. Both of these groups need input from the development team in order to ensure that the game's marketing and PR campaigns are the best they can be.

It is crucial to involve the marketing department early in the development process; they have access to a great deal of information about competing games, focus testing, sales, and industry trends. Marketing input is valuable in the concept phase, especially when brainstorming the game's hook and core game loop.

Sometimes, the relationship between marketing and development can be less than harmonious. This usually happens because marketing and development have different perspectives on the game. Marketing usually measures success with tangible metrics, like sales figures or review scores, so all of their decisions are driven by what they think will sell more games. Thus, they are heavily biased towards viewing the game as a commercial product. The development team, while understanding how sales figures and reviews are good for the bottom line, are still heavily indexed towards delivering what they consider to be the most enjoyable player experience, which can be hard to quantify. They view the game more from the lens of a creator—while commercial success is great, the quality of the experience is even more important. Understanding how these groups view the game can help them work better together.

To facilitate communication with marketing, establish a single point of contact on the development team whose job it is to work with the marketing team. This helps to prevent confusion and frustration on both sides since marketing has a clear point of contact through which they can route all their requests. The development team contact can then review the requests, figure out what is needed, prioritize work, and keep confusion and redundant work to a minimum. This also creates a tighter communication loop between the marketing and the game team.

It is equally important for the game team to keep marketing up to date on any changes in the game. Even though things change very quickly in development, keep marketing in the loop so they always have the latest information about the game. It's not good if marketing starts talking publicly about a game feature only to find out later that it has been removed. Misunderstandings about product features can create ill will among the fans, so this needs to be avoided whenever possible. Marketing is part of the same team, so treat them like any other department or vendor you are working with.

While the game is in development, marketing is actively publicizing the game and building up anticipation with the players. This means that marketing needs support from the development team in the form of key art, screenshots, demos, trailers, and other game-related items. If these requests are not built into the development schedule, it can cause havoc and stress for the development team to deliver them. Ideally, the producer and marketing manager will work together to create a list of all the support and assets marketing needs from the development team. As with anything else, if the team is aware of these needs in advance, it will be much easier for them to anticipate and plan for them.

19.2.1 What's Needed

The marketing team is usually separated from the development team, so it is easy to forget that they need status updates and other pertinent information about the game. To begin with, marketing should be involved in some capacity in the entire game development process, from concept to launch. The importance of marketing increases as the game gets closer to launch. However, if you utilized marketing input from early on in the process, the game is better positioned for sales success when it launches.

Schedule a weekly sync with marketing, and put it on the calendar. This ensures at least one touch point each week at which marketing and production can get up to speed on what's going on and the status of any marketing requests. The types of information that marketing needs are:

- **Development schedule:** This includes major milestones, submission dates, proposed launch dates, and so on. Even though the development schedule will change, marketing needs a rough idea of what key dates they are planning around. They will create their own marketing schedule and need to update it whenever the development schedule changes.
- **Game documentation:** This includes information about the game's story, characters, and key features. Marketing will use this information to determine the target audience. Based on this audience, they may also request some changes in the game narrative so it is more appealing in advertisements.
- **Platform information:** Marketing should be involved in decisions about what platforms the game will launch on. They may also request exclusive content for each platform. For example, there may be a player character skin that is only available on Sony platforms and a different skin that is exclusive to Xbox platforms.
- **Prototype:** Make sure marketing has access to the prototype. This is the best way for them to experience and learn about the game. Ideally, you should also invite marketing to any type of team-wide playtests. The more the marketing team can play the game, the better their understanding of the features and selling points will be.
- **Cheats and Walkthroughs:** If marketing is demoing the game at a conference or for journalists, they may need cheats or game walkthroughs. These things allow them to quickly jump to key parts of the game they want to highlight for any marketing purposes.

19.2.2 Focus Groups

During the concept phase, marketing may arrange for focus testing of the game. This will result in feedback from the target audience on the game's concept, features, story, and characters. This feedback could indicate that an iteration or change is needed before further progress can be made in the development process. Focus testing is usually done by an external test group. Marketing usually takes point on setting up these focus tests, with input from the development team.

Often, developers find it useful to receive direct feedback from the target audience, particularly if the game in development represents a major change to the direction of a franchise or is an entirely new type of game. In this case, the team may have specific questions they want asked in the focus group. They may also want to observe the focus in real time in order to get the raw feedback (before it is synthesized into the focus testing report).

When formal focus testing is not possible, the developers might choose to arrange informal focus testing on their own. In this case, it is important that the participants sign nondisclosure agreements (NDAs) before they are shown anything about the game. When conducting informal focus testing, establish the exact objectives beforehand. Make sure that there is enough hardware for all participants, and be sure to establish some methods for gathering information about the testing, such as a questionnaire that the participants need to fill in.

If done with intent, focus tests can be extremely helpful in finding the right game concept or refining something about the game that hasn't quite hit the mark. They can also create more confusion, especially if the feedback from the participants in the focus group contradicts itself. Because feedback gained from the focus group is subjective and not quantifiable, it's best to view it more as a way to get feedback from your target audience.

19.3 Marketing Assets

There are a large variety of marketing assets that need to be created for the game's marketing campaign. If the company is large enough to have a creative services group, this group will be responsible for creating these. If the team is small and doesn't have the luxury of a creative services group, artists on the development team will likely be tapped to create them. If the development team is expected to double as a creative services team, plan to hire at least one artist whose primary function will be to work with marketing and to create assets for whatever materials are needed. Some examples of what will be needed are social media banners and profile images, website images and content, gameplay trailers (both cinematic and gameplay capture), and other types of advertisements. Deadlines for these deliverables should be factored into the development schedule so no one is caught off guard with any surprise requests.

Anticipate marketing needs ahead of time, and be proactive about creating a set of game assets that can be used in a variety of ways. The types of game assets that marketing finds useful are:

- **Screenshots:** These are used by websites and magazines to promote the game. Taking a quality screenshot can require some time as the image needs to have action and provide an idea of what the gameplay experience is like. It's a good idea to take screenshots on a weekly basis and just have them on hand for whenever marketing might need them.
- **Raw Gameplay Footage:** Gameplay footage is used to create game trailers and shorter videos that can promote the game. As with screenshots, it is useful to set up a consistent schedule for capturing gameplay footage. Marketing will need it.
- **Key Art:** Think of key art as the main image that can best market the game. This is usually the image that is used for any packaging or digital storefronts. Key art can be time-consuming to create since it will go through several rounds of revisions with the development and marketing teams. It also needs to be high resolution and highly polished.
- **Demo Builds:** Marketing will need some version of the game they can demo at conferences and trade shows. Depending on the state of the game's development, you may want to restrict access to certain parts by turning off functionality in the user interface (UI) or stripping the functionality from a demo build. Plan ahead for these requests so you don't disrupt the team's work too much when they have to create a separate version of the game for a trade show.

19.4 PR Events

The PR department works with the media to get publicity for the game in the form of articles, reviews, video features, and so on. The PR team sets up interviews and press tours, and prepares the development team for interviews. They may also schedule media training for key members of the development team. This training helps people feel more at ease when giving interviews, especially in front of a camera.

The key people who the PR group interfaces with are journalists and influencers. Journalists will do stories for web, video, and print about the game. Influencers usually promote the game via a social media platform, such as Twitter, Twitch, or YouTube. Influencers are not necessarily professional journalists; therefore, their influence can sometimes be stronger since people trust them to provide an honest opinion and an authentic reaction about the game.

The PR plan will include some of the following events:

- **Press Tours:** This is when key people on the development team talk to the press about the game. In order to be efficient with time and information, a press tour is scheduled so that multiple media outlets can talk with these people over the course of a few days. The press tour usually occurs just before the game launches so that the journalists can get their content and reviews written and ready to publish the day it comes out.
- **Conferences:** The PR department works shoulder to shoulder with marketing during conferences. The PR folks will be demoing the game to

the journalists and key influencers in the hopes that one of these outlets will promote the game.

- **Giveaways:** The PR folks are also the ones who determine what type of promotional items or swag should be created for the game. This swag is sent to media connections and influencers to promote it.

19.5 Conclusion

A solid marketing and PR plan is important to the success of the game. Work closely with these departments during development so you are aware of what they will need when it comes time to promote the game. If you don't plan ahead for marketing and PR needs, the team's schedule and work output can be negatively impacted if they have to drop what they are doing on the game to create a piece of content for marketing and PR. This chapter provides a high-level overview of the types of things that are needed. For an understanding of how to create a full marketing and PR plan, consult *A Practical Guide to Indie Game Marketing* by Joel Dreskin (2015).

CHAPTER 20

Releasing to Players

20.1 Introduction

A game launch requires more than just a completed and tested version of the game. As discussed in the previous chapters, there are many activities that occur outside of the game development team that must be completed before its official launch. Many of these items are not handled directly by the development team, such as securing software ratings or the copyrights for licensed content, which is why involving other departments, such as localization, marketing, legal, PR, and publishing, in the overall game development process is important. Typically, the bulk of the releasing and publishing tasks will fall to someone on the production team as there are a lot of pieces to coordinate and manage. And while the producer may not make the final decision on whether a game is ready for release or not, they do ensure that all the important tasks are completed and that the stakeholders have all the relevant information they need to sign off on the game's release.

Once the game is released, there are still post-release tasks to tackle, including fixing critical issues that prevent players from enjoying the game, managing feedback from the player community, and planning additional content releases. A plan needs to be defined for this live services of work before the release, or the development and publishing teams won't be prepared to address any of these areas quickly and effectively. A bad game launch can severely impact the success of a game, so planning out the release process and its expectations is as important as planning out the game's art, engineering, and design. This chapter contains an overview of key things to be aware of during the post-release and live operations phase in order to help you define a release roadmap for the game's launch and post-release activities.

20.2 Is It Ready?

The development team is in the final bug-fixing phase, the game is localized, and marketing events are in full swing—does this mean the game is ready for release? It depends: are all licenses and copyrights finalized; have third parties signed off on the game; are the software ratings finalized; and, most importantly, have the stakeholders reviewed and approved the game for release? These questions, and a few more, need to be answered before a game can be deemed ready to launch. Because there are so many different departments that need to sign off on the release, clearly defining and communicating the release process is critical. If a process is not in place, you may find yourself in the uncomfortable position of delaying a release for something small, but critical, that wasn't ready in time.

Begin by looking at all the major areas of publishing to determine what needs to be approved and who provides the sign-off for each. The following are some key areas to review and include on a release checklist:

- **Testing:** Refer to Chapter 18 for more information on testing your game. During the release process, you must work with the QA and development teams to define and implement a process for addressing all the bugs that must be fixed before launch. In addition, publishing, customer support, and community management should be involved in these discussions to make sure that they are aware of known issues that will ship with the game. Use your bug priority/severity system to clearly define which bugs will be addressed and which won't when the game ships. For example, you may determine that all Priority 1 and 2 bugs must be fixed, while this is not necessary for bugs Priority 3 and 4. Having a clearly defined system makes it much easier to communicate the state of the game's launch readiness across all departments. At this point in the process, you may also have lively discussions about which bugs must be addressed and which can be fixed in a patch. Again, have a good process in place for tracking any bugs for a patch, and make sure this is clearly communicated across all departments.
- **Software Ratings:** Refer to Chapter 14 for more information on software ratings. The game must be submitted and have all necessary software ratings before it is launched. If you are launching on a digital storefront, confirm with them what ratings are required to launch on their platform.

Since it can take anywhere from 10 to 30 days to secure software ratings, don't leave this until the last minute. Ideally, you will be able to submit the game for a rating after it is content and code complete. It's not common, but it has happened that a launch was delayed because the game didn't have final ratings certificates. Most digital storefronts will require the official ratings certificate before approving the game for launch. Make sure to add the ratings submission timeline to your release roadmap so there is enough time for this process.

- **Legal:** Refer to Chapter 3 for more information on handling licensing, copyrights, and other agreements that should be in place before the game launch. If you are licensing an IP, this piece is extremely critical, especially if the license holder needs to approve the final version of the game before it is launched. In some cases, it may take the license holder a week or more to approve the game, so plan accordingly when you are creating the final release schedule.

Talk to people in these key areas, and use what you learn to put together a full release checklist. The checklist should clearly define each action that must be completed before the game is launched. Publish this checklist, and keep it updated so that everyone involved in the process has a clear understanding of what's been completed and what's still outstanding. Once the checklist is complete, the game should be cleared for launch.

The stakeholders on the project must be engaged in the release process and will likely need to complete specific items on the release checklist. Requiring all the stakeholders to sign off on the launch is very helpful since it ensures that everyone with a key decision about the game is well-aware of what is being released (including any known issues or special circumstances). Some of the key stakeholders are as follows (although you may have other people to add, depending on circumstances):

- **Development Team:** Typically, the leads on the development team work in conjunction with QA and publishing to determine if all the necessary features are ready for launch and if all the key issues have been addressed. During the release process, the development team should be playing the build as much as possible to ensure that all is working as expected, and there are no last minute feature adjustments or critical bugs to address. The opinion of the development team is considered by publishing and the executive team when making a decision about launching the game.
- **QA Team:** The QA team should run through the full test plan a final time and provide a formal report of what the results were to the stakeholders. By this point in the process, the QA team should know the game inside and out. They are the best sources of information on what the known issues are and thus can best advise on how these issues are going to impact player experience. For example, how often will players come across an issue, and what percentage of players are likely to experience it? This information can help the stakeholders determine whether fixing an issue is critical or can just be listed on the known issues list (which is discussed later in this chapter).

- **Publishing Team:** The publishing team consists of marketing, PR, community, customer support, and any other group that is involved in launching the game. During this phase of the process, they should be playing the final version of the game and bringing red flags to everyone's attention. They will be involved in any key decisions about whether the game should be released or not.
- **Third Parties:** This group consists of any third parties that are involved in launching the game. For example, IP holders will need to sign off on the final version. This also includes any platform holders, such as Sony, Microsoft, or Nintendo, and any digital storefronts, such as Steam or the Epic Games store. As discussed earlier in this book, you will need to submit the games to third parties and digital storefronts for approval, and they will need 5–10 days to provide this final approval and then set up the game on the appropriate storefront.

20.3 Release Notes

When the game is launched, it is good practice to publish publicly facing release notes. The release notes serve two purposes; which purpose they serve depends on what version of the game is released. For the game's initial launch, these release notes will consist of "known issues," along with a way for the player to either avoid or correct them. These are bugs that are still in the game that players might encounter while playing. In theory, most of the known issues are minor and won't severely impact player experience but are really just annoying when encountered. Publishing the known issues list hopefully reduces the number of CS requests since the players can consult the list for their issue and implement the proposed solution without calling customer support. Work with the QA team to create a list of known issues from the database of unresolved bugs. You won't need to list every single issue, just the key ones that players are likely to encounter while playing the game.

After the game's initial launch, updates may be released to patch existing bugs, add new features, or add new content. In this instance, you will publish release notes that detail anything that was added or changed by the update (including any bug fixes) and include a known issues section.

20.4 Monitoring Game Health

The game is launched, and players are enjoying it! The team can breathe easy and move on to their next project...or can they? The reality is that players are likely to encounter issues within the first few weeks of the game that may need to be addressed with a patch. In order to do this most effectively, work with the development and publishing teams to create a Live Operations team (also known as LiveOps). A LiveOps team consists of people from customer support, community management, development, and publishing who work together to monitor issues and determine when to release patches and other game updates to the players.

Consider this scenario: a single-player game has an issue where a player can't progress past a specific objective, and this can't be resolved with a work-around. This is a critical issue that must be patched as quickly as possible.

Another scenario: a live multiplayer game crashes each time a player tries to join a friend's game. The crashes are happening so frequently that it is causing lag and performance issues for all of the players. The problem is getting worse each hour, and the publisher decides to take the game offline in order to resolve the problem.

You can deal with both of these scenarios more effectively if you have a LiveOps process in place that is comprised of a team of people that have specific responsibilities for monitoring issues, implementing solutions, and resolving player-impacting situations in a timely manner.

This system should incorporate data from customer support and community management, and include ways to communicate about the player-impacting issues, both internally and externally to the players. How quickly you respond to player-impacting issues is important to maintaining the health of your game. This section gives an overview of the different areas that are involved in the live operations of the game.

20.4.1 Customer Support

Once a game is launched, Customer Support (CS) becomes the first line of defense for addressing any player-impacting issues. Help customer support prepare for dealing with these issues by including them in the release plans and discussions of known issues. There are a few ways in which you can help CS prepare to deal with issues that will occur after the game is launched:

- **Provide CS with builds of the game so they can play the game and become familiar with it:** Troubleshooting issues is much easier if the CS agent is familiar with the game and the known issues.
- **Assign a designer or QA tester to work with a CS person to develop FAQs:** The designer can assist CS in writing explanations for how certain features work in the game. Testers can help CS write up information on known issues and work-arounds. The CS agents can use this information to create standard FAQs that will be published to the players. These can also be incorporated into the troubleshooting flowcharts that CS agents may use when assisting players with an issue.
- **Include CS in LiveOps status updates or daily meetings:** Including CS in these meetings provides them with accurate information about the daily status of the live game more quickly. They can also provide data and information on how many people have contacted them about a particular issue, which is useful in determining the timing of any patch releases.

CS can provide assistance to players in a variety of ways, and each of these have different levels of involvement. The preferred (and most cost-effective) method is to provide a way for players to troubleshoot and solve the issue without contacting the CS department. The easiest way to do this is to set up a public website that lists common CS issues and solutions. Players are responsible for diagnosing the issue, searching for it on the website, and then applying the solution. If this doesn't work for the player, their next step is to contact the CS department via phone, email, or chat support. Each of these contact methods has various costs, so you will want to consider what method works best within your budget, time, and team constraints.

If there are player issues that don't have a work-around, CS collects data on these issues to get a better understanding of how widespread it is. The development team will use this data to find a solution, then work with the publishing team to determine if it is necessary to patch the issue or sufficient to just add it to the known issues list.

20.4.2 Community Management

Community managers spend a lot of time interacting with the player community, and they are also a primary line of defense if the players run into any problems with the game. Players are likely to post about problems on forums, Reddit, Discord, and other social media platforms. The community manager will monitor all these channels to gain an understanding of what issues players are encountering and how this is impacting their enjoyment of the game. You can help community management prepare for the game launch by including them in status updates, providing builds of the game during development, and listening to the feedback they are providing to you from the players. However, keep in mind that players who are vocal in the community may not always represent the majority of the player base. Therefore, before you make any changes to the game based on feedback in the forums, analyze the data collected by the game metrics to determine if the issue is something experienced by most players.

20.4.3 Metrics and Analytics

Metrics and analytics are a useful tool for collecting information from the game that allows you to answer questions about player engagement. You can use the answers to these questions to create updates to the game that enhance the players' experience and enjoyment. There are numerous types of data you can collect from the game, including how long people are playing the game, what UI buttons are most frequently interacted with, which characters and weapons are most popular, how many players complete a particular objective, and so on. Because of the vast amount of information that can be collected from the game, start by defining which questions you want to answer, and then use these answers to determine which analytics to add. Some examples are:

- How long does the average gameplay session last?
- What in-game activities are most popular with the players?

- How often do players use a particular feature? Which leads to another question—do players know how to access a particular feature?

Questions help determine which analytics are the highest priority, and you can add more analytics to the game whenever you do an update. Ideally, the developers who created and implemented a particular game feature will include analytics as part of the development process. They can anticipate the types of questions that will be asked and implement some basic, but key, analytics during the initial feature implementation.

Keep in mind that in addition to collecting data, you need to have a process in place for parsing and analyzing this data; otherwise, the data collection will not be very useful. On a large development team, you may have a data analyst who focuses solely on collecting and analyzing the data, and then generating reports that the development, marketing, and publishing teams use to make decisions about how well the game is performing and what future game updates should contain.

20.4.4 Releasing Updates

Once you've gathered the player feedback, received reports from CS and community, and reviewed these in conjunction with the data, you should have a fairly clear picture of what bug fixes, feature enhancements, and content to include in updates for the game. As discussed earlier in this chapter, crash bugs and critical issues that impact the majority of the player base will need to be addressed quickly. In a case where a critical issue needs a quick fix, it is best to stay focused on generating a fix for that particular issue and getting it out the door as quickly as possible. Don't get sidetracked by attempting to cram in less critical bug fixes if time is of the essence. The less critical bugs can always be included in a future update.

In situations where players are communicating about a gameplay issue or a feature they don't like, you will want to synthesize feedback and data from all the sources mentioned above and then determine if the issue needs to be addressed. If it does, work with the development and publishing teams on an appropriate timeline for this. For example, you might decide to release an update 3 weeks after the initial game launch that includes a fix for the issue the players didn't like as well as fixes for 5 known issues, an iteration based on player feedback for one of the UI screens, and a new item for the player character to use (also based on player feedback). If you know the players will need to download an update to fix an issue they are unhappy with, it's useful to take advantage of this and include a few other things that will improve their experience. Again, you want to be very focused on what fixes and content are included in an update so that you can avoid feature creep (unfortunately, feature creep is a constant risk, even with patches!).

Things to keep in mind when doing game updates are:

- **Keep the players informed about which issues will and won't be addressed:** You can build a lot of goodwill with players by acknowledging their feedback and providing information on how it is being used to make the game better. Ways you can do this include setting up a public-facing database, Trello board, or website that provides information on what's being fixed, what's not being fixed, and what's being added. This gives community management a framework and process for communicating accurate information back to the player. As discussed previously in this chapter, there should be a clear process in place for determining which things will be included in game updates.
- **Respond to players in a timely manner:** Players want to make sure their voice is being heard. So, as decisions are made about which issues to include in an update and how to handle them, don't keep the players in the dark about what's happening. An acknowledgement that the development team is investigating an issue and more information will be forthcoming is a nice way to build trust with the player community.
- **Releasing an update needs to have a release process similar to the one used for the initial game:** Just because an update takes less time to create and is likely less complex than a full game, don't cut corners by skipping a formal release process. It's very easy to introduce new and unintended issues in an update because it wasn't thoroughly tested. There have been cases where something used as placeholder art was released to the public and caused issues because the art was either inappropriate or didn't have the correct licensing permissions.
- **Think about the impact the update has on the player:** For example, is the update several gigs? If so, how long will it take the player to download? What happens if the player doesn't install it; will they be able to play with people who do have the update installed? How often are updates released? Will players get frustrated if they have to download an update every week? Does the update require downtime for the game? If so, how long will the game be offline?

COLIN THOMPSON, VIDEOGAME INDUSTRY SUPPORT DIRECTOR. GOOD CUSTOMER SUPPORT

The most important principles of good customer support are an interconnected set of values and operational successes that are blended to provide a positive support experience:

- **Empathy:** A customer support agent of any stripe needs to be able to connect in a thoughtful way with their audience. Whether they're troubleshooting a PC game installation on old hardware, evaluating a policy exception refund, or communicating a game's behavioral expectations following an infraction, a good customer support professional should be able to bridge why the customer is seeking support and how to best leverage a solution that will keep them on the "fan" end of the spectrum.

- **Grit:** Customer Support work can be monotonous, and 8 hours of angry emails or phone calls can carry serious weight. A Customer Support professional needs a good daily support system across their colleagues, communication platforms, and leadership, but they also need a solid foundation in tenacity—the ability to leverage their best across the mundane, the exception, and the escalation.
- **Strength of process:** At the core of things, Customer Support professionals engage with customers with issues or questions, whether it be via phone, email, live chat, or across a counter. The success rate of positive resolutions (or transformed outcomes) is greatly supported by a robust process. The more framework, policy, opportunities for latitude, product knowledge, and expertise the CS agent has at their disposal, the better the outcome can and should be.
- **Clarity:** Any outward-facing communication, whether it be a 1:1 email, phone call, text, tweet, Facebook post, or Reddit thread, must be clear in form, structure, grammar, and tone. A good support team with solid training materials, expectations, and hiring practices in the areas of writing, comprehension, and communication will succeed.
- **Presentation:** Are your support paths clear, cogent, and thoughtfully designed? Do your contact forms contain relative picklists or options to capture all the information needed for a CS agent to rapidly diagnose or resolve? Is your support website clean and branded? Is your support ticket system configured to organize and prioritize effectively? Are your support channels aligned to be effective? Are you setting clear support experience expectations on quality of information and response time frame? The answer to all of these has to be "Yes" in order to execute successfully.

20.5 Conclusion

This chapter provided a high-level overview of the release process. Start by clearly defining who needs to be involved in approving the game for release, which will include some combination of the development leads, QA, and the publishing team. These groups must work together and define a release process that includes checks and balances for all the things that need to be double-checked before the game is launched. Work with this group to put a process in place for dealing with any critical issues and player feedback after the game is launched. If there is a game-stopping bug, you want to know ahead of time how you can quickly create a fix and release it to the players.

PART 7
Appendices

The appendices have been divided into the following categories:

Glossary: *It provides definitions of game production terms and acronyms.*

Resources and Tools: *It provides useful websites, software, and books that relate to game production and the topics discussed in this book.*

Biographies: *It provides information on the people who were featured in sidebars throughout this book.*

Appendix A: Acronyms

AI	Artificial intelligence
API	Application Programming Interface
AR	Augmented reality
CS	Customer support
DLC	Downloadable content that adds new content to a game
IP	Intellectual property
MMO	Massively multiplayer online game
NPC	Non-player character
PR	Public relations
QA	Quality assurance
RITES	Rapid iterative testing and evaluation
RNG	Random number generator
SDK	Software Development Kit
TRCs (aka TCRs)	Technical requirements checklist
UI	User interface
UX	User experience
VR	Virtual reality

Appendix B:
Resources and Tools

B.1 Funding

Altered Ventures: www.altered.vc/

Chucklefish: https://blog.chucklefish.org/funding/.

Fig: www.fig.co

Game Founders: www.gamefounders.com

Indie-Fund: http://indie-fund.com/

Indiegogo: www.indiegogo.com

London Venture Partners: www.londonvp.com

Makers Fund: https://makersfund.com/

Kickstarter: www.kickstarter.com

Small Business Administration: www.sba.gov

FDIC Money Smart for Small Business: www.fdic.gov/consumers/consumer/moneysmart/business.html

B.2 Grants

Unreal Dev Grants: www.unrealengine.com/en-US/unrealdevgrants

National Endowment for the Art (Artworks Media Art Grants): www.arts.gov/grants-organizations/art-works/media-arts

European Games Developer Federation: www.egdf.eu/funding/

IndieCade Foundation: http://indiecade.org/

Entertainment Software Association: www.esafoundation.org/application.asp

Lego Education: https://education.lego.com/en-us/grants-and-funding

National Science Foundation: www.nsf.gov/funding/aboutfunding.jsp

Institute of Education Sciences: https://ies.ed.gov/sbir/

Games for Change: www.gamesforchange.org/

B.3 Platform Development

Android Developers: https://developer.android.com/distribute/console/

Apple Developers: https://developer.apple.com/

Microsoft Developers: www.xbox.com/en-US/developers

Nintendo Developers: https://developer.nintendo.com/

Sony Developers: https://partners.playstation.net/

Steam: https://partner.steamgames.com/doc/home

B.4 Design and Prototyping

Design Kit: www.designkit.org/

d.School at Stanford University (Design Resources): https://dschool.stanford.edu/resources/

Google Noto Fonts: www.google.com/get/noto/

Game Accessibility Guidelines: http://gameaccessibilityguidelines.com/

Game UX Master Guide: https://gameuxmasterguide.com/

United States Copyright Information: https://copyright.gov/

United States Patent and Trademark Office: www.uspto.gov/

B.5 Project Management

Asana: https://asana.com/

Basecamp: https://basecamp.com/

Confluence: www.atlassian.com/software/confluence

Google Sheets: www.google.com/sheets/about/

HacknPlan: https://hacknplan.com/

Hansoft: www.perforce.com/products/hansoft

JIRA: www.atlassian.com/software/jira

Microsoft Project: https://products.office.com/en-us/project/project-and-portfolio-management-software

Monday: https://monday.com/

Pivotal Tracker: www.pivotaltracker.com/

Project Manager: www.projectmanager.com/

Shotgun: www.shotgunsoftware.com/

Smartsheet: www.smartsheet.com/

Trello: https://trello.com/

Project Management Institute (PMI): www.pmi.org

Scrum Alliance: www.scrumalliance.org/

B.6 General Production

Slack: https://slack.com/

Discord: https://discordapp.com/

SAG-AFTRA: www.sagaftra.org

XLOC: www.xloc.com/

PremiumBeat: www.premiumbeat.com/

B.7 Game Industry

Academy of Interactive Arts and Sciences: www.interactive.org

Entertainment Software Association: www.theesa.com/

Gamasutra: www.gamasutra.com/

GameDev.net: www.gamedev.net

Game Rankings: www.gamerankings.com/

International Game Developers Association: www.igda.org

Metacritic: www.metacritic.com/

Moby Games: www.mobygames.com/

Newzoo: https://newzoo.com

SIGGRAPH: www.siggraph.org

Indie Game Business (Twitch): www.twitch.tv/indiegamebusiness

Indie Game Business (YouTube): www.youtube.com/channel/UCjPItT-16WxnP9vyBq6Nqrg

B.8 Conferences

Consumer Electronics Show (CES): https://cesweb.org

D.I.C.E. Summit: www.dicesummit.org

Game Developers Conference: www.gdconf.com

E3: www.e3expo.com

Montreal International Game Summit (MIGS): www.facebook.com/MontrealGameSummit/ or www.migs18.com

Pax Dev (PAX): http://dev.paxsite.com/

B.9 Game Development Books

Dreskin, Joel, *A Practical Guide to Indie Game Marketing*, Routledge, 2015.

Dunlop, Renee, *Production Pipeline Fundamentals for Film and Games*, Routledge, 2014.

Hodent, Celia, *The Gamer's Brain: How Neuroscience and UX Can Impact Video Game Design*, CRC Press, 2017.

Fullerton, Tracy, *Game Design Workshop: A Playcentric Approach to Creating Innovative Games*, Fourth Edition, CRC Press, 2018.

Keith, Clinton, *Agile Game Development with Scrum*, Addison - Wesley Professional, 2010.

Lewis, James P, *Project Planning, Scheduling, and Control: The Ultimate Hands-On Guide to Bringing Projects in on Time and on Budget*, Fifth Edition, McGraw-Hill, 2005.

Lynch, Michael and Adrian Earle, *Surviving Game School and the Game Industry After That*, Boca Raton: CRC Press, 2008.

McConnell, Steve, *Rapid Development: Taming Wild Software Schedules*, Microsoft Press, 1996.

Millington, Richard, *Buzzing Communities: How to Build Bigger, Better, and More Active Online Communities*, FeverBee, 2012.

Schell, Jesse, *The Art of Game Design: A Book of Lenses*, Second Edition, CRC Press, 2014.

Schultz, Charles P. and Robert Denton Bryant, *Game Testing All in One*, Third Edition, Mercury Learning and Information, 2016.

Schwaber, Ken and Mike Beedle, *Agile Software Development with Scrum*, Pearson, 2001.

Tozour, Paul, *The Game Outcomes Project*, http://gamasutra.com/blogs/PaulTozour/20141216/232023/The_Game_Outcomes_Project_Part_1_The_Best_and_the_Rest.php, 2014.

B.10 Leadership Books

Lewis, James P., *Project Leadership*, McGraw-Hill Education, 2002.

Lewis, James P., *Team-Based Project Management*, AMACOM, 1997.

Kouzes, James M. and Barry Z. Posner, *The Leadership Challenge*, Sixth Edition, Jossey-Bass, 2017.

Bennis, Warren, *On Becoming a Leader*, Third Edition, Basic Books, 2009.

Covey, Stephen R., *The 7 Habits of Highly Effective People*, Free Press, 1989.

Brooks, Jr., Frederick P., *The Mythical Man-Month*, Addison-Wesley Professional, 1995.

Buckingham, Marcus and Curt Coffman, *First, Break All the Rules: What the World's Greatest Managers Do Differently*, Gallup Press, 2016.

DeMarco, Tom and Timothy Lister, *Peopleware*, Third Edition, Addison-Wesley Professional, 2013.

Spaulding II, Seth, *Team Leadership in the Game Industry*, Cengage Learning PTR, 2009.

Catmull, Ed and Amy Wallace, *Creativity Inc.: Overcoming the Unseen Forces that Stand in the Way of True Inspiration*, Random House, 2014.

Other Recommendations from Our Experts

Chuck Hoover

Be open to reading about all sorts of different fields, from psychology to business, leadership, and even quantum mechanics, to hone your craft.

Some quick recommendations:

- Collins, Jim, *Good to Great: Why Some Companies Make the Leap and Others Don't*, Harper Business, 2001.
- Stone, Douglas and Shelia Heen, *Difficult Conversations: How to Discuss What Matters Most*, Penguin Books, 2010.
- Hock, Dee, *One from Many: VISA and the Rise of Chaordic Organization*, Berrett-Koehler Publishers, 2005.
- Stone, Douglas and Shelia Heen, *Thanks for the Feedback: The Science and Art of Receiving Feedback Well*, Penguin Books, 2015.

Matt Immerman

The best resources for game production aren't really about game production at all. Some of the best lessons I've learned have been focused on communication and human behavior. As you grow in your career doing production, you'll find that you spend less and less time in software such as JIRA or Excel and have replaced the time you used to spend doing those things with communicating information. You'll eventually transition from day-to-day tasking to running meetings, managing conflict, messaging changes across departments and disciplines, messaging with clients and partners, communicating project status to studio leadership, and so on. Communication is what is really at the core of what production does. My recommendation is to watch any TED talk or Game Developers Conference (GDC) talk you can find focused on communication, and get your hands on any books that focus on team building and culture management. It's also helpful to just delve into the history of companies that you feel have strong cultures, and research the kinds of things they did/do.

Jay Powell

We have a Twitch show live twice a week that discusses the business and marketing side of the industry. www.twitch.tv/indiegamebusiness

We also maintain a curated list of lectures from conferences around the world. We break them down by topic, and you can find them all here: http://bit.ly/PowellGroupYouTube

Ben Smith

I feel I learned more about making games from reading Donald Norman's *Design of Everyday Things* (Basic Books, 2013) than from any development postmortem published by *Game Developer Magazine*. This is because making a game is about making a product that people use.

Brian Sowers

It's not a production-oriented book, but *Game Coding Complete, Fourth Edition* by Mike McShaffry and David Graham (Cengage Learning PTR, 2012) was one of the first books that introduced me to the realities of developing production-ready code.

Colin Thompson

For focused CS reading, I commonly recommend Tony Hsieh's *Delivering Happiness: A Path to Profits, Passion, and Purpose* (Grand Central Publishing, 2013). Zappos.com is a gold standard in any service-focused industry, and there's a wealth of good wisdom and practice in his book.

Appendix C: Biographies of Interviewees

Ray Crowell

Ray Crowell is a 2× founder, ethnographer, investor, and economic ecosystem builder working at the intersection of design and innovation to solve complex challenges. As Director of Venture creations, he currently launches alumni-led start-ups at the Savannah College of Art and Design (SCAD). From homeless to Harvard, decorated military veteran to award-winning venture developer, Ray has continuously excelled as an entrepreneur, innovator, leader, and peer-to-peer knowledge transfer pioneer. He has developed continuous innovation strategies for Fortune 500 companies; has mentored industry-leading start-up accelerator programs; and advises big data, additive manufacturing, and artificial intelligence companies on information architectures, data visualization and optimization, infrastructure protection, and user adoption. Ray has served as a Harvard Kennedy School Fellow, studied legislative operations at Georgetown, and received executive business education at Notre Dame.

Jason Della Rocca

Jason Della Rocca is a game industry entrepreneur, funding advisor, and cluster expert. As the cofounder of Executions Labs, he was a hands-on early-stage investor in over 20 independent game studios in North America and Europe. Between 2000 and 2009, he served as the executive director of the International Game Developers Association (IGDA). As a sought-after expert on the game industry, Jason has lectured at conferences and universities worldwide. More about Jason via http://dellaroc.ca/.

Stephanie Deming

As Co Founder and President of XLOC, Stephanie is focused on enhancing the customer experience for all clients while strengthening and expanding XLOC's business and strategic relationships. Over the course of her career, she's worn many hats that now benefit XLOC customers, from software development producer and production consultant to operations executive, for worldwide, award-winning educational and entertainment leaders, including Activision, Electronic Arts, Capcom, and 2K Games. With over 15 years of localization expertise, Stephanie has successfully sim-shipped hundreds of language versions of high-profile titles, including the Call of Duty®, Guitar Hero™, Tony Hawk™, and NBA2K™ Series; Rock Band™; League of Legends®; BioShock®; and more. Stephanie holds degrees in both Psychology and Sociology from the University of California, Santa Barbara.

Chuck Hoover

Chuck is the General Manager of Facebook Reality Labs Pittsburgh, working on the future of VR and AR with an amazing team. Before joining Facebook, he spent 12 years as the Chief Production Officer (CPO) of Schell Games, where he led the production team and managed relationships with clients ranging from Disney to Microsoft, Google, Universal Studios, Yale, and EA, among others. Prior to that, Chuck was a producer for Electronic Arts and a graduate of Carnegie Mellon University's (CMU) Entertainment Technology Center. An appetite for creating world-class experiences in the game and entertainment industry has influenced Chuck both in and out of the workplace. In addition to being the founder of the Game Leadership Workshop, Chuck is also Adjunct Faculty at Carnegie Mellon University's Entertainment Technology Center graduate program, teaching Production and Leadership.

Celia Hodent

Celia Hodent is recognized as a leader in the application of UX and cognitive science in the game industry. She holds a PhD in psychology and has over ten years of experience in the development of UX strategy and processes in video game studios. Through her work at Ubisoft (e.g., Rainbow Six franchise), LucasArts (e.g., Star Wars: 1313), and as Director of UX at Epic Games (e.g., Fortnite), she has contributed to many projects across multiple platforms, from PC to consoles, mobile, and VR. Celia is also the founder of the Game UX Summit, advisor for the GDC UX Summit, and author of *The Gamer's Brain: How Neuroscience and UX can Impact Video Game Design* (CRC Press, 2017). She currently works as a freelance Game UX Consultant, helping studios increase their games' likeliness of being engaging and successful.

Matt Immerman

Matt Immerman has served as a Producer on Killer Instinct, Deadpool, Skyrim Switch, Fortnite, and Dreadnought, among other titles. He is a huge Disney nerd, gamer, wrestling fan, cinephile, and avid cook. Kingdom Hearts and God of War were the games that really made him to pursue a career in this field. After studying Radio/Television and Film at the University of Central Florida for undergraduation, he was accepted into the Florida Interactive Entertainment Academy (FIEA) for his Masters in Interactive Entertainment Production. He can be contacted at mattimmerman@gmail.com.

Ashley Jennings

Ashley Jennings has worked as a Technical Artist at Hi-Rez Studios, where she led the Tech Art department for the world's #1 action MOBA, SMITE. Before working on AAA games at Hi-Rez Studios, she received a master's degree in Digital Media from Georgia Institute of Technology. Her focus is in software engineering, 3D animation pipelines, and Unreal Engine development.

Jay Powell

Jay is the Founder of The Powell Group, a consulting firm specializing in business development, licensing, and marketing in the video game industry. Over the past 20 years, Jay has negotiated countless deals for licensing, development, and distribution. During his career, he has had the privilege of working on behalf of companies including Haemimont Studios, Paradox, DICE, Starbreeze Studios, and Invictus Games. He has also built relationships with publishers and media groups such as Amazon, National Geographic, Disney, Cartoon Network, MTV, Nickelodeon, Microsoft, and Sony.

Chris Schweitzer

Chris gained his first project management experience working in the theme park industry at Universal Orlando Resort. Over the course of 12 years at Universal, he worked within their Entertainment division on many different seasonal projects (2003–2012 Halloween Horror Nights, 2008–2011 Macy's Holiday Parade at Universal, 2009–2011 Mardi Gras Parade at Universal) as well as in daily entertainment operations as an Entertainment Coordinator for 3 years (Universal Studios Animated Characters, Island of Adventure Seuss Animated Characters and "Oh The Stories You'll Hear" Show, Poseidon Adventure, and The Eighth Voyage of Sindbad) and behind the scenes as a Talent Coordinator and Scheduling Specialist for 5 years. Chris started his transition into the game industry by obtaining his Masters of Interactive Entertainment from the Florida Interactive Entertainment Academy (FIEA) Master's program in Orlando, FL. At the end of 2015, he joined Epic Games as a Production Assistant on Fortnite. Over the course of almost 3 years, he rose up to Associate Producer and supported the Art and Animation team of Fortnite through the launch of both the Save the World and the Battle Royale game modes.

Ben Smith

Ben Smith spent 14 years working his way up from the very bottom at EA, finishing his production career at Electronic Arts as a Senior Producer in the EA Partners (EAP) group. During his time with EAP, Ben worked on the Battlefield Franchise with Digital Illusions CE (1942 expansions, Vietnam, 2), Kingdoms of Amalur Reckoning with Big Huge Games, Rage with iD Software (briefly, before the publishing rights were moved to Bethesda), and many other projects. Ben left EA in 2014 to pursue exciting opportunities outside game development.

Brian Sowers

Brian Sowers has been developing games since he picked up a book on QBASIC in 8th grade. He's been a professional in the industry for over 10 years, starting as a Tools and Framework Engineer for the Gamebryo game engine. Since then, he has worked on console games, mobile, and VR/AR, and recently crowdfunded his own board game. He moonlights teaching game design and programming at a local community college, and is an avid lover of indie games.

Daniel Taylor

Gaming has always been a passion for Daniel since he was a teen. He knew from then on that when he grows up, he wanted to make video games. As soon as he turned 18, he started applying for QA jobs. He has now been in the industry for over 18 years and has worked on close to 25 titles. He started in QA for the first 3 years and has been in production ever since.

Colin Thompson

Colin is a bourbon-appreciating, meat-grilling, outdoors enthusiast, mage-main, and PC-building-fan who regularly wavers between writing a book about CS high/low experiences and writing a screenplay for a video game industry romantic-drama-medical-reality sitcom, drawing from 12-and-counting years in the video game industry as CS people and process leader. He's happy to discuss any of the above at his ill-advised (a lot of Colin's out there sign up for crazy stuff with his address) but conveniently short email address, colin@outlook.com.

References

Ashcroft, Brian, "Bethesda Censors Fallout 3 for Japan," available online at https://kotaku.com/5082637/bethesda-censors-fallout-3-for-japan, 2008.

Cooper, Tristan, "5 Weird Ways Germany Has Censored Video Games," available online at www.dorkly.com/post/80945/germany-censorship, 2016.

Della Rocca, Jason, "Funding What When," available online at GDC Vault: https://gdcvault.com/play/1024953/Funding-What, 2018.

Digital Media Wire, "Korea Slaps Curfew on Gamers," available online at: https://digitalmediawire.com/2011/11/28/korea-slaps-curfew-on-gamers/, 2011.

Doran, George T. "There's a S.M.A.R.T. Way to Write Management's Goals and Objectives," *Management Review. AMA FORUM*. 70, no. 11(1998): 35–36.

Entertainment Software Association, 2017 Annual Report. www.esaannualreport.com/a-letter-from-michael-d.-gallagher.html.

Entertainment Software Association, 2018 Sales Demographic and Usage Data. www.theesa.com/wp-content/uploads/2018/05/EF2018_FINAL.pdf.

Gates, Christopher, "Games That Were Forced to Change Internationally," available online at www.svg.com/97026/games-forced-change-internationally/, 2017.

Hall, Meredith, "Choosing a Project Management Tool for Game Development," available online at: www.gamasutra.com/blogs/MeredithHall/20180629/321013/Choosing_A_Project_Management_Tool_For_Game_Development.php, 2018.

Hodent, Celia. *The Gamer's Brain: How Neuroscience and UX Can Impact Video Game Design*. Boca Raton, FL: CRC Press, 2017.

Isbister, Katherine, and Noah Schaffer. *Game Usability*. New York: Morgan Kaufman, 2008.

Matulef, Jeffrey, "Natural Selection 2 Dev's Subnautica Is Out Now on Steam Early Access," available online at www.eurogamer.net/articles/2014-12-17-natural-selection-2-devs-subnautica-is-out-now-on-steam-early-access, 2014.

Maxwell Chandler, Heather, and Stephanie Deming. *The Game Localization Handbook: Second Edition*. Jones & Bartlett Learning, Burlington, MA, 2011.

Pokémon GO Wiki, "Pokemon GO Game Updates," available at http://pokemongo.wikia.com/wiki/List_of_game_updates, 2018.

Project Management Institute, *A Guide to the Project Management Body of Knowledge* (PMBOK® Guide), 2013.

Smith, Graham, "The First Moments of Minecraft," available online at www.pcgamer.com/the-first-moments-of-minecraft/, 2012.

Steamworks Documentation, "Early Access," available online at https://partner.steamgames.com/doc/store/earlyaccess.

Index

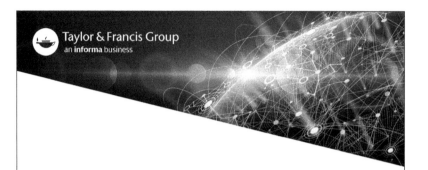